The Art of Contrarian Trading

Founded in 1807, John Wiley & Sons is the oldest independent publishing company in the United States. With offices in North America, Europe, Australia, and Asia, Wiley is globally committed to developing and marketing print and electronic products and services for our customers' professional and personal knowledge and understanding.

The Wiley Trading series features books by traders who have survived the market's ever changing temperament and have prospered—some by reinventing systems, others by getting back to basics. Whether a novice trader, professional, or somewhere in-between, these books will provide the advice and strategies needed to prosper today and well into the future.

For a list of available titles, visit our Web site at www.WileyFinance.com.

The Art of Contrarian Trading

How to Profit from Crowd Behavior in the Financial Markets

CARL FUTIA

WILEY

John Wiley & Sons, Inc.

Published by John Wiley & Sons, Inc., Hoboken, New Jersey.
Published simultaneously in Canada.

For general information on our other products and services or for technical support, please contact our Customer Care Department within the United States at (800) 762-2974, outside the United States at (317) 572-3993 or fax (317) 572-4002.

Wiley also publishes its books in a variety of electronic formats. Some content that appears in print may not be available in electronic books. For more information about Wiley products, visit our web site at www.wiley.com.

Library of Congress Cataloging-in-Publication Data:

Futia, Carl, 1948–
   The art of contrarian trading : how to profit from crowd behavior in the financial markets / Carl Futia.
      p. cm.—(Wiley trading series)
     Includes index.
     ISBN 978-0-470-32507-0 (cloth)
    1. Investments—Psychological aspects.   2. Speculation—Psychological aspects.
3. Investments—Decision making.   I. Title.
    HG4515.15.F87 2009
    332.6—dc22

                                         2008053438

Printed in the United States of America

10 9 8 7 6 5 4 3 2 1

Contents

Preface   xi

CHAPTER 1   Can You Beat the Market?   1

The Speculator's Edge   1
Lending a Helping Hand to Investors   2
Uncovering Market Mistakes   4
Looking at the Evidence   5
Market Timing   6
Catch-22   7

CHAPTER 2   Market Mistakes   9

Efficient Markets   9
Roller Coasters and Stock Markets   10
Do Stock Prices Fluctuate Too Much?   12
A Look at Behavioral Finance   14
Behavioral Finance and Exploitable Market Mistakes   16
No Free Lunch Redux   17

CHAPTER 3   The Edge   19

A Theory of Market Mistakes   19
To Get Along, Go Along   21
Go Along and Create a Mistake   22
The Social Calculus of Crowds   25
The Vision of a Contrarian Trader   27

CHAPTER 4   The Wisdom and Follies of Crowds   31

Can a Crowd Be Wiser Than Its Members?   31
The Need for Collective Wisdom   32
Independent Decisions in the Financial Markets   34
Forecasting Market Psychology   36
Information Cascades into the Whirlpool of Speculation   38

**CHAPTER 5   The Life Cycle and Psychology
of an Investment Crowd   43**

Prologue   43
The Cycle of Birth and Death   44
The Stock Market Bubble of 1994–2000   46
It's Different This Time: The New Information Economy   48
Shattered Dreams: The Bear Crowd of 2001–2002   49
Popular Instincts and the Search for Certainty   51
The Pied Pipers of Investment Crowds   54
The Mental Unity of Investment Crowds   55
Suggestibility, Volatility, and Disintegration   59

**CHAPTER 6   The Historical Context for Market
Mistakes   61**

Mature Investment Themes and Market Crowds   61
Mistakes versus Fair Value   62
Market Data Sources   63
The Deadly Mistake   64
When Is the Stock Market (Extremely) Overvalued?   65
When Is the Stock Market Undervalued?   67
The Peak Oil Bubble   70

CHAPTER 7   How Crowds Communicate   71

What Do Information Cascades Tell Investors?   71
The Role of the Mass Media   73
A Word about Personal Flexibility and the Future
of Media   76

Monitoring the Markets   76
Studying the History of Bubbles and Crashes   77

CHAPTER 8   Constructing Your Media Diary   79

Gaining the Edge   79
How My Diary Made a Difference in 2002   81
Get Ready to Cut and Paste   83
Excerpts from My Media Diary: November 2005   86
Excerpts from My Media Diary: June 2006   89
Interpreting Magazine Covers   92

CHAPTER 9   Important Investment Themes   97

Telling the Market's Story   97
New Eras   98
Effect of War and International Political Crises on
    the Stock Market   100
Financial Crises Create Crowds   102
New Industries and Companies   104
Commodity Booms   106
Interest Rate Movements and the Bond Market   107
Using Your Media Diary to Track Investment Themes   107

CHAPTER 10   Interpreting Your Diary: Market
               Semiotics   109

Media and Information Cascades   109
Your Media Diary: A Living History of Information
    Cascades   110
Semiotics: The Study of Signs   110
The Most Important Sign: The Price Chart   112
Magazine Cover Stories   114
Newspaper Headlines   116
Front Page Stories and Editorials   118
Crystallizing Events   118
The Weight of the Evidence   119
More on Market Semiotics   120

CHAPTER 11   The Grand Strategy of Contrarian
Trading   123

Contrarian Investment Planning   123
Contrarian Trader's Investment Portfolio   125
The Investment Goal of the Contrarian Trader   126
A Warning about Capital Gains Taxes   128
Contrarian Trading Strategy #1: Don't Speculate   128
Contrarian Trading Strategy #2: Don't Invest with the Crowd   129
Contrarian Trading Strategy #3: Contrarian Rebalancing   129
The Aggressive Contrarian   130
A Long-Only Strategy for the Aggressive Contrarian Trader   131
More Aggressive Contrarian Trading Strategies   134

CHAPTER 12   The Great Bull Market of 1982–2000   137

Prologue   137
The 1987 Crash   138
Interlude: The 1929–1932 Crash and Bear Market   140
The S&L Crisis, the 1987–1990 Bull Market, and the 1990
  Bear Market Crowd   141
Rally without Joy, 1991–1994   143
The Stock Market Bubble Inflates, 1995–2000   145
The Aggressive Contrarian Faces the 1987 Crash   147
The 1990 Low   149
Long Term Capital Management Goes Bust   150

CHAPTER 13   Collapse of the Bubble: The
2000–2002 Bear Market   153

End of the Great Bull Market   153
Contrarian Rebalancing during the 2000–2002 Bear Market   154
The Long Way Down Again   154
Contrarian Rebalancing during the Crash   155
The Aggressive Contrarian during the 2000–2002
  Bear Market   157
A Wall Street Wreck   158
The Summer Rally   160

The March 2001 Plunge   162
Terrorists Attack on 9/11   164
End of a Bear Market   164
Transition to a New Bull Market   166

CHAPTER 14   The Postbubble Bull Market
             of 2002–2007   169

Escaping the Bear's Claw   169
What Bull? Looking for Signs of a Bullish Information
  Cascade   170
The Story of Google's IPO   172
The Housing Bubble   175
Aggressive Contrarian Trading during the 2002–2007
  Bull Market   177
April 2005—A Buying Opportunity   181
June 2006—Another Buying Opportunity   182
Aggressive Contrarian Trading in Early 2007   183
July–October 2007   186

CHAPTER 15   The Panic of 2008   189

The Conservative Contrarian during the Panic   189
The Mortgage Mess   191
The Debt-Deflation Spiral Takes Hold   193
Lenders of Last Resort   194
The Credit Crisis and the Contrarian Trader   195
Bull Market Top and the First Step Down   195
The Bear Stearns Failure   198
Fannie and Freddie   199
The Crash: Bankruptcy of Lehman Brothers   201

CHAPTER 16   Vignettes on Contrarian Thought
             and Practice   205

The Psychology of the Stock Market   206
The Godfather of Contrary Opinion   206
Opinion Polls: What Do You Think   207

Is the Odd Lotter Always Wrong? 209
A Forecasting Giant of the Past 211
Paul Montgomery, the Magazine Cover Contrarian 212
Irrational Exuberance and Other Bubbles 212
Value Investing—A Back-of-the-Envelope Approach 214

About the Author **218**

Index **219**

Preface

W hy is it so difficult to beat the stock market?
It is easy to see that the market gives us plenty of chances to buy low and sell high. Just look at the history of the past 10 years, 1998 to 2008. During that time the Standard & Poor's (S&P) 500 index has fluctuated between 752 and 1,565. There have been five distinct, substantial swings across this range. The brief panic in 1998 arising from the Russian credit default and the failure of a big hedge fund, Long Term Capital Management, dropped the S&P nearly 20 percent, from 1,187 to 957. Those fears quickly evaporated, and the subsequent climb in prices capped a stock market bubble that was unprecedented in the financial history of the United States. The S&P rose to a high of 1,527 in March 2000, an advance of nearly 1,400 percent from its 1982 low of 102.

The biggest thrills of this stock market roller-coaster ride were yet to come. The S&P dropped nearly 50 percent during the following two years. At the index's October 2002 low of 777, investors gasped at the shocking collapse of the Internet stocks and feared that corporate accounting statements were meaningless. But the downward rush in stock prices during the preceding two years seemed to generate just the momentum needed to push the market back up to the top of its next hill. During the subsequent five years the S&P more than doubled to a closing high in October 2007 of 1,565.

As the stock market began to edge downward from its 2007 peak, no one could imagine the terrors that lay ahead. Within a year the panic of 2008 had destroyed financial institutions around the world. The rest teetered on the edge of collapse. On November 20, 2008, the S&P closed at 752 after careening downward 52 percent from its high a year earlier. Many people feared that even worse was to come.

In this book I tell you why it is so difficult for the average investor to profit from these roller-coaster swings in stock prices. I explain why it is almost impossible to consistently buy low and sell high and thus do better than the benchmark strategy of the buy-and-hold investor. Along the way

I hope to help you make an informed choice of your personal investment strategy.

You may decide that attempting to beat the market is not really a good choice for you. The emotional strain involved may just not be worth the effort. Self-knowledge like this is invaluable, worth far more than the price of this book.

Or you may choose to learn the art of contrarian trading. If so, I think you have chosen a difficult path, but I also think you have in your hands the only book in print that can help you achieve this goal.

I am a contrarian trader. I have learned my art the hard way, by making plenty of mistakes, by unknowingly becoming part of the crowd at the wrong time. You see, the reason stock prices move up and down so much is that we all like to join crowds, social groups of like-minded people. When such crowds form around investing themes in the stock market, they push stock prices too high or too low relative to fair value. Why? Crowds suppress the dissenting views of nonmembers and amplify the consensus views of their members. Crowd members act together, not independently, and when this happens the market price strays substantially from fair value.

Economic experts believe that stock prices are much more variable than warranted by fluctuations in corporate profits and dividends. I think that the constant formation and disintegration of investment crowds is responsible for this excessive variability and for the wide range over which stock prices tend to fluctuate.

Another way of putting this is to say that investment crowds are responsible for the pricing mistakes made by Mr. Market. Mr. Market is the subject of an investment parable told by the father of value investing, Benjamin Graham. Mr. Market is at your elbow each day telling you what he thinks your investment portfolio is worth. Many days his estimate seems plausible and justified by business conditions. On many other days Mr. Market lets his enthusiasm or fears run away with him, and the value he proposes seems little short of silly. Investment crowds are responsible for Mr. Market's periodic bouts of enthusiasm or fear.

If investment crowds are responsible for the pricing mistakes made by the stock market, then it logically follows that you can do better than a buy-and-hold investor if you can detect those situations in which an investment crowd has driven a stock or the entire market too high or too low relative to fair value. The method for doing this that I propose in this book rests on a simple observation.

Crowds develop and grow during a communication process called an *information cascade*. During an information cascade the print and electronic media focus public attention on recent, dramatic movements in markets and the associated profits and losses of investors. This in turn encourages people to put aside their natural skepticism and adopt the investment theme the media are highlighting. As the investment crowd thus grows larger, it pushes the market even further away from fair value and toward a substantial valuation mistake.

I think a contrarian trader can learn to take advantage of Mr. Market's periodic bouts of enthusiasm and fear by tracking information cascades in the media. I will show you how to do this by keeping a media diary. In the final third of this book I'll illustrate the use of the contrarian trader's media diary during the turbulent years beginning with the 1987 crash and continuing through the panic of 2008.

I warn you that the journey toward becoming a contrarian trader will be a difficult one with an uncertain end. Most people are simply not cut out to be contrarian traders, for they love the companionship and approval of their fellow investors too much. But if you are prepared to step away from the crowd, to make wise investment choices that the crowd will think silly or ill-advised, then this book is for you. You may also want to follow my contrarian trading views in real time. For these you can look to my blog, which currently can be found at www.carlfutia.blogspot.com.

Each of the following 16 chapters begins with a brief outline of its content. Here I want only to give you a general picture of this book's structure and the way in which it explains the process of contrarian trading.

Chapters 1 to 5 develop the foundation on which our method will rest. We answer the question of why some speculators win but most lose, and in so doing we identify the successful speculator's characteristic edge. We will see why investment crowds are responsible for market mistakes and discuss the characteristic behavior of such crowds.

Chapters 6 to 11 explain a practical approach to contrarian trading. Here we learn about the contrarian trader's principal tool, his media diary. We discover how the information contained in a media diary can be interpreted and then coordinated with a statistical view of a market's current and past swings. We also develop specific contrarian trading strategies, one for a conservative and another for an aggressive contrarian trader.

In Chapters 12 to 15 we apply the techniques explained in the preceding chapters to the stock market. I kept my own media diary in real time during the years 1987 to 2008. I think you will be surprised to see how effectively it identified the many valuation mistakes the stock market made during those years.

Chapter 16 contains a small number of very brief essays and notes I wrote for my own benefit as I learned to be a contrarian trader. It explains the development of the theory of contrary opinion, highlights the contributions key individuals made to the theory, discusses briefly several books every contrarian should read, and offers comments on back-of-the-envelope value investing for the contrarian trader.

You will notice that this book contains not a single stock market chart. There is a good reason for this. When you see a chart accompanying an explanation of a stock market technique, you also generally also see how things turned out. This makes the result of a good investment decision seem inevitable and obvious. But every real-life decision is made under conditions of great uncertainty, at a time when it is not at all obvious whether your choice will yield a subsequent profit or instead yield a loss. To convey more of the feeling of uncertainty that accompanies real investment decisions, I have chosen to focus attention only on the facts that could be known at the time the investment choice was made. This is best done without the use of charts as illustrations.

There is another reason to exclude charts from the discussion. When presented with a chart, the human eye is naturally drawn to its salient features. For a stock market chart these are usually the high and low points of prices. But one important message of this book is that the contrarian trader is not in the business of predicting stock market highs and lows or of making correct forecasts of any kind. Instead his focus is on a single objective, that of achieving a higher return than that earned by the buy-and-hold strategy. He does this by adopting an investment strategy that leans against the crowd. This does not require him to buy near low points or sell near high points in prices. It only demands that his average selling price exceeds his average buying price by an amount sufficient to compensate for risk and for the time value of money.

Writing this book has been an adventure and a pleasure. If you can take from it even one idea that improves your investment results, then I shall be doubly rewarded. Now let us begin our uncertain journey.

CARL FUTIA
November 26, 2008

CHAPTER 1

Can You Beat the Market?

The speculator's edge • traits needed for an edge • the right stuff • markets need speculators • lending a helping hand • fair value • market mistakes • uncovering mistakes • corporate profits and fair value • statistical models for profit forecasting • such models are useless • investors don't live in Lake Wobegon • evidence from mutual fund performance • technical analysis and market timing won't give you an edge • the catch-22 of investing • the No Free Lunch principle • the art of speculation • most people should not speculate • but if you have the right stuff, read on!

THE SPECULATOR'S EDGE

Can you beat the market? I'm going to do my best to convince you that the answer to this question is *no*. This surely is a novel way to start a book about speculation! Of course the name of the speculative game is beating the market. And, yes, I want you to read this book about beating the market from cover to cover and tell all your friends to do the same. But I also want you to read these chapters with your eyes wide open to the dangers and pitfalls of speculation. There is no easy money waiting for you in the financial markets. So here, right up front, is the most important thing I have to say to you: *Don't speculate unless you are sure you have an edge. Without an edge you can't beat the market.*

What do I mean by an edge? An edge is a talent or skill or some specific knowledge that will give you an advantage over other investors and speculators. Sad to say, a high IQ, great educational credentials, or a substantial net worth are *not* edges in the game of speculation. Neither is the willingness to work hard and to keep trying after repeated failures. These things may make you a success in your profession or trade and a valued member of your community. But they won't guarantee you success in the world of speculation.

You should know that the biggest part of any speculator's edge does *not* come from a superior scientific or statistical knowledge of market behavior. If it did, you could build your edge the same way you acquire skills in any profession—by study and practice. But have you noticed that no college or university offers a major in speculation? There is a good reason for this. A speculator's edge arises from two personal traits that can't be taught and that people either have or don't have. The first is flexibility of mind and spirit, the ability to adapt easily and quickly to changes in market conditions and habits. The second is the willingness to think for oneself and to risk hard-earned money by "fading" (investing opposite to) popular opinion. This means that you will usually take market positions that most people (your husband or wife especially!) will see as unwise or even foolish. Doing this day in and day out requires emotional toughness that few people can muster. It also requires a certain arrogance—a firm conviction that you know what you are doing and that most other people in the market don't. Do you have the right stuff to be a successful speculator?

I think you will agree that this is an unusual explanation of the nature of the speculator's edge. In our technological society, it's natural for people to believe that speculative profits arise from the use of superior methods or from some arcane knowledge of market behavior. But this isn't true. The essence of successful speculation cannot be found in specialized knowledge of market behavior or of trading technique. You can't learn to be a successful speculator by reading books (this one included!), by taking courses, or by attending seminars.

However, if you do have the right stuff to be a speculator, then you can move your game to a higher level by applying the methods I explain in the following chapters. The financial markets need skilled speculators. Capitalism couldn't survive without them. To see why, just keep reading.

LENDING A HELPING HAND TO INVESTORS

What is a speculator? What is his mission on capitalism's battlefield of creative destruction? Lewis and Short (my always-at-hand Latin dictionary) defines the verb *speculor* to mean "the action of watching, observing, examining or exploring." So a speculator is a lookout, a scout, an explorer, and an investigator.

A financial speculator explores the terrain ahead of the army of long-term investors. This army is advancing toward a very uncertain future, a consequence of Joseph Schumpeter's perennial *gale of creative destruction*, which always accompanies the development of a capitalist economy. Long-term investors must be assured of being able to buy and sell at a *fair price*, and this despite the enormous uncertainty that is in capitalism's very nature. If long-term investors believe that markets won't give them a fair shake, they will lock up their investment capital, and the machinery of capitalism would then grind to an impoverishing halt.

How does a speculator help ensure that long-term investors get a fair shake? Every speculator is on the lookout for mistakes the market has made in pricing a stock, bond, or commodity. A market mistake is a situation where the current market fails to accurately reflect all that is known about the probable earning power of the company or the supply-demand balance for the commodity. A speculator profits by spotting market mistakes and helping to correct them by buying when the price is too low and selling when it is too high.

A market mistake is a deviation from the *fair value price*. The phrase *fair value* is a plain-and-simple term for what economists call the *equilibrium price* (i.e., the price that will equate supply with demand). Economics teaches that the equilibrium price is an accurate reflection of what is known about the prospects of the stock or commodity in question. As such, the equilibrium price is a very good thing. People who buy or sell at the equilibrium price are getting a fair shake; they aren't being unfairly exploited by more knowledgeable investors.

It is important to remember that the concept of fair value can be difficult to pin down. In the next chapter we briefly discuss one method for calculating fair value: *discounted future dividends*. In Chapter 5 we discuss another: the *q ratio*, first developed by the economist James Tobin. Both of these methods are designed to give very long-term, multiyear estimates of the fair value price. But generally both methods are too unwieldy to be of much use to a professional speculator. We discuss more practical ways to estimate fair value in Chapter 6.

It should come as no surprise that markets make mistakes. Usually these mistakes are only short-lived, minor ones, but on occasion a market makes a really big, long-lasting mistake. Mistakes can take the form of a shortsighted reaction to a surprising corporate or economic development. Or a mistake can arise because of a mass delusion or mania. In either case, the price of the stock or commodity rises too high or falls too low relative to any reasonable assessment of fair value.

A speculator's economic function is to be on the lookout for these market mistakes and to help correct them. He does this by buying when the price is below fair value and by selling when it is above. The speculator's buying and selling thus helps to nudge the market price closer to fair value. In this way speculators perform a valuable service for longer-term investors. They help ensure that market prices more often and more closely reflect the best possible assessment of future economic prospects.

UNCOVERING MARKET MISTAKES

How does a speculator know that the market is making a mistake? You can be sure that there is no neon sign to that effect posted in front of the stock exchange. You won't see "XYZ ON SALE TODAY" or "ABC NOT WORTH AN ARM AND A LEG" running across the message board at 42nd and Broadway in New York City.

Most investors approach the problem of identifying market mistakes from an economic and statistical perspective. Basic economic considerations suggest that the fair value price for a company's stock should be determined by discounting to the present the profits the company is likely to earn over some reasonable time interval, say 10 years. You can try to estimate of these profits by modeling the industry and the economy using state-of-the-art statistical and economic tools. Or you could buy this information from someone who can do this modeling for you. In either case this profit estimate will determine an estimate of the fair value price for the stock. Detecting a market mistake is then just a matter of comparing this estimate of the fair value price with the current market price.

This certainly is a logical approach to the problem of uncovering market mistakes, at least in the stock market. Economists agree that the fair value for a corporation's common stock is the price that reflects all the information currently available about the company's future earning power, dividends, general economic conditions—everything that might be relevant to estimating the likely future dividends and capital gains an investor could expect. Investors who adopt this approach will purchase stocks that are trading below their estimates of fair value and sell stocks if they are trading above such estimates. Here is the key question: Is there any reason to believe that this method for detecting market mistakes will allow an investor to earn above-average returns?

You may find my answer to this question shocking. I believe that it is *impossible* to earn above-average returns on your investment portfolio by using statistical estimates of economic fair value. Why? Well, the key phrase is *above-average returns*. One can certainly use statistical and business knowledge to construct models for estimating fair value of a common stock that have some reliability. But you must keep in mind that speculation is a very competitive business. Many investors, money managers, and economic consultants are doing this same thing. They are all competing for the profits that can be earned by making superior estimates of a stock's fair value price.

Sadly, unlike the children of Lake Wobegon, who are all above average, investors cannot all achieve above-average investment results. Remember that lots of people have the knowledge and statistical skills to build good corporate earnings forecasting models. If building such models led to superior investment results, people would rush in and adopt this methodology. But by doing so they would collectively move market prices in the direction of their fair value estimates. This would narrow the deviation of the market price from the fair value estimates to the point where this investment technique would yield only average results. There is so much competition among model builders and the investors who pay for these models' forecasts that neither group can earn above-average returns, either by building models or by using the forecasts the models produce to guide their investment strategy!

LOOKING AT THE EVIDENCE

Perhaps I have already convinced you that competition makes it hard to speculate successfully by doing corporate profit modeling. But if not, you might counter by saying that the world in which we live is nothing like the freely competitive world of theoretical economics. Perhaps all that is needed is to build the better mousetrap, the super-duper, high-tech profit-forecasting model that will beat all others to the pot of gold. I think there is very good reason to be skeptical of this possibility. If resources and technical skills would guarantee success in the battle for investment profits, we should find that investment professionals, those who ought to have access to the best profit-forecasting models, produce better than average investment results. So let's look at the actual investment results achieved by professional money managers to see if this is true.

In a 2005 article in the *Financial Review*, "Reflections on the Efficient Market Hypothesis: 30 Years Later," volume 40, pp. 1–9, Burton Malkiel examined the performance of professional money managers in the United States and other developed countries. His data on mutual fund performance reveal three important facts. First, most actively managed stock market mutual funds underperform their benchmark index, the Standard & Poor's (S&P) 500. Over a single-year time span, 73 percent do worse than the index, and this percentage increases to 90 percent if one considers performance over a 20-year time span. Second, passively managed S&P 500 index funds do about 2 percent better per year than do actively managed stock market mutual funds. Most of this difference is accounted for by the higher fees actively managed mutual funds charge their shareholders. Finally, there is little consistency from year to year in performance relative to the benchmark by any given mutual fund. So it is impossible to tell in advance which mutual funds will do better than the benchmark using only their past performance as a guide.

Malkiel's conclusions are typical of those reached by financial economists when they examine the performances of professional money managers. From this body of research I think we must conclude that models that estimate fair value using economic and business data will *not* give you any advantage over other investors. If they did, we would expect to see above-average investment performance by stock market mutual funds, because their managers have access to the best earnings forecast models. We would also expect such market-beating performance to persist from year to year for specific mutual funds, because it is the mutual fund management firm that pays for the models and these models would be available to any manager who works for the management firm.

But we see none of these things. The conclusion to be drawn from this evidence is simple enough. If you are trying to identify the market's mistakes by using statistical models to estimate future profits, you are barking up the wrong tree. Models that forecast corporate profits can't help you beat the market, because everyone uses them. After all, this sort of approach to stock market valuation is taught in every business school. How could it give you a chance to earn above-average returns if every professional money manager knows and uses it?

MARKET TIMING

There is an even more striking conclusion to be drawn from the persistent underperformance of mutual fund money managers as a group. The logic that leads one to conclude that statistical forecasting models that forecast corporate profits can't be used to achieve market-beating investment performance has to apply to other approaches as well.

This broader category of essentially valueless methodologies includes what are popularly known as technical analysis and market timing. The idea behind technical analysis is that a market's price action reveals to the careful observer what other investors have learned about fair value. For example, investors who estimate fair value using economic and business data (so-called fundamentalist investors) reveal these estimates to the watchful and skilled market technician via the buying and selling they do to take advantage of their models' estimates. In this way a market technician believes he can piggyback his analysis upon the efforts of the fundamentalist investors. When he does this, he amplifies the effects of fundamentalists' buy and sell decisions.

In the standard technical analyst tool kit one finds various forms of price chart interpretation, momentum and moving average trading strategies, and overbought-oversold oscillator methods. These tools are too widely known and studied to help you earn above-average returns on your investments. Any advantage they might confer is soon competed away in the profit-seeking rush of technical analysts to adopt them. Of course one cannot rule out the possibility that there *are* market-beating technical methods. One can only deduce that you will not read about them in a book!

A market timer is someone who attempts to beat the market by predicting the swings in market prices ahead of time and acting on these predictions. Technical analysis typically plays a big role in most market timers' decision processes. But market timing is in general a fruitless activity for the same reason that technical analysis fails.

Think about market timing like this. If a market timer is to be successful he must be right twice in a row—he must first buy low and then sell high. So let's suppose our hypothetical market timer is quite skilled and has developed a method that predicts and takes advantage of the direction of a market's upcoming move 70 percent of the time (most methods I have seen don't come close to this success rate). The probability that this market timer is right two consecutive times is $.70 \times .70 = .49$. So even if his method guesses right 70 percent of the time, only 49 percent of the time will he improve his position over the alternative of doing nothing. For this reason the odds are that a market timer's efforts will simply make his portfolio more volatile without increasing his average returns. Even a skilled market timer will have difficulty beating the market.

CATCH-22

We have just encountered what I call the catch-22 of investing: Any statistical methodology that directly (fundamentalist approach) or indirectly (technical analysis approach) estimates fair value and that is widely used cannot help you beat the market. Economists call this the *No Free Lunch principle*. Competition among investors leads to a situation in which knowledge in the public domain can't lead to above-average investment returns. There is no information you can find in a book on investing or trading (this one included!) or you can learn at an investment seminar that will by itself help you do better than the market. Notice that this also means that it is even impossible for you, an average investor, to purchase superior investment performance by entrusting your money to a professional money manager.

So where does the No Free Lunch principle leave us? One thing seems obvious. Developing an edge over other investors cannot simply be a matter of reading some books, getting a good education, or having a high IQ. An edge cannot arise from mastery of statistical and analytical skills you can learn from books or in business school courses. The reason is simple: Lots of people do this, and what lots of people do won't make you an above-average investor.

I think that to develop an edge you must start by abandoning preconceived ideas. You are making a good start if you have read this far. You must learn to be suspicious of popular opinion and conventional wisdom. Indeed, the entire art of speculation consists of choosing the right moment to invest in a way opposite to that suggested by popular opinion. An edge can be found only by living by one's wits in a world where survival and prosperity are daily question marks. I have seen firsthand that maintaining this kind of edge extracts an emotional and mental toll that very few people can pay. For the vast majority, an investment edge is just not worth the effort it takes to acquire and maintain it. It makes no sense for most people to speculate in the financial markets.

Well, I have done my best to convince you that you should not speculate. But if you still think you have the right stuff, you will find a lot of useful information and suggestions in the rest of this book. I'll try to explain what you must do to hone your speculative skills. I can summarize my message very simply: Become a professional contrarian!

CHAPTER 2

Market Mistakes

Efficient markets? not! • *markets make mistakes* • *"no free lunch" means that mistakes are hard to identify* • *roller coasters and stock markets* • *do stock prices fluctuate too much?* • *Shiller's work on stock market volatility* • *efficient markets theory can't explain volatility* • *behavioral finance* • *why might market mistakes persist?* • *the unknown unknown* • *the last one to know* • *the lunatic factor* • *markets do not make systematic mistakes* • *Fama's work* • *No Free Lunch redux* • *looking for the edge*

EFFICIENT MARKETS

In Chapter 1 I explained that a speculator's job is to discover market mistakes and then help to nudge the market price back to fair value. I boldly asserted that markets make lots of mistakes. But you should know that there are respected theories in financial economics that assert that markets never make mistakes. These theories say that markets are strongly efficient, that at every moment the market accurately reflects all that can be deduced from economic analysis and technical market methods about today's fair value market price.

If markets really were efficient in this strong sense, there would be no room for speculators to make a profit. In this chapter I want to explain why I think markets are *not* efficient in this strong sense. I want to argue that, as a matter of fact and not opinion, markets rarely trade at the fair value, economic equilibrium price. I want to convince you that at least in

9

principle there are many opportunities for speculators to make a profit. To do this, we'll have to take a close look at the reasons markets spend extended periods of time trading well above or well below fair value. This investigation will carry us into the realm of behavioral finance, investor sentiment, and crowd behavior. To keep things simple, I am going to focus on the mistakes made by markets for common stocks in the United States, although all financial markets worldwide are mistake-prone as well.

Keep in mind that the No Free Lunch principle tells us that markets do not make lots of *statistically exploitable* mistakes. In other words, financial markets' mistakes show no statistical regularities and can be used to predict and identify these mistakes as they are happening. The reason for this bears repeating: There are large numbers of speculators and investors on the lookout for market mistakes, and they are willing to use any plausible statistical method to uncover these mistakes. Competition among speculators will reduce the returns earned by their statistical methodologies to the returns earned by the buy-and-hold strategy. The No Free Lunch principle predicts that every mistake a market makes will be a surprise at the time it is happening. To the vast majority of investors, market mistakes will be visible only in hindsight. So market mistakes will be very hard to detect and exploit at the time they occur. Sadly, a speculator cannot profit from 20/20 hindsight, so the No Free Lunch principle is telling us that successful speculators are a rare breed—people who have skills and characteristics that cannot be taught or easily discovered. *It is my thesis that the successful speculator's edge rests on his ability to stand apart from the crowd and to act opposite to the crowd's beliefs and expectations.*

ROLLER COASTERS AND STOCK MARKETS

When the financier John Pierpont Morgan (1837–1913) was asked for his stock market forecast he replied, "Stocks will fluctuate." There is more wisdom in his reply than meets the eye. Morgan understood the implications of the No Free Lunch principle, because he made no attempt to predict whether the stock market was about to move higher or lower. He spoke as if he believed that all the factors that might influence the market's movements were already reflected in the level of current prices. Future price changes would therefore be responses to new and currently unknowable information. But he also emphasized that stocks would "fluctuate." We shall soon see that this is an enduring characteristic of the stock market, and indeed of all financial markets.

Do you have fun riding roller coasters? Frankly, they are not my cup of tea, but my children love them. I think stock markets are a lot like roller coasters. Prices always seem to be in motion—up or down. At the start of a bull market, stock prices, like the start of a roller coaster's ride, move slowly but steadily higher. They seem to be climbing a steep hill pulled by improvements in underlying economic conditions and corporate profits. As the market reaches the top of the hill, its advance slows, flattens out, and then prices gradually soften. Soon the market is hurtling downhill as if pulled by gravity, its riders screaming in panic. Fear replaces optimism, but just when the stock prices appear ready to plunge to zero and economic depression seems imminent, the market springs upward. It is as if the very momentum of the previous stomach-churning drop has combined with an invisible turn of the track to push prices higher once more. The path to the next bull market peak will no doubt take the market through several hair-raising twists, turns, and loops. It will be lots of fun, but everyone knows that another terrifying drop lies dead ahead. Its all part of the roller-coaster experience.

Imagine having to ride a roller coaster whenever you had to travel to work from home. How would you feel if a roller coaster was the only available mode of transportation you had? I suppose you could get used to it. But you would be traveling many more miles (many of them in the vertical direction!) than you do now in your car. Not only would your travel times lengthen, but (at least for me) just getting to the grocery store would be a nerve-racking experience.

Investors have no choice but to ride the market roller coaster. Its ups and downs seem designed to defeat all but those with the strongest stomachs. And, just like a roller coaster, the market's movements are in a certain sense artificial. At least from an economic perspective, they are not justified by ups and downs in underlying economic conditions and corporate profits. Instead they reflect something that seems inherent in the very nature of the process that prices corporate assets.

Professor Robert J. Shiller is among the word's experts in the study of the behavior of speculative markets. In March 2000, with an exquisite sense of market timing in the publishing world, the book for which he is justifiably famous, *Irrational Exuberance* (Princeton University Press), shook the world of Wall Street. In it Shiller argued that the great stock market boom that had started in 1982 was displaying all the signs of a bubble, that every indicator of economic value showed that investors were *irrationally exuberant*. They were placing unreasonably high valuations on prospective corporate profits and dividends. We all know what happened next. In March 2000 the S&P 500 began a drop that eventually carried it 50 percent lower by October 2002. The NASDAQ Composite index, home to the

Internet and technology highfliers of 1998–2000, dropped 80 percent during the same time. Some fluctuation!

Yet the bull market of 1982–2000 and the ensuing three-year bear market were by no means unprecedented events, as Shiller shows in *Irrational Exuberance*. He is in a position to know. Indeed, Professor Shiller's entire career had been devoted to the study of speculative markets and to investigating whether market fluctuations are in any sense determined and justified by economic developments and changes in corporate profits. The results of his investigations were published 11 years earlier in his book *Market Volatility* (MIT Press, 1989). They provide important information about the frequency and extent of the stock market's mistakes.

DO STOCK PRICES FLUCTUATE TOO MUCH?

In Chapter 4 of *Market Volatility* Shiller adopted the standard economic hypothesis for determining the fair value of the stock market. This says that the long-term fair value price for the Standard & Poor's Composite 500 stock market index should be taken to be the present discounted value of future dividend payouts. This standard approach to asset valuation would apply not just to common stocks but to any other asset (e.g., bonds, real estate. etc.) that is expected to yield a regular sequence of cash payouts over the foreseeable future. Of course, at any point in time one doesn't actually know what these future dividends will be, say over the next 30 years, but Shiller's economic model assumes that you do. You might object that such an assumption is ridiculous on its face. But it turns out that the discounted stream of dividends is very predicable and grows at a nearly constant rate. So in this sense Shiller's "perfect foresight" assumption is a reasonable one because dividend payouts for the stock market as a whole are quite predictable.

Having this estimate of the stock market's fair value price in hand, Shiller then compares it with the actual level of the S&P Composite 500 index. Both these numbers change from year to year, and Shiller compares the variability of the S&P Composite over time with the variability of the discounted stream of futures dividends. He finds that prices are in the long run about four times as volatile as the discounted stream of dividends. Moreover, the correlation between the changes in the level of the S&P Composite index and the changes in the value of the long-run stream of dividends is very low. This is surprising, at least to economists. Efficient markets theory predicts that stock market prices should show less variability than discounted dividends, and that changes in stock market prices should be highly correlated with changes in the discounted value of dividends.

What should we make of these facts? At an intuitive level at least, most investors would find Shiller's conclusions unsurprising. Indeed, they might marvel that anyone would suggest that the discounted stream of future dividends should determine fair value in the stock market. "After all," they would say, "we care far more about earnings growth than dividend payouts, and our profit forecasting models take this difference into account." But such a response misses the point. The fact is that economy-wide earnings and economy-wide dividends move in lockstep over time. True, any individual company may be seen as a "growth opportunity" or as a "steady dividend payer" by individual investors, but this is a distinction without a difference when looking at the economy as a whole and when trying to understand the source of price fluctuations in the S&P Composite index. If stock prices are *not* determined by the long-run dividends and earnings generated by corporations in the U.S. economy, *what does determine them?* In this situation I believe that the sage of Omaha, Warren Buffett, would accept the broad outline of Shiller's approach. Buffett has often quoted Benjamin Graham's saying that in the short run the stock market is a voting machine, but in the long run it is a weighing machine. By this he means that the value of a company's common stock is determined in the long run by the company's ability to earn profits and pay out dividends to its shareholders.

Some economists have criticized Shiller's calculations by observing that the growth of dividends from year to year is better described as a random walk than as a process that fluctuates around a known trend. If this is true, one would in general expect more volatility in stock prices than Shiller's model would predict. (In technical terms these economists are saying that the series of dividends is not stationary, contrary to Shiller's assumption.) But it turns out that even when this different statistical model of the behavior of dividends is adopted, the stock prices still fluctuate far too much relative to long-run dividend fluctuations.

The basic conclusion of Shiller's research is that the efficient markets model does not do well in explaining stock market volatility. This no doubt cheers investors who have grown weary of economists' employing efficient markets theory as a club to beat them into accepting the futility of trying to beat the market. It is clear from Shiller's data that the stock market as a whole makes lots of mistakes—the S&P Composite index fluctuates in a wide range around fair value as measured by discounted future dividends. But those who would take satisfaction from this defeat of the efficient markets theory should be wary. The No Free Lunch phenomenon still rules the investment world. Stock markets may indeed make many mistakes, but it is generally impossible to recognize these mistakes when they occur! But might thinking outside the box of standard financial theory and looking at different sorts of data help us identify and exploit the mistakes of the sort Shiller detected?

A LOOK AT BEHAVIORAL FINANCE

To answer this last question we have to take a look at the reasons stock market prices might deviate from fair value. This will take us into the realm of what is known as behavioral finance, a branch of economics. Classical economics studies the behavior of markets in which people buy and sell using all the information they have in a statistically appropriate way. But what if human psychology or computational limitations prevents this? What if a significant number of investors, for whatever reason, fail to use information available to them correctly? How would this affect the behavior of the stock market? Must it inevitably cause the market to make mistakes? Behavioral economics addresses these sorts of questions.

Richard Thaler is a professor at the University of Chicago and a widely recognized expert in behavioral finance. Together with his co-author, Nicholas Barbaris, Thaler wrote a recent survey of behavioral finance that appears as Chapter 1 in *Advances in Behavioral Finance, Volume 2* (Richard Thaler, ed.; Princeton University Press, 2005). Thaler and Barbaris discuss the many reasons why investors might psychologically be unable to make good statistical use of the information they have. Indeed, they point to the ample experimental evidence showing that this is a pervasive phenomenon, that people fail to use a sound statistical approach when making choices under uncertainty.

However, as Barbaris and Thaler point out, the fact that a segment of the investor population acts irrationally in this sense does not necessarily imply that markets make mistakes. After all, if some people make statistical errors and consequently drive the price of a stock away from its fair value price, shouldn't a rational investor be able to take advantage of this mistake by taking the opposite action and profiting as the price returns to fair value?

To this question the behavioral economist answers "perhaps," but the classical economist answers "always." Here lies the essential difference between behavioral theories of financial markets and the classical efficient markets hypothesis. Let's examine the reasons why rational investors might not be able to correct the mistakes made by irrational investors.

Every trading and investment strategy has its associated costs and risks. Costs arise from the process of buying and selling itself (brokerage commissions, bid-ask spreads, etc.) as well as from the expense of gathering and processing information correctly. Risks arise from the usual uncertainties associated with asset pricing as well as from institutional factors resulting from the way markets are organized. A simple example of this is short selling. If a rational investor recognizes that a stock is selling above its fair market price and he wants to participate in this selling, he may not be able to sell the stock if he does not already own it. To do so he must borrow the shares from a willing lender, and this not only requires the cooperation of two parties but the payment of interest on the loan of the shares. Moreover, the market for borrowing these shares may be very thin and may expose the short seller to added risk of a squeeze by the lender. Thus, even if the shares can be borrowed, the costs and risks of short selling are not symmetrically placed with those of buying the stock in question. For this reason alone, one might expect the stock market to be more prone to make mistakes of overvaluation than of undervaluation.

But there are three other kinds of risk associated with attempts to correct market mistakes—risks that are rarely considered, probably because experienced speculators don't usually put their thoughts on paper.

The first is the risk of the *unknown unknown*. This is just a snappy way of describing what the economist Frank Knight called *uncertainty* in his 1921 book *Risk, Uncertainty, and Profit*. Knightian uncertainty, nowadays called unquantifiable risk, is a situation in which we cannot even imagine the things we don't know (hence the term *unknown unknown*). And even if we can imagine them, we have no way to attach probabilities to them. A good example of Knightian uncertainty developed during the panic of 2008 market turmoil arising from the subprime lending mess. We'll discuss this episode in greater detail later. For now I just want to point out that no one then had a grip on just how much toxic waste (a technical term used by financial types to describe assets that cannot be sold) was to be found on the balance sheets of a number of big banks and brokerage firms, nor on how such securities could be valued. Consequently, the markets for all kinds of securities took a tumble and buyers were hard to find—all because no one could even estimate the magnitude of a problem that had never arisen before. This is a classic case of the danger of the unknown unknown.

The second kind of risk I like to call "the last one to know" risk. When I think a market is making a mistake, the first thought that comes to my mind is: "What if other people know something I don't?" My experience has been that every investor has the same fear of being the last to know. We will see that this plays an important role in causing markets to make mistakes. It certainly makes it difficult for the average investor to play any role in correcting these same mistakes.

The third risk is just as significant as the other two, perhaps more so. It is the risk associated with what I call the *lunatic factor*. Years of experience have taught me to ask, upon seeing what looks like a market mistake, whether the lunatics have taken over the asylum. It is important never to underestimate the buying or selling power of a crowd of market lunatics who are acting under the influence of some financial delusion or emotion, whether greed or (more commonly) fear. When the lunatics take over the market asylum, any market mistake can and probably will get a lot worse before it is corrected. In such a situation, rational calculation of underlying economic factors must yield to attempts to outguess the thinking processes and behavior of the lunatics. In such circumstances the market price can be nearly indeterminate, and the risks inherent in attempting to correct market mistakes are inordinately high.

We see then that there are costs and risks associated with the effort to correct a market mistake. If these are substantial, we would expect the mistake to persist and even get worse before it is corrected.

BEHAVIORAL FINANCE AND EXPLOITABLE MARKET MISTAKES

Behavioral finance gives us reason to believe that markets can trade at levels different from the fair value price. So, certainly one can then expect that there will be plenty of market mistakes that an interested speculator can exploit. But wait a minute! Have we forgotten the catch-22 of investing? How does the No Free Lunch principle affect this situation? If a speculator is to correct a market mistake, he must first have some way of identifying it as it happens. Is there some statistical method that enables us to recognize the mistakes predicted by the theory of behavioral economics when they occur?

If we take the No Free Lunch principle seriously (and I do), then we are forced to a sad conclusion. Despite the insights generated by behavioral finance into the behavior of real investors, the effects on market prices of these departures from rational behavior cannot be predictable. They cannot exhibit any statistical regularity that can be exploited by a speculator. But we can't be satisfied with deducing this using pure reason alone. Let's look at the evidence.

In his paper "Market Efficiency, Long Run Returns, and Behavioral Finance" (*Journal of Financial Economics* 49 (1998), 283–306) Eugene Fama investigates the claims that behavioral finance has found evidence that undermines the efficient markets hypothesis. He observes that the classical efficient markets hypothesis is rarely, if ever, compared statistically with an explicitly formulated alternative. In other words, the behavioral economists who point out that the efficient markets hypothesis fails to statistically explain certain market phenomena rarely offer any specific statistical model as an alternative. The predictions of behavioral finance are rarely made in a form that can be systematically compared with market data. Fama tries to make such comparisons in his paper. He finds that the empirical literature on market mistakes does not reach any unified conclusions as to the nature and direction of these mistakes. In other words, there is no behavioral theory that predicts the exact kind of mistake a market will make in a particular context.

Fama concludes that while the classical efficient markets theory has its weak spots, no one has come up with any theory, behavioral or not, which is more successful in explaining the behavior of financial markets. In other words, he confirms the No Free Lunch principle.

NO FREE LUNCH REDUX

Where does this leave us? We have seen that there can be little doubt that markets make mistakes. They fluctuate far more than does any reasonable notion of fair value. Markets underreact and overreact to news and to economic developments. But the No Free Lunch principle guarantees that these mistakes will be very hard to exploit systematically using available statistical techniques. *There can be no theory of market mistakes that both confronts the data successfully and can be exploited by a typical speculator to earn above-average returns.*

Discouraging as this state of affairs may be to a prospective speculator, I think that one can progress only by confronting it squarely and thinking about its implications. The No Free Lunch principle is telling us that success in speculation must rest on personal traits, on abilities outside the reach of the majority of investors. It must also rest upon some arcane understanding of market behavior and of the behavior of investors and other speculators. Lewis and Short define the Latin adjective *arcanus* to mean a thing that is hidden, concealed, secret, or private. To beat the market, one must develop and exploit a kind of skill that is inaccessible to most people. To discover the nature of this skill, we must turn our gaze inward. We must focus on human nature and the social relations that are the warp and woof of the world in which we live. It is here in the speculator's relationship to crowds, in his ability to identify them, and in his ability to stand apart and act differently from them that his edge may be found.

CHAPTER 3

The Edge

A theory of market mistakes • investment crowds • a theory most people cannot exploit • the source of a speculator's profit • to get along, go along • Keynes the speculator • dangers of succeeding unconventionally • the value of social groups • go along and create a mistake • social groups in the world of investments • investment themes • peak oil • life cycle of an investment crowd • the boom and bust of 1996–2002 • the social calculus of crowds • the vision of a contrarian trader • a contrarian trader's edge

A THEORY OF MARKET MISTAKES

In this chapter and the next we are going to develop a theory of market mistakes. Our theory will identify social interactions among investors as the probable cause of price movements away from the fair value price. We will see that the cooperative organization of industrial society encourages the formation of social groups whose focus is on this or that financial market. I think these groups can be aptly named *investment crowds*. The word *crowd* is intended to convey the idea that the group's members show an unusual unity of purpose, thought, explanation, and expectation. A crowd is not simply a collection of individuals, each of whom makes choices independently of the other people in the crowd. Instead, crowd members imitate each other. Indeed a crowd is a kind of social *black hole* because it relentlessly attracts people into its orbit of thought and action.

We focus our attention in this chapter on the general fact that investment crowds are like other social groups because they make it easier for their members to survive and prosper in society. The human species stands out among earth's creatures in its instinctive drive and ability to form and cooperate in large social groups. Indeed, it cannot be far from the truth to assert that this cooperative instinct is responsible for the rapid development of human society over its relatively short recorded history. Our motto could be that *social groups make life easier and safer.* Everyone knows this to be true. Consequently people are willing to join social groups and are even willing to suffer inconvenience or other costs to be members. Among these costs are a certain sacrifice of independence in thought and action. Every member of a social group cedes to the group some part of his autonomy.

This perspective has particular implications for investment crowds. Even though individual investors may have the resources and skills required for rational calculation, such calculations play only a minor role in the life of the crowd. Moreover, people may willingly join investment crowds even when an inevitable consequence is below-average investment performance arising because on average the crowd's members buy above fair value and sell below it. The rewards of membership in investment crowds are usually not financial ones.

If our theory is to be of value, it must offer us guidance as speculators and investors. It must identify observable phenomena that are associated with market mistakes *at the time they occur*, not just in hindsight. These phenomena will be discussed in detail in subsequent chapters. For the moment I am content to emphasize the following point: *It is the ability to identify an investment crowd, to determine the crowd's position in its life cycle, and then to act rationally on these deductions that constitutes a speculator's edge.* A speculator is successful only to the extent that he is willing to be *antisocial* in the investment context.

Straightaway we run into a problem. The No Free Lunch principle asserts that there can be no theory of market mistakes *that can be exploited by the typical speculator* to earn above-average returns. How can I reconcile this with my intent to develop a *comprehensible* theory of market mistakes based on the action of investment crowds? Won't any such theory enable the average investor on the street to beat the market?

The resolution of this conundrum will be found in the observation that our theory *cannot* be exploited by the typical speculator. More than 40 years of observations of markets and investors have convinced me that most people cannot exploit the implications of any crowd-based theory of market mistakes. The reason is simple: To do so would require them to sever many of the social bonds that connect them to the investment community. It would require them to become antisocial in the investment world, setting themselves apart from investment crowds instead of being *a part* of them. I believe that the social bonds associated with investment crowds are valued by investors not primarily for financial reasons but rather for the satisfaction found in making connections with people with common interests. In fact, I believe that it would be irrational for most people to sacrifice the satisfaction arising from crowd participation on the altar of financial gain. Thus, from an economic point of view, it makes sense to regard this financial cost to a typical individual (the opportunity cost of below-average investment results) of participating in investment crowds as the source of a speculator's profit.

TO GET ALONG, GO ALONG

> *Worldly wisdom teaches that it is better for reputation to fail conventionally than to succeed unconventionally.*
> —John Maynard Keynes, *The General Theory of Employment, Interest, and Money*

This observation by John Maynard Keynes appears amidst a brilliant analysis of investor expectations and their role in speculative activity in the stock market. Few people know that Keynes himself was a very successful speculator when he wasn't contributing to debates on macroeconomic policy. For a brief description of Keynes' roller-coaster experiences in the markets, I recommend that you read Chapter 21 of *Hedgehogging* by Barton Biggs (John Wiley & Sons, 2006).

Why might failing conventionally be better for one's reputation than succeeding unconventionally? We need not go far to discover the reason. It is a true (and therefore trite) observation that human beings are social animals. Success achieved by acting contrary to social conventions, contrary to beliefs and values shared by one's fellows, necessarily diminishes a person's standing within his communities and in the larger society. Antisocial behavior is rarely if ever rewarded.

Social groups naturally form among individuals with common interests. They may be biologically related, share vocations, live near one another, have similar personalities, and so on. But there is another side to this coin. Anyone whose behavior is seen to be outside the norm for his group, who develops a reputation for being different, runs the risk of being cast out to the group's fringes. Having to live on the fringes of the group (or entirely outside it) can make performing the day-to-day tasks required for survival difficult or even impossible. The group can exist and protect its members only if they cooperate with one another. Thus membership in social groups entails obligations as well as benefits. Among these obligations are acceptance of group beliefs and the willingness to act in conformity with group expectations. Put another way, group membership is open only to those who are good cooperators.

Eccentrics are by definition people who are not good cooperators. As Keynes observed, doing anything unconventionally is dangerous for one's reputation and is potentially harmful to one's good standing in a social group. For this reason our social antennae are finely tuned to pick up signals from our friends and associates that we are somehow not meeting group expectations for our behavior and opinions. When we pick up these warning signals we instantly feel uncomfortable, and with good reason. Survival and prosperity depend on being accepted as a member in good standing in all of our social groups.

People who are good at going along with other members of their social groups get along well in life and in the worlds of work and business. They are well connected and are generally the first to gain valuable information about new opportunities available to group members. There is good reason for this. *Social relationships are highways for new ideas and for life-sustaining information about our environment.* In each social group there are explorers and innovators, people who are the first to notice a new opportunity to improve their lives in the economic, social, or political sphere. The news about these new opportunities moves along the highway formed by their relationships with other members of their social groups. In this way all members of a group can benefit from the information that is gathered by only a few. The information highways formed by social bonds make it possible for the entire group to adapt quickly and respond successfully to new and possibly life-threatening circumstances.

We see then that the development of strong social bonds confers a number of evolutionary advantages. Acting conventionally and conforming to group norms and expectations for behavior and belief strengthen an individual's bonds with the group. It is no surprise, then, that Homo sapiens and his ancestors have survived on this earth for millions of years precisely because individuals are born with the instinctual needs and skills for forming and strengthening these social bonds. People value social bonds for their own sake because they understand, if only at an intuitive level, that strong social bonds can assure their survival and their prosperity.

GO ALONG AND CREATE A MISTAKE

The world of finance and investments is a microcosm of society itself. Within the world of finance there are many overlapping social groups. We are interested in a particular sort of social group, the investment crowd.

One identifying mark of an investment crowd is that it consists of individuals whose attention is focused around an *investment theme*.

An investment theme is a *system* of belief asserting that some asset is likely to yield investment returns that are well above (or below) average. Investment themes are generally associated with a specific class of assets (stocks, bonds, commodities, real estate, etc.); with the stock of a specific company (e.g., Google); with the stocks in a specific industry group or related groups (technology, dot-coms, telecommunications, energy, etc.); or with specific commodities (e.g., oil, gold, silver, soybeans, wheat, corn).

I have emphasized the word *system* because the investment theme of a crowd must always have an underlying economic logic that is easy to state and appeals to ordinary people. It is even better if the internal logic of the investment theme squares with facts people can personally experience. This system of belief must lead naturally to the conclusion that the market on which the crowd is focused will yield superior investment returns. This weightiness of the crowd's theme is essential for it to be persuasive. It is what makes the crowd capable of attracting new members and permits the crowd to grow large enough to cause a market to make a substantial mistake.

Not all market-investment-themed social groups that can be found in the world of finance become investment crowds. For this to happen, a trigger or precipitating event is needed. Generally this precipitating event is a big or sustained change in the market price of the asset on which the group is focused. This change has to be in the direction the group's theme has predicted. When the market price changes in a dramatic and predicted fashion, the group begins to attract the attention of investors and the general public who had not been aware of this investment theme. The price change has presumably made early adherents to the investment theme wealthy. This adds enormous credibility to the logic of the investment theme.

It is at this point that an investment-themed social group begins its transformation into an investment crowd. To the outside world the group appears smart and successful, and lots of people want to be part of a rising and prominent social group. The natural social process of imitation kicks in, and the pressure to conform to a visibly successful investment strategy rises. These forces join to create an investment crowd whose members exhibit a unity of thought and action not typical of a large, randomly chosen group of individuals who participate in a given market.

A good example of this phenomenon is the *peak oil* investment crowd. Peak oil believers assert that worldwide production of crude oil will reach its peak sometime during the first decade or two of the twenty-first century. The implication is that crude oil prices have nowhere to go but upward. One important reason a large social group has grown around the peak oil theme is that ordinary people experience its implications every time they fill up their automobiles' gas tanks. This reinforcing personal experience is a very important factor that helps transform an investment-themed social group into an investment crowd. The theme's logic has to be something that can be concretely experienced by ordinary individuals, not just by investment professionals.

Crude oil traded as low as $11 per barrel in 1998 after falling from a high price of $40 in 1990. The peak oil theme had only a small number of adherents in 1998, although its logic was as strong then as it is now, 10 years later. But it was only after the price had moved up more than 400 percent to a new high above $40 in 2004 that the peak oil theme began to attract significant numbers of adherents and an investment crowd began to form around this theme. This investment crowd is still growing as I write this in July 2008 with oil around the $130 level.

Notice that the peak oil social group began its transformation into an investment crowd only after the price of crude oil had moved up 400 percent over a period of six years. *This is the single most useful clue that an investment crowd is in the process of forming.* Even though the underlying economic logic of peak oil made as much sense in 1998 as it did in 2004, it took a dramatic price advance in crude oil to new historical highs to convince people that the logic was correct and potentially profitable. *The price change itself was taken as confirming evidence for the validity of the theme.*

This is a nearly universal characteristic of investment crowds. Any social group's growth is fed by the success of its founding members. An investment crowd's growth is stimulated by the financial success of its early adherents. They have gotten rich from a dramatic upward move in the price of some asset. The financial success of early innovators provides the fuel to drive the new investment theme along the highways of social connections and thus increase the numbers of converts to the theme's logic. An investment crowd forms as the group attracts adherents who have no particular expertise or experience with the theme's asset.

It is at this juncture that the formation of an investment crowd causes the market to begin its departure from fair value. New members of the crowd accept the investment theme as proven to be correct because of the big change in market price they have observed. They no longer attempt independent assessments of the relationship of price to fair value and instead accept the onward and upward assertion of fellow crowd members at face value. This willing suspension of independent thought by crowd members is the explanation for the market mistake associated with the crowd. *As the crowd's size grows, its collective market position forces the market price much higher than any reasonable estimate of fair value.* The resulting bubble may well keep the market price too high for a sustained period of time if the group's social bonds are strong and continually reinforced. But eventually all such bubbles must deflate as the underlying forces of economic competition assert themselves and drive the profitability of the associated businesses down to normal levels.

This pattern of the life cycle of an investment crowd can be seen in several other investment crowds that formed in the stock market during the boom and bust of 1996–2002. During these years several investment crowds formed around the themes of Internet retailing, telecom growth, and computer equipment/software. Belief in the transformative power of the Internet, the computer, and telecommunications was strong, and the stocks of new companies associated with these themes soared even when no evidence of profits existed. The wild fluctuations associated with the resulting stock market boom gave birth to a day-trading crowd. Its members bought and sold stocks several times each day hoping to outguess their fellows about the effects of the latest news on their favorite stocks and to profit from the wide intraday fluctuations that were common at the time.

That these crowds force the stock market into a mistake of general overvaluation is no longer disputed, although at the time most people refused to acknowledge this possibility. Once a crowd has attracted all the adherents it can, an inevitable process of disintegration begins. When a large investment crowd disintegrates, the market that is its focus typically moves from overvaluation to undervaluation with no stop in between. Remember the roller coaster!

This process is well illustrated by the sequel to the 1996–2000 boom. During the 2000–2002 bear market in stock prices, the NASDAQ Composite index (home to the Internet, computer, and telecom stocks) fell from the 5,000 level to 1,100, a drop of almost 80 percent. The stocks of the old bricks-and-mortar economy did not escape this washout. Their home, the S&P 500 index, fell 50 percent during the same bear market.

The demise of these investment crowds was so traumatic that in reaction another investment crowd formed in 2002. Its theme was that everyone associated with Wall Street was a crook and that stock prices had to go even lower than they had already fallen. The 2000–2002 bear market experience made this logic seem very plausible, and as a result many otherwise sane investors dramatically reduced the common stock portions of their portfolios. The beliefs of this crowd kept stock prices too low relative to fair value during the second half of 2002. But this crowd, too, began its inevitable disintegration in 2003. Over the next five years the market averages doubled.

THE SOCIAL CALCULUS OF CROWDS

Why must the social groups associated with investment themes so often turn into investment crowds and force prices well above or below fair value? Why must investment crowds be a common feature of the financial landscape? I have argued that people want and need to belong to social groups. The incentive to join successful groups is strong. After all, such groups play important roles in alerting their members to new opportunities for social and economic advancement. And usually one can make a lot of money (at least for a while) by investing with the investment theme of a group. But more than this, membership in a successful group can be its own reward. People often find satisfaction and gain prestige among their friends and family through their membership in socially and financially prominent groups. One need only recall the kudos collected by dot-com investors and entrepreneurs, venture capitalists, and even day traders during the 1999–2000 stock market bubble in the United States.

These considerations imply that people should be willing to pay a price for their membership in an investment crowd. As long as this price is seen to be less than the benefit associated with group membership, the crowd will grow. What are the costs of group membership? And how do these balance against the financial and nonfinancial rewards of group membership?

For investment crowds, the primary cost of group membership manifests itself only near the end of a crowd's life cycle. Once the crowd's investment theme has driven market prices too high or too low, the inevitable return of the asset price to fair value causes the crowd's late joiners to incur substantial investment losses. And it has been my observation that the majority of members of any investment crowd join only after the asset is priced above fair value (for a bullish investment theme) or below fair value (for a bearish one). It is important to remember that this sort of cost is unique to investment crowds and is not generally associated with membership in any other type of social group. For this reason it is not likely to be anticipated by people who have little experience as members of investment crowds.

Against these costs must be laid the benefits of crowd membership. As I have said, social approval and prestige are the principal benefits. But one must keep in mind that investment crowds develop precisely because the group's early joiners and innovators achieved very much above-average investment returns. These above-average returns act as a kind of social beacon lighting the night of investment uncertainty. Every crowd member is attracted by this beacon and motivated superficially by the prospect of duplicating this above-average investment performance.

Of course such optimistic expectations will result in disappointment for the majority of the investment crowd, those who adopt the investment theme late in the crowd's life cycle. For this reason the pursuit of an investment theme is often said to reflect ill-informed or even economically irrational choices by many individuals. Many economists would adopt this view but I do not accept it.

First of all, I think the typical investor is likely to join only a single investment crowd in his investment lifetime. The drop in asset value as the crowd disintegrates is traumatic and leads the investor to a vow never to repeat the mistake again. Thus most members of any substantial investment crowd are novices—not repeated joiners of multiple crowds—and so have no statistical basis upon which to predict the outcome of their crowd membership. Secondly, as I have emphasized there are nonfinancial considerations that enter into the calculus of choice for people in this context. Joining social groups and maintaining membership ties are generally good things in themselves. A person's network of social groups is the warp and woof of his life in society. Consequently, the life strategy of joining successful and prestigious social groups is one that we all naturally adopt. That this may often prove to be a costly error when joining investment crowds does not much diminish its value as a generally successful survival strategy in society.

We see then that people have a strong incentive to join investment crowds, not just in the hope of achieving superior investment returns but also because joining prominent and prestigious social groups is a good survival strategy in all social realms. Investment crowds differ from many other social groups in that they generally have limited life spans. Moreover, the majority of members in such groups are likely to suffer significantly below-average investment results. Yet the cost of below-average investment performance—if it can be recognized and calculated at all—can be seen as largely offset by the prestige and satisfaction associated with joining prominent and (temporarily) successful social groups. And it is the opportunity cost of this below-average investment performance that is the source of a speculator's profit.

THE VISION OF A CONTRARIAN TRADER

Why is it important to understand investment crowds? I have argued that large investment crowds are associated with significant market mistakes, situations in which the price of a stock, bond, or commodity is forced too high or too low relative to its fair value. If this is true, then a speculator can potentially earn above-average returns by exploiting this connection. One need only watch for the emergence of an investment crowd. As the crowd grows, it makes sense to invest in harmony with the crowd's investment theme. But eventually the crowd grows so large that it forces the market price well past fair value. At this point the investor needs to either step aside from the crowd's theme investment or even invest in an opposite theme.

This is the strategic vision of the *contrarian trader*. I use the word *trader* here instead of the word *investor* because I believe that market mistakes are generally temporary ones. A contrarian trader does not intend to hold an investment over several bull and bear cycles. Instead he is focused on taking advantage of a market price that is above or below fair value and will later abandon his position when the market returns to its fair value price. There is no such thing as a long-run investment for a contrarian trader. His business is exploiting market mistakes arising from the growth of an investment crowd but then stepping aside from his investment as the life cycle of the crowd inevitably returns price to fair value.

To implement this contrarian trading strategy, one must become skilled in discovering emerging and/or popular investment themes and in evaluating the strength and stage of development of the associated crowd. One must learn to understand the role the news media play in reinforcing and popularizing investment themes. In addition, one must develop the skills needed to place this information in its proper market context. In other words, one must learn to compare the market performance of the investment theme's asset to historical norms and to the performance of other markets. Subsequent chapters explain how you may begin to develop these skills.

Why does the contrarian trader have an edge on the average investor? How is it possible for him to earn above-average returns? Why doesn't the No Free Lunch principle apply equally to the contrarian strategy discussed in this book? What is the source of the contrarian trader's or investor's edge?

The simple fact is that a contrarian trader must by definition be a nonconformist to be successful. This is the key to understanding the difficulties and the opportunities associated with a contrarian stance toward markets.

I have argued that every person is born with an instinct to join social groups and cultivate social bonds with other individuals. Such instincts and social skills endow individuals with an evolutionary advantage. For this reason one expects and observes that people are far more comfortable accepting the conventional wisdom of their social groups and acting in accord with such conventions. This is true of investment crowds no less than of groups that form the larger society in which we all live. Yet a contrarian trader must place himself *apart* from investment crowds. By choice he becomes a kind of social outcast in the world of investments, the very world to which he has chosen to devote so much time, energy, and money. Few people can comfortably live with this sort of emotional dissonance. And this internal conflict is always felt most acutely when the financial stakes are highest, when the groupthink phenomenon associated with investment crowds is most intense.

This is why there are so few contrarian investors, even among professional money managers. Every professional money manager knows that it is better "to fail conventionally than to succeed unconventionally." Why? Because every investment strategy fails on occasion, but if his investment strategy is unconventional as well, its failure will get the manager fired. Nonconformists are always on a very short leash.

It is his ability to suffer the internal conflicts and the social isolation associated with a contrarian investment stance that is the source of a contrarian trader's edge. In economic terminology this is a very high barrier to entry into the speculator's profession. One must be able to think clearly and to act on one's contrarian conclusions in the face of a market that for the moment seems determined to reduce the value of one's portfolio. Very few people can do this. For this reason the No Free Lunch principle does not preclude above-average market returns for the contrarian trader. There are so few contrarian traders that the market returns gained by pursuing this approach will remain above average and will not be competed away as long as society rests upon a foundation of strong social bonds among its members.

CHAPTER 4

The Wisdom and Follies of Crowds

Another side to collective behavior • a crowd can be smarter than any of its members • when can this happen? • the danger of self-fulfilling prophecy • the importance of independent judgment • Surowiecki's book on the wisdom of crowds • three criteria for collective wisdom • what about the stock market? • failure of the independent decision-making criterion • when markets have better information than individuals • why belief in a market's collective wisdom will lead to collective folly • Keynes on the nature of speculation • forecasting market psychology • conventional belief that tomorrow will be pretty much like today • market prices liable to change dramatically in response to factors that are of no long-run significance • descent from collective wisdom into the whirlpool of speculation • information cascades • a theory of fads, fashion, custom, and cultural change • information cascades and investment crowds • value investors bring the information cascade to a halt • fragility of information cascades and investment crowds

CAN A CROWD BE WISER THAN ITS MEMBERS?

In this chapter we take a different look at the phenomenon of crowds. In Chapter 3 I argued that investment crowds arise from an inherently social process. People instinctively want to be part of prominent and successful social groups. Moreover, an investment crowd implicitly promises new

31

members above-average investment returns similar to those that were achieved by the crowd's initial core group of believers. This implicit promise is backed up by the very visible, predicted change in the price of the crowd's favorite asset, which has made the crowd's original members look smart and successful. At this point the forces of conformity and imitation that encourage people to join successful and prominent social groups kick in. The crowd grows to the point at which its size creates a market mistake.

When described in this way, members of an investment crowd may appear to be acting irrationally (i.e., contrary to their own perceived interests). And this may be true. The pressures to conform to group behavior and to accept the social and promised financial benefits attached to participation in a successful group may well overwhelm individuals' capacity for rational calculation. The consequent market mistake may then be taken for evidence of the folly of the investment crowd's behavior.

But there is another side to the collective behavior of social groups. Crowds may sometimes exhibit a kind of collective wisdom instead of the collective folly I have ascribed to investment crowds. It is a general principle of scientific inquiry that to understand a phenomenon, in our case the activities of investment crowds, it often helps to study the polar opposite of the same phenomenon. The polar opposite of an investment crowd is a crowd that exhibits a kind of collective wisdom. A collectively wise crowd operating in the stock market would cause prices to hover consistently near fair value. This of course is the prediction of standard economic theory. Economists generally see markets as crowds of independent individuals that exhibit the collective wisdom found in the market equilibrium price. This price is collectively wise in that it accurately reflects all that is known about the current and prospective economic situation.

So when might we expect a large group of individuals, a crowd in the colloquial sense, to exhibit collective wisdom? When might the same group show collective folly? By answering these questions we can gain insight into the nature of investment crowds and discover why they are associated with market mistakes.

THE NEED FOR COLLECTIVE WISDOM

Let's begin by looking more closely at the nature of the collective wisdom that determines prices in financial markets. If this arises from information about underlying economic conditions that investors investigate independently from one another, I think we would expect the resulting market price to be a good assessment of fair value. In this case the market is likely to act wisely. But if instead investors' wisdom consists essentially of their *perceptions of other investors' information, beliefs, and actions*, we have a problem. In this case the door is opened to self-fulfilling prophecy—herd behavior.

First consider the situation in which individual investors act on private information about economic conditions. Presumably this information comes from a combination of personal experience and research. Of course people may make mistakes when they assess current conditions, when they try to judge future conditions, and when they try to translate these judgments into an appropriate investment policy. But if investors make these judgments and investment decisions independently from one another, their mistakes are very likely to cancel out. The average investment choice then is likely to reflect a more accurate assessment of future conditions than does any individual's choice.

In this situation, investors' *collective judgment* is better than the judgment of any single individual. The fact that people are diverse in their thinking processes, in the information they have, and in their ability to choose good investments ensures a diversity in the type of mistakes they will make. And this diversity in mistakes means that, collectively, they don't make any mistake at all!

This is an amazing phenomenon and one very difficult to accept. But you don't have to take my word for it. A few years ago James Surowiecki wrote a book entitled *The Wisdom of Crowds* (Random House, 2004). He examined situations in which groups of people had to make individual choices or predictions. The prototype is the game of guessing how many marbles are in a large glass jar. No individual is likely to make a very accurate guess. But time and time again the *average guess* of the number of marbles turns out to be amazingly accurate. The group's collective knowledge is superior to that of any of its members!

Surowiecki recounts many examples of this phenomenon in his book and does so in a very entertaining and illuminating way. But he does more than just entertain. He identifies three characteristics of situations in which we can expect a group of people to make a collectively wise choice. First, the knowledge base of the group must be diverse, and the more diversity in knowledge and experience among the group's members the better. Second, individuals in the group must make their choices without regard for the choices made by other group members. Finally, there should be a definite point in time at which the reward for choosing well is distributed among group members. This reward should be connected with some objectively observable external event and have nothing to do with the internal workings of the group decision process. When these conditions are met, either by chance or by design, Surowiecki asserts that the collective wisdom of the group will yield an average choice or decision superior to any that an individual group member is likely to make.

In Surowiecki's work we find the key to understanding why economic theory can make successful predictions even though each individual consumer, investor, or businessperson may have biases and make mistakes. In situations where people act independently from one another, deviations from rational behavior (the mistakes and biases of individuals) will tend to cancel out. In these sorts of market situations, each market participant knows his own interests and collects his own information about underlying economic conditions. As a group, market participants act competitively and therefore independently, making choices without regard to the choices made by others. The rewards for choosing well are entirely appropriated by each individual and accrue at a definite point (or points) in time. In such circumstances one can reasonably expect to see mistakes made by individuals offset one another so that the group as a whole makes no mistake at all. The collective wisdom of the marketplace produces a price that accurately reflects fair value. So we should think of classical economics as the study of collective action in situations in which collective wisdom can manifest itself.

INDEPENDENT DECISIONS IN THE FINANCIAL MARKETS

Let's continue along Surowiecki's path to see if we can expect the stock market to be wise. Can we expect it to exhibit the wisdom of crowds? Remember that crowds are likely to show collective wisdom when their members have diverse information, make decisions independently from one another, and expect foreseeable payoffs for their choices at some definite point in time.

Certainly stock market investors as a group have access to very diverse information. Indeed all the information relevant to corporate earnings prospects is available in the economy somewhere to someone. And for the most part, stock market investors make decisions independently from one another without any formal and very little informal mutual consultation. So the stock market seems to satisfy two of Surowiecki's criteria.

It is the third of Surowiecki's criteria whose failure opens the door to the rise of investment crowds and causes collective wisdom to make only occasional appearances in the stock market. The stock market game never ends. Indeed, this important characteristic distinguishes equity ownership from bondholders' interest in a corporation. Dividend and interest payments are predictable. But capital gains are not, and these are an important component of stock market returns. In fact, it is the pursuit of capital gains that motivates many if not all investors. And capital gains arise only when one can expect that at some foreseeable time in the future other investors will price an asset differently from the way they are pricing it now. This pursuit of capital gains is the reason that markets for long-lived or perpetual assets are particularly vulnerable to the follies of collective behavior. No capital gains, no investment crowd! To pursue capital gains and avoid capital losses, investors must anticipate the beliefs and actions of other investors. But if this happens, individuals will no longer make investment choices independently, causing the catastrophic failure of Surowiecki's second criterion, too.

There is another way of seeing why Surowiecki's independent action criterion will fail in the stock market and thus make the emergence of collective folly likely. Suppose for the sake of argument that stock markets generally price corporate assets at fair value and that in this way the market reflects the collective wisdom of investors. *This situation is necessarily very unstable.* For if the stock market's estimate of fair value is better than the estimate by any single individual, it follows that an investor should trust the market's estimate more than his own. After all, *the market has better information than he does!* But if the investor prefers the market's information over his own, he is then acting in concert with other investors, not independently from them. Even worse, why should an individual investor even bother to take the trouble to construct an independent assessment of fair value? After all, he won't be using it!

Think about what this means. If the stock market exhibits the wisdom of crowds, then individual investors will correctly see that the market price contains more information than they have individually. So each investor will no longer have reason to collect and analyze information for his own use. But how then can the market price reflect information that no one bothers to collect? It is as if people were asked to guess the number of marbles in a jar without ever seeing the jar itself! One would not expect collective wisdom to emerge in such a situation.

We see then that if investors actually believe the stock market trades near fair value, we can conclude that the stock market will probably not trade near fair value. If all investors decide to rely on the market price for information about underlying economic conditions, the stock market will no longer be moored to those conditions.

Economists have found a way of resolving this stock market catch-22. They call it the theory of *rational expectations*, and the advocates of this theory hold that we are likely to see the economy settle into what is called a *rational expectations equilibrium*, although I prefer the term *collective wisdom equilibrium*. This is a way of resolving the paradoxical nature of collective wisdom in a market situation. When the stock market is in a collective wisdom equilibrium investors use their private information but supplement it with information they glean from the market price itself. Everything works out happily in the end. But does it?

Economists know that a collective wisdom equilibrium can be quirky and fragile. The market price might even wind up being influenced by factors (like the phases of the moon) that are irrelevant to the corporate profits. This fragility arises precisely because everyone knows that the market price is the best single summary of what everyone else knows about future prospects. For this reason external events can cause the market price to become unmoored from economic reality. People can begin to believe unreasonable things simply because the market price tells them to, a distressing echo of "The devil made me do it." After all, isn't the market wiser than any individual? If enough people believe in the collective wisdom of markets, then we perforce enter the world of collective folly.

The fragility that attends a collective wisdom equilibrium is evident in the frequency with which investment crowds form and disrupt the asset pricing process associated with such an equilibrium. But even though I have chosen to describe this outcome as collective folly, I do not believe that it necessarily arises from individual folly. I believe that members of an investment crowd may have good reasons for adopting the crowd's beliefs as their own. It may be perfectly rational for an individual to heed the crowd. To see why this can happen, we return to the writings of perhaps the single most influential economist of the twentieth century.

FORECASTING MARKET PSYCHOLOGY

John Maynard Keynes, himself an experienced and successful speculator, has defined speculation as *the activity of forecasting the psychology of the market.* (The quotations in this section can be found in Chapter 12, sections 5 and 6 of his 1936 treatise *The General Theory of Employment, Interest, and Money.*) Keynes goes on to elaborate on his definition of speculation. He observes that the energies and skill of the professional investor are often occupied with "foreseeing changes in the conventional basis of valuation a short time ahead of the investing public." Such an investor is concerned not about what a stock is worth to the man who "buys it for keeps but rather with what the market will value it at, under the influence of mass psychology, three months or a year hence."

Why might a professional investor be more interested in forecasting short-run fluctuations instead of long-run changes in fair value? In Keynes' view, this short-run focus arises precisely because market prices are observed to fluctuate far more than is justified by the arrival of new information about likely long-run corporate and economic performance.

Consequently, investors are naturally focused on possible short-run capital gains and losses. And professionals' livelihoods depend more on their short-run performance relative to that of other professionals.

But Keynes is well aware that this elicits another question: Why do prices fluctuate so much in the short run? This fact Keynes explains by observing that markets normally operate on the basis of a widely held convention—that "the existing state of affairs will continue indefinitely." It is this convention, Keynes believes, that is the foundation upon which beliefs about future market returns are constructed. But he asserts that such a convention is necessarily fragile and likely to be disrupted by any unexpected economic drama played out on the national or world stage: "A conventional valuation which is established as the outcome of the mass psychology of a large number of ignorant individuals is liable to change violently as the result of a sudden fluctuation of opinion due to factors which do not really make much difference to the [long-run] prospective yield."

The word *psychology* is itself of interest here. It refers to the collective mental state of investors. The implication is that investor psychology is in principle something distinct and separate from objective economic facts. Keynes makes this clear when he elaborates on his views by saying:

> [T]he professional investor is forced to concern himself with the anticipation of impending changes, in the news or in the atmosphere, of the kind which experience shows that the mass psychology of the market is most influenced. And again: the actual private object of the most skilled investment to-day is to "beat the gun," as the Americans so well express it, to outwit the crowd, and to pass the bad, or depreciating, half-crown to the other fellow.

In a subsequent paragraph, Keynes adopts his famous beauty contest metaphor for speculation. In Keynes' description of the contest, a prize goes to the observer of the beauty contest whose choice of the most beautiful contestant most closely corresponds to the average choice made by all the other observers. He says:

> Each competitor has to pick, not those faces which he himself finds prettiest, but those which he thinks likeliest to catch the fancy of the other competitors, all of whom are looking at the problem from the same point of view. It is not a case of choosing those which, to the best of one's judgment, are really the prettiest, nor even those which average opinion genuinely thinks the prettiest. We have reached the third degree where we devote our intelligences to anticipating what average opinion expects the average opinion to be. And there are some, I believe, who practice the fourth, fifth and higher degrees.

Keynes also sees a natural tension between *enterprise* and *speculation* in every financial market. He observes that there are indeed large profits to be made in the long run by enterprising individuals who operate unperturbed by the speculative ebb and flow of market psychology, who "invest on the best genuine long-term expectations that can be framed." Keynes further notes:

> *[I]t makes a vast difference to an investment market whether or not they [long-run, enterprise-type investors] predominate in their influence over the game-players. . . . Speculators may do no harm as bubbles on a steady stream of enterprise. But the position is serious when enterprise becomes a bubble on the whirlpool of speculation. When the capital development of a country becomes a by-product of the activities of a casino the job is likely to be ill-done.*

This is the theme of all of Keynes' writing on the behavior of investors. His experience as a speculator taught him that every market's collective wisdom equilibrium is fragile. It is prone to disruption by the forces of short-run speculation arising from changes in mass psychology. It is perfectly rational for investors, professional or not, to pay careful attention to short-run changes in psychology. Their livelihood and net worth depend on it. But speculation about changes in investment psychology can easily lead to a disruption of a collective wisdom equilibrium—to a situation in which enterprise becomes a bubble on a whirlpool of speculation.

INFORMATION CASCADES INTO THE WHIRLPOOL OF SPECULATION

Let's now examine the process by which a collective wisdom equilibrium in the stock market can dissolve in a whirlpool of speculation. Surprisingly, economists have some important things to say about these departures from collective wisdom.

Suppose we look closely at the behavior of investment crowds. They share one important characteristic: The members of every investment crowd are certain that the crowd's size is evidence of the correctness of the crowd's beliefs. So many people can't be wrong! An investor outside the crowd is impressed not just by the crowd's investment success but by the unanimity of its beliefs and expectations. Experience reinforced by an instinctive belief in collective wisdom then causes him to put aside his skepticism. He believes the crowd's members must collectively know more than he does. In this way the crowd gains one more member.

But it is the nature of an investment crowd that its shared beliefs are not simply the average the independent beliefs of the crowd's members. Remember that an investment crowd grows because outsiders prefer to replace their own beliefs with what they think are the more accurate and wise beliefs of the crowd. In this way the crowd's shared belief is like a cosmic black hole. It is a powerful conviction, usually supported by well-known facts, which is an irresistible attraction for individuals and which overwhelms their personal knowledge and experience.

Surprisingly, this behavior need not be irrational on its face. It has been studied by economists. It goes under the name of an *information cascade*. The original source for this idea is a paper by Sushil Bikhchandani, David Hirshleifer, and Ivo Welch (BHI) that was published in the *Journal of Political Economy* in 1992 (pp. 992–1026) under the title "A Theory of Fads, Fashion, Custom, and Cultural Change as Information Cascades."

Simply put, an information cascade is a situation in which an individual imitates the behavior of others without regard to his own information. He does so because he believes that his own information is inferior to the information of those he chooses to imitate. The idea of successive imitation, that a cascade is a *sequence* of choices made over time by different people, is important here. And it is the sequenced cascade of imitation that I believe chronicles the life of any investment crowd.

Why should an individual choose to imitate the actions of others? Sociologists have studied this phenomenon carefully. Among the explanations they offer are the preference for conformity (which has high survival value for an individual who wishes to maintain strong social bonds), as well as the fact that a strong group can enforce sanctions on deviants. But as BHI point out, the sociological explanations aren't sufficient to explain why mass behavior is so often fragile is the sense that small shocks can result in big changes.

Information cascades are fragile precisely because the collective information contained in the cascade can be seen as a pyramid standing upside down on its point or vertex. A very little information held by a few individuals right at the start of the cascade induces a great number of individuals to abandon their own collectively more substantial information and instead imitate the early innovators. Any small piece of information that subsequently is seen by some member of the cascade to contradict the information upon which the cascade is built can cause the entire structure to tip over and collapse.

Here in the theory of information cascades we again encounter the theme of fragility in market and group behavior. Changes in collective behavior and mass psychology can occur rapidly and for no obvious reason. The best way to think of this phenomenon is to compare it to the spread of an epidemic. A wonderful discussion of epidemic-related aspects of collective behavior can be found in the book *The Tipping Point* by Malcom Gladwell (Little, Brown, 2000). His book is subtitled *How Little Things Can Make a Big Difference*, and it has a lot to say about the reasons people imitate each other, each illustrated by illuminating examples.

Let's see how the theory of information cascades sheds light on the behavior of investment crowds. In the theory of cascades, a person imitates the actions of those who have preceded him in the cascade because he believes that they know something he does not know. Moreover, this belief in the superiority of other people's information can be an objectively correct one, a belief founded on the best statistical use of one's own information.

An investor who is not yet part of an investment crowd generally knows a number of things. He knows that the crowd is focused on an asset whose price has changed a lot in a relatively short period of time. Indeed, this price change may well be what has attracted our hypothetical investor's attention in the first place. Our investor also knows the beliefs and forecasts shared by the crowd, which he has learned from its current members. To be persuasive, these must be grounded in facts that are public knowledge. There has already been a big price change in the asset, and this lends more credence to the crowd's beliefs. Yet another element of persuasion may be the financial gains made by friends and acquaintances of our investor who are already members of the crowd.

It is not surprising that in such a situation an investor may rationally choose to make the crowd's beliefs his own and join the information cascade. He determines that the members of the crowd know or understand something he doesn't and that he will gain financially by adopting the crowd's investment theme. This crowd cascade can continue so long as the crowd's successful investment stance persuades new investors to join. But remember that most members of the crowd have voluntarily chosen to ignore their own private information as they cascaded into the crowd. This is a ticking bomb that will inevitably blow the crowd apart. As soon as the investment performance of the crowd falters or convincing, contradictory information becomes available to crowd members, the cascade starts to run in reverse. At that point the crowd's members will no longer weight the crowd's beliefs more heavily than their own. The investment crowd disintegrates, vanishing like a wisp of smoke in the wind.

Here we reach the critical point in our analysis of investment crowds. We know that a crowd built by an information cascade is a fragile one. Information that contradicts the crowd's theme can stop the cascade and cause the crowd to disintegrate. What kind of information might be most effective in reversing the cascade of new members into the crowd? I think the answer will be obvious after a little reflection. The crowd's growth is fed by the success of the crowd's investment theme. Without evidence that prices are moving in the direction predicted by the crowd's theme, the cascade would stop. Prospective crowd members would no longer weight the crowd's information more heavily than their own. The market's action itself can halt the cascade.

But for the market to move against the combined buying or selling power of an investment crowd, some sort of countervailing coalition of speculators and investors must develop. This can happen only if the market price has been driven far enough from fair value by the crowd's activities to make investing opposite the crowd's theme an attractive and reasonably safe proposition. It is important to note that it isn't necessary for yet another crowd to form in opposition to the first one. All that is required is that the divergence between price and fair value created by the crowd's activities attracts enough value investors with an opposite view that the movement of price away from fair value is halted.

Because an information cascade is so fragile, the growth of an investment crowd is likely to halt as soon as the above-average returns to its investment theme fail to materialize. This will happen as a natural consequence of the significant divergence of the market price from fair value that has resulted from the crowd's investment activities. And as soon as the crowd's growth stops, there will then be a trickle of members who lose faith in the crowd's theme. As they leave the crowd, the market price will slowly begin to drift back toward fair value. At that point the information cascade that built the crowd will begin to run in reverse and the trickle of disillusioned members will become a flood.

A market affected by information cascades and the investment crowds cascades build will experience many episodes of significant overvaluation and undervaluation. The fact that market prices fluctuate so much more than can be explained by long-term valuation factors tells us one thing: Cascade-induced valuation mistakes are the rule, not the exception, in financial markets. These mistakes are investment opportunities for a contrarian trader.

How can the contrarian trader recognize an information cascade in the making? What clues should he look for to detect an emerging investment crowd and the investment opportunities it creates? In the next chapter we start to answer these questions by building a detailed description of the life cycle of a typical investment crowd.

CHAPTER 5

The Life Cycle and Psychology of an Investment Crowd

The cycle of birth and death • cosmological analogy • business competitors and value investors eventually cause the death of the crowd • once the crowd disintegrates, a new crowd often starts to form in response to the extended movement of prices • crowd formation causes (and in turn is caused by) excessive price volatility • bearish crowds are different from bullish ones • the 1994–2000 stock market bubble • stock market valuation and Tobin's q ratio • it's different this time • the new information economy • shattered dreams • the bear crowd of 2000–2002 • the quest for certainty • the conflict between science and certainty • every opinion has its rationale • instinctual belief • the need for affirmation • pied pipers lead the crowd • mental unity of crowds • intolerance of contrary views • examples from the 1994–2000 bubble • Julian Robertson, Stanley Druckenmiller, and Gail Dudack • Allan Sloan and America Online (AOL) • social and financial pressure on unbelievers • price volatility and homogeneous thinking in crowds • price volatility is one sign that a crowd is mature

PROLOGUE

In this chapter I collect the strands of fact and theory we've developed in the preceding chapters. I will weave them into a tapestry that chronicles the life and death of a typical investment crowd. Investment crowds differ from one another in numerous details, but they all develop through the stages depicted on this tapestry. To make things as concrete as possible,

I am going to use the stock market crowds of 1994–2002 to illustrate the typical pattern of an investment crowd's life and death. Once this cyclical picture of the life of an investment crowd is completed, we will turn to a study of the internal life of an investment crowd. By this I mean the study of the psychological attitudes of those who join the crowd and the nature of the individual rationalizations that permit the information cascade to develop. Knowledge of these individual patterns of thinking can be very valuable for identifying information cascades and the investment crowds that grow from them.

THE CYCLE OF BIRTH AND DEATH

How do investment crowds get started? There is no single right answer to this question. But I think it is accurate to say that most investment crowds find their genesis in the deaths of other investment crowds. I like to use a very apt cosmological metaphor to help understand this process. Investment crowds are the stars of the financial universe. The stars in the Milky Way and in the much larger cosmos have limited lifetimes, which typically end in a massive explosion called a supernova. But new stars are being born (i.e., starting their own process of nuclear fusion) all the time. What is the source of the material that is the stuff of a new star? Well, it is just the cosmic debris left by the explosions of old stars!

In much the same way, investment crowds burn brightly in the financial universe and are responsible for much of the observed price fluctuation. But they have finite lifetimes (a few months to a few years). The inevitable disintegration of any investment crowd causes a big run-up or drop in prices and lots of commotion and confusion in the marketplace. But the debris associated with the disintegration of a crowd is the stuff from which the next crowd forms. The change in price associated with the disintegration of an investment crowd is powerful advertising. It attracts the attention of investors, especially of those whose portfolios have been directly affected by the rise or fall in asset value.

Let's examine this process more carefully. To keep things concrete, you might want to keep in mind as an example the price of a common stock or of some market average.

Imagine that a bullish investment crowd has driven the average or the stock price well above fair value. Every investment crowd's lifetime is limited by the natural economic forces of supply, demand, and competition. Once price is far enough above fair value, willing sellers appear as if out of the woodwork. New business competitors arise, and there may be a capital investment boom in the relevant industries. This shift in supply conditions steadies the price above fair value and eventually causes it to drop. The fragility of every information cascade guarantees that this process will feed on itself, eventually leading to the complete disintegration of the bullish crowd.

But this dramatic drop back toward fair value attracts the attention of another group of investors. The fear of financial loss unites them into a bearish crowd and leads to the articulation of their bearish investment theme. Their activities force price well below fair value. Typically this is a very temporary situation. Price excursions below fair value are generally shorter in duration than those above fair value. Once the fear of financial ruin dissipates, prices return fairly quickly to fair value. The movement is reinforced by the natural economic forces if they have had time to operate and if the bearish market mistake is large enough. The return to fair value accompanies the disintegration of the bearish information cascade and sets the stage for the birth of a new, bullish investment crowd.

Now, the next bullish investment crowd does not form when price is below fair value. Instead the rise in price from far below fair value back toward fair value advertises a bullish environment. It is this price movement that stimulates the birth of a bullish crowd. Some investors have hit the jackpot because of this run-up in prices. If this jackpot is big enough to attract the attention of the media and of other investors, a bullish investment crowd will form. The bullish crowd is most likely to form at the point where price has returned to but is not yet above fair value.

We have before us a cyclical picture of the self-reinforcing life cycles of investment crowds. This picture offers an explanation of the connection between investment crowds and excessive stock market fluctuations and volatility. Bullish and bearish investment crowds in turn drive the market price above and then below fair value. Each such swing sets up the conditions that eventually lead to the formation of another crowd with the opposite market orientation.

So far I have depicted bullish and bearish investment crowds pretty much as opposite sides of the same coin. It is tempting to believe that there is a pleasing symmetry that controls the way both sorts of crowds form, grow, and dissolve. But as anyone with experience in the financial markets will testify, this isn't true. In fact, the growth of a bullish crowd generally proceeds at a more leisurely pace than does the growth of a bearish crowd. Bullish crowds last longer, and the mistakes they force upon markets tend to extend over longer periods of time. In contrast, bearish crowds form and dissolve over relatively short time spans, and the market mistakes they cause are for the most part of comparatively short duration. The reasons for this asymmetry are not very well understood. It may arise from the fact that there is no specific limit to how high a price may climb, but no price can drop below zero. In any case, we will find that this difference between bullish and bearish crowds is itself evidence pointing to the essential characteristic of all investment crowds: Their members eventually behave as a herd—a mass of individuals whose behavior is governed by instinct, suggestibility, and imitation, not by reason.

THE STOCK MARKET BUBBLE OF 1994–2000

Bullish investment crowds get started when the market is trading near fair value. The birth of the crowd is triggered by the substantial advance in prices that occurred as the market returned to fair value from a position well below fair value. The phenomenon is nicely illustrated by the birth of the investment crowd that gave us the stock market bubble of 1994–2000.

The stock market boom of 1994–2000 in the United States was the culmination of an 18-year advance, an unprecedented bull market that began in 1982. At its low in 1982 the Dow Jones Industrial Average stood at 777. On the final trading day of 1994 the average closed at 3,835, almost 400 percent higher than in 1982. As the market continued its advance in 1995, many experts believed that the averages were already trading well above fair value and on this basis predicted an imminent crash. But were prices *really* above fair value then?

As every investor knows, assessments like this are hard to make. But I have found that, at least as far as long-term trends in the U.S. stock market are concerned, it is very helpful to seek guidance from the famous q *ratio*, which was invented by the Nobel Prize-winning economist James Tobin. Tobin believed that to determine the extent to which the stock market is under- or overvalued, it makes sense to compare the value the stock market places on corporate assets with the current cost of replacing these assets (their so-called replacement value). It is this ratio of stock market value to replacement value that Tobin christened q.

The best explanation of the q ratio I have found in print appears in the book *Valuing Wall Street* by Andrew Smithers and Stephen Wright (McGraw-Hill, 2000). In it they explain the q ratio and apply it to practical valuation problems. A simple synopsis of the theory behind the q ratio goes like this. When q is substantially above 1.0 it is cheaper to buy real assets, build factories, buy equipment, and start businesses than it is to buy the same stream of income in the stock market. Thus a q above 1.0 stimulates a boom in real economic investment and this leads to above-average economic growth. A q below 1.0 means that it is cheaper to buy a given stream of income in the stock market than it is to earn it by making real investments in the economy. Thus a q below 1.0 acts as a brake on the economy, or at least leads to below-average economic growth.

Thus one expects a q ratio substantially above 1.0 to accompany an economy-wide investment boom, which arises because the stock market is overvalued. In such a situation investors want to buy capital equipment and form new corporations, then sell their interest in the stock market which values this interest well above its cost. In contrast, a q ratio well below 1.0 should be associated with weak demand for new capital goods. The stock market is substantially undervalued and making real investments yields an instantaneous stock market loss since the market values them at less than cost.

Here is a remarkable fact: At the end of 1994, after a nearly 400 percent rise in stock prices measured from the 1982 low point, Tobin's q ratio was just barely above 1.0! Over the preceding 110 years q had varied from a low value of 0.4 to a high value of 1.9. In 1994, q stood at 1.1. By contrast, in 1982 q stood at 0.5, the lowest value seen since 1932 in the depths of the Great Depression. So we see that, at least in terms of Tobin's q ratio, a 12-year, 400 percent advance in stock prices had only returned the market to fair value by the end of 1994!

This long advance had made a big impression on investors. To see how it changed people's thinking about the stock market, I highly recommend reading *Bull!* (HarperCollins, 2004), a book by Maggie Mahar that chronicles the stock market boom and bust from 1982 through 2002 in fascinating detail.

Mahar reports that in 1995, for the first time since the early 1970s, U.S. households held more wealth in the stock market than in real estate. I date the emergence of the bull market investment crowd from 1995. This crowd's theme was that buying shares in mutual funds and holding them was the sure way to amass wealth and achieve early retirement. The universal expectation of this crowd was that stocks would return 10 to 20 percent yearly in perpetuity. During the next five years money poured into mutual funds. People who had never invested in stocks committed their life savings to the market. The q ratio rose from 1.1 in 1994 to an unprecedented peak of 2.6 in the year 2000. The 2.6 reading was the highest q had ever been in the 120 years for which data had been available! It is not then surprising that the 1998–2000 period saw an enormous capital goods boom, which vastly increased capacity in the telecom, computer equipment, and Internet services industries.

The birth of this investment crowd in 1995 occurred when the stock market was priced at fair value, but only after a long rise in prices over the preceding 12 years from a level well below fair value. This very powerful stimulus no doubt played a role in determining this crowd's unusual longevity and the size of the mistake it forced upon the market. That aside, this is a classic illustration of the circumstances attending the birth of most investment crowds. But investment crowds can develop in other ways as well, and such crowds also played an important role in the 1994–2002 boom and bust.

IT'S DIFFERENT THIS TIME: THE NEW INFORMATION ECONOMY

In Chapter 4 we saw that an information cascade begins when some investors decide that other investors know more about a particular investment opportunity than they do themselves. In such circumstances it can be rational for a person to imitate another's actions even when his own private information and proclivities tug him in the opposite direction.

So it is natural to expect that an information cascade is especially likely to develop in response to a genuinely new and different investment opportunity, one that is completely outside the realm of most investors' personal experience. And this is exactly what is happening when we hear talk about new industries and new technologies that promise to revolutionize the economy. The unfamiliarity of the new investment opportunity can make it difficult to tell if the market price of an initial public offering or of the stock of a company in an unfamiliar industry is near fair value. Such circumstances make it easy for business and investment cheerleaders to assert that the price is at or even below fair value and thus to encourage the growth of an investment crowd.

The 1994–2000 stock market boom was accompanied by a popularization of the phrase the *new economy*. This referred to the confluence of trends toward *globalization* on the one hand and the growing use of *information technology* (embedded in communication and computer equipment) to revolutionize the way business is done. In the new economy, productivity growth was thought to be unusually high. This permitted high economic growth and high employment accompanied by low inflation, a situation that Goldilocks herself would envy.

The new economy environment of 1994–2000 not only encouraged the growth of the mutual fund stock market crowd but also supported the emergence of smaller investment crowds, which focused on particular industries or companies. Since information technology was supposedly revolutionizing economic relationships, old thinking about the relationship of fair value to earnings potential became suspect. These newcomers to the corporate world understood things that old-time investors did not. Conditions were ripe for the development of information cascades, and develop they did. Soon investment crowds took hold in the stocks of companies like Amazon, America Online (AOL), Apple Computer, Dell Computer, eBay, Enron, Intel, Lucent Technologies, MCI WorldCom, Microsoft, Oracle, Priceline.com, Qwest Communications, Silicon Graphics, and Yahoo!, to name just a few. These telecommunications and dot-com companies rocketed the NASDAQ-100 index to a gain of almost 400 percent from late 1998 to early 2000.

The very newness of the businesses these companies saw themselves in made it easy to convince normally skeptical investors that traditional valuation standards no longer applied. As the resulting information cascade gained momentum, the enormous amount of money made by entrepreneurs and early investors gave added credence to this theme. That it all ended badly is just the ever-repeating story of investment crowds and stock market information cascades.

SHATTERED DREAMS: THE BEAR CROWD OF 2001–2002

So far we have looked at the birth of the bubble crowds that formed during the stock market run-up from fair value in 1994 to extreme overvaluation in 2000. These bullish investment crowds grew from cascaded dreams of a new economy. When these bubbles burst, the cascade of dreams morphed into a cascade of fear and recrimination. This built the bear market crowd that dominated the U.S. stock market during 2001–2002.

I have explained the process by which the typical bearish crowd develops. The disintegration of the preceding bullish crowds triggers the birth of new bearish crowds. This generally happens only after price has returned to the vicinity of fair value.

Remember that the fair value price is only a signpost on the road to the inevitable undervaluation that will be forced by the growth of the bearish investment crowd.

Where was fair value in 2001 for the U.S. stock market? At the peak of the bull market in 2000, Tobin's q ratio stood at a historical high of 2.6, exceeding by a very wide margin its previous high of 1.9. The ratio was clearly behaving differently than it had over the past 120 years by leaving its normal range of fluctuation between 0.4 and 1.9. This posed a problem for anyone trying to use q in real time, because it raised measurement reliability issues. Perhaps the numbers used to calculate q didn't have the same economic significance they had in the past?

These uncertainties forced me to temporarily abandon q as an estimator of fair value for the U.S. stock market in 2001–2002. The q ratio may yet prove to be of great use, but the jury is out on the current significance of its readings to investors. This sort of circumstance illustrates the importance of having multiple methods for estimating fair value. When one or another method seems to be out of whack for some reason, one has alternative measurement available. Here is a simple alternative method I like for estimating long-term fair value. It uses only market price data, not economic data. As an empirical matter, the U.S. stock market has followed a cycle of about 48 months from trough to trough over the period that began in 1929. So as a rough-and-ready estimate of fair value, I like to use the 48-month, simple moving average of the month-end reading of the S&P 500 stock market index. (Recall that this moving average is computed by adding up 48 consecutive monthly closes and dividing the answer by 48.) The 48-month length of the moving average is selected to minimize the effects of the normal 48-month rhythm is stock prices.

Let's get back to the story of the 2001–2002 bearish investment crowd. In March 2001 the S&P 500 touched its 48-month moving average, my long-term estimate for fair value, for the first time since 1982. The index had traded above this fair value estimate for more than 18 years! The moving average stood at roughly 1,210 in March 2001, and the index itself dropped to 1,084 that same month and then rallied to 1,315 by May 2001.

The return to fair value from a point of overvaluation will leave investors with losses. Indeed, newspaper and magazine commentary during late 2000 and early 2001 held unanimously that the dot-com and technology bubbles had burst. This event was dramatically recorded by the NASDAQ Composite stock market index, home to most of the bubble stocks. At its 5,132 high in March 2000, this index was trading more that 150 percent above fair value as measured by its 48-month moving average. One year later the NASDAQ Composite had dropped as low as 1,619, about 35 percent below the moving average estimate of fair value at the time and a stomach-churning 69 percent drop from its high a year earlier.

The shock of a 69 percent drop in the technology sector was transmitted instantly to investors, because they had poured money into technology mutual funds during the 1999–2000 bubble years at unprecedented rates. The natural response to such destruction in portfolio values is fear of further loss, a search for means of escape, and the identification of scapegoats and evildoers to be held responsible for the damage. These are the potent ingredients from which the theme of nearly every bearish investment crowd emerges. Bearish crowds tend to develop quickly because most members already have experienced financial loss. The information cascade that develops on these foundations gives new members of the crowd reason to fear that more erosion in asset values lies ahead. Such persuasion is easily accomplished. It relies on the universal convention that guides people in markets and in life: *Tomorrow will be pretty much like today.* But in the case of a bearish investment crowd, today is filled with financial pain. Tomorrow can only be worse, especially because the crooks responsible for the current distress have not all been caught. The means of escape becomes obvious: sell. Once an investor has sold out, he is even more convinced that worse is to come in the market, for otherwise his actions will appear foolish.

I will discuss the 2001–2002 bearish stock market crowd in more detail in subsequent chapters. Suffice to say here that by mid-2002 it had become a very visible and dominating investment crowd. By that time the NASDAQ Composite index was trading more than 50 percent below its moving average estimate of fair value and nearly 80 percent below its 2000 high. The S&P 500 was trading 38 percent below its fair value estimate, down about 50 percent from its 2000 high at 1,553.

POPULAR INSTINCTS AND THE SEARCH FOR CERTAINTY

As a bullish crowd disintegrates, price drops back toward fair value. When a bearish crowd disintegrates, price rallies upward toward fair value. In both instances a big, unexpected price change advertises the death of the crowd. It also attracts the attention of the rest of the financial world. People ask, "Why did prices drop so much?" They wonder, "How come the market rallied so far in the face of bad news?"

Investors always want answers. In this respect they are simply being human. It is man's inclination to ask and to answer the question *why* that distinguishes him from animals lower in the food chain. Scientists grapple with the *why* question every day. That's their business. But, as every scientist knows, the most powerful device humans have invented for getting answers, the scientific method, requires a suspension of judgment about this answer or that one. Instead the scientist proposes a theory to explain observed events and then carefully compares it with the empirical evidence. Sometimes the data prove the theory is plain wrong. Or, if he is lucky, the scientist might find that the data are entirely consistent with the theory's predictions. But these outcomes are not common. Usually the comparison of data with theoretical predictions has an ambiguous result, so the scientist must go back to his desk or lab to reconsider his ideas and research strategy. The ship of scientific inquiry spends little time near the sheltered shore of certainty.

In their everyday affairs people do not use the scientific method to explain events. They have neither the time nor the skill. In his book *Instincts of the Herd in Peace and War* (orig. pub. 1919; reprinted by Cosimo Classics, 2005), the London surgeon and sociologist Wilfred Trotter observes:

"In matters that really interest him, man cannot support the suspense of judgment which science so often has to enjoin. He is too anxious to feel certain to have time to know." With little time to know (i.e., to apply the scientific method) and a low tolerance for ambiguity, the typical investor must rely more on instinct than on science to explain market movements.

What do I mean by the word *instinct*? Nowadays psychologists and sociologists don't believe that any human behavior is instinctual in a narrow technical sense, that is, in the same sense that certain animal behavior may be described as instinctual and biologically based. But I think this term can still be useful in describing the nature of rationalizations people use to explain their beliefs and actions. This is precisely the way Trotter uses it in his book. He cites Volume 2 of William James' *Principles of Psychology* (1890, reprinted by Dover Books in 1950 and available digitally on the Internet) to explain how instinctual behavior in Trotter's sense appears to human introspection. He defines an instinctive action or belief as one appearing so grounded in common sense that any idea of discussing its basis appears "foolish or wicked." An instinctual action is obviously the right thing to do. Only a foolish or ill-intentioned person would dare dispute an instinctual belief.

Of course instinct in this sense is not a biological phenomenon and so is unlike animal instinct. Instead it is analogous to a religious belief or a belief that is axiomatic, based on assumptions that are never questioned. Instinctual beliefs in Trotter's sense often arise when people transfer their experiences and behavioral responses and beliefs from one realm of activity to another. But an even more important mechanism for belief transmission and acquisition is the social group and the crowd.

People prefer the comfort and certainty of instinctive belief to the ambiguity associated with scientific procedure and knowledge. Trotter points out that in everyday life:

> *[individuals] make vast numbers of judgments of a very precise kind upon subjects of very great variety, complexity, and difficulty. . . . The bulk of such opinions must necessarily be without rational basis . . . since they are concerned with problems admitted by the expert to be still unsolved, while as to the rest it is clear that the training and experience of no average man can qualify him to have any opinion upon them at all.*

Trotter continues:

> *It is clear at the outset that these beliefs are regarded by the holder as rational, and defended as such, while the position of one who holds contrary views is held to be obviously unreasonable.*

To be sure, no one I have ever met has admitted that his beliefs are for the most part instinctual in this sense. Far from it. We all think our beliefs are rational, often self-evidently so. Trotter notes this phenomenon:

> *[I]t should be observed that the mind rarely leaves uncriticized [its] assumptions ... the tendency being for it to find more or less elaborately rationalized justification for them. This is in accordance with the enormously exaggerated weight ascribed to reason in the formation of opinion and conduct.*

If most of our beliefs are instinctual, it is natural to wonder about their source. How do such beliefs arise? How do we acquire them? Certainly some are generalizations from individual experience. But we all hold beliefs about politics, national affairs, economics, local affairs, sports, and so forth, and these realms are for the most part outside of our personal experience.

Most of our beliefs and their rationalizations are adopted from the social groups in which we participate. We take the very fact that many people whom we know hold these beliefs to be evidence for their validity. This mechanism for belief formation has something of the flavor of an information cascade. But to describe it in cascade terms ascribes too much rationality to the process of belief acquisition. Trotter expresses this same idea more colorfully when he compares society to a herd of animals, but a herd endowed with a voice, a power of suggestion:

> *[B]elief in affirmations ... sanctioned by the herd is a normal mechanism of the human mind, and goes on however much such affirmations may be opposed by evidence. ... [R]eason cannot enforce belief against herd suggestion. ... [T]otally false opinions may appear ... to possess all the characters of rationally verifiable truth.*

This is not to say that all or even most of our beliefs that have a purely social basis are necessarily wrong or irrational. Indeed, scientifically verifiable beliefs often acquire the sanction of the herd, the crowd, or the social group and are thus transmitted to those who have no access to or understanding of the scientific method. This sanction generally takes a generation or more to acquire, but one need go no further than the examples of Darwin's theory of evolution or Einstein's relativity theory to see this process in action on a large scale.

THE PIED PIPERS OF INVESTMENT CROWDS

The drop in the market price back to fair value during the death of a bullish crowd and the rise in price back to fair value during the death of a bearish crowd generally attract a lot of attention. Investors want an explanation of a dramatic and unexpected price change. This demand for explanation naturally creates its own supply. I liken the rationalizations that emerge in these situations to the Pied Piper of Hamelin. The rationalizations rarely if ever have any scientific basis. Instead, the music of the pipe first attracts attention because it sounds like a plausible, indeed logical, explanation of an otherwise mysterious price movement. The reasoning appears instinctually obvious to its growing number of adherents. But eventually the piper exacts a toll from his audience, a price that far exceeds the few coins rational calculation would have offered. The investment crowd follows the piper to its inevitable doom brought about by the economic forces that limit the size of market mistakes.

During the big move in crude oil prices from $40 in 2004 to $140 in 2008, the pied piper of peak oil played a very seductive tune. Peak oil advocates asserted that world production of crude oil was bound to start an inevitable decline for purely geological reasons early in the twenty-first century. The obvious conclusion was that crude oil prices had nowhere to go but up. Other theories competing with peak oil reinforced expectations of a steady upward march in crude oil prices. One of these was that the accelerated economic growth in China and India was creating unusual and expanding demand for all natural resources, not just for oil. Another was the *devil theory* of markets, which attributes all big moves to the machinations of speculators. Here were three pied pipers that enabled the bullish crude oil crowd to grow to enormous size by mid-2008.

The new economy bubble of 1994–2000 had its own pied pipers. This bubble inflated on the basis of the new information economy, the acceleration of globalization, and the associated rise in productivity. Demand for telecom bandwidth was said to be unlimited. The Internet was to provide a whole new business model in which profits played but a small role. One interesting aspect of the bubble was that many of the pied pipers were actual people. They had names everyone in the bubble crowds recognized: Jack Grubman, Frank Quattrone, Abby Joseph Cohen, Mary Meeker, Henry Blodget, Maria Bartiromo, Ralph Acampora, and Alan Greenspan.

The bear crowd of 2001–2002 had its own pied pipers, but they were not as plainly visible as the ones that had enabled the preceding bubble. The bear crowds that form amidst the debris of a bubble typically blend the characteristics of lynch mobs and repentant sinners: We had it coming for believing in the patent nonsense of the bubble investment themes; they led us astray and cheated us, and now they must pay the price. The crowd searches for scapegoats, and those it finds become inverted pied pipers, repelling listeners with the dissonant music of their pipes. They are offered as exemplars of unsound and even stupid investment policies. This process of tearing down the edifice of belief that supported the bubble continues until only discouragement and fear for the future control investor attitudes.

THE MENTAL UNITY OF INVESTMENT CROWDS

So far we have seen that investment crowds get started after the market price returns to fair value following a significant excursion away from fair value. The price movement that arises from the return to fair value attracts public attention. Investors' human aversion to ambiguity and uncertainty, coupled with their limited capacity for scientific thinking, leaves them vulnerable to pied piper explanations for the run-up or the drop in prices. These explanations are always plausible and exhibit a certain internal logic. This is what makes them seductive tunes for the pied piper's pipe. If the tune promises a significant continuation of the price move that has already been observed, then an investment crowd will be born and start to grow.

Now we will discuss the view from inside a developing investment crowd. How do people in a crowd act? How can we distinguish an investment crowd from any random group of individuals? I am going to offer my own answers to these questions, but much of what I say can also be found in Gustav Le Bon's 1895 classic *The Crowd*. The analysis of crowd motivation and behavior you can find in his book makes it required reading for any contrarian trader.

The most important characteristic of any crowd is what Gustav Le Bon calls the crowd's *mental unity*. The attention and sentiments of all crowd members are focused in a single direction or on a single phenomenon. The mental unity of an investment crowd is externally manifested in the crowd's *investment theme*. An investment theme is a basket of explanations and of the forecasts that seem to be their obvious consequences. An investment theme identifies an asset or a class of assets, and explains why the price of these assets has changed so much recently (during the return to fair value) and why price will continue to change in the same direction. The pied pipers of the financial world are the early advocates of these investment themes. We have already seen examples of investment themes:

those that unified the bubble crowds of 1994–2000 and the bear market crowd of 2001–2002.

An investment theme begins to attract adherents as its true believers publicize their views and as the market price continues to move in the direction they forecast. This is the beginning of an information cascade. Newcomers are persuaded by the arguments of the true believers to ignore their own information (if they have any) and accept the information upon which the cascade builds. The mental unity of the crowd begins its development in this way. But there is much more to a crowd's mental unity than simply its investment theme.

The essence of life within a crowd is constant reinforcement and affirmation of the crowd's beliefs. Crowd members communicate with one another, either directly as individuals or indirectly through the print and electronic media. Crowd leaders are always visible and always courting publicity. They never forgo the chance to "talk their book," to urge newcomers to accept the crowd's investment theme.

This constant repetition of a crowd's investment theme is the single most important characteristic of life within an investment crowd. Life within any crowd (not just an investment crowd) is like life within an echo chamber. All one hears is a repetition of the investment theme and confident pronouncements about profits to be earned by its followers. Soon even the logic supporting the theme is forgotten—or reduced to easily remember cliché. The mere fact that crowd members experience so much affirmation of their belief (albeit only from other crowd members) is taken as more evidence of the correctness of the crowd's theme.

Both Le Bon and Trotter observe that the affirmative messages that build crowd unity are not usually appeals to the intellect of crowd members. Instead they are appeals to emotion, to stereotypes, to dreams or fears. The language of persuasion and crowd solidarity is the language of drama, not science.

Affirmation and repetition build the mental unity of an investment crowd. As the crowd's mental unity develops, members of the crowd begin to resemble one another in their preferences, beliefs, and actions. Crowd members sense an increase in the power of the crowd, and this encourages each of them to be more of a risk taker. Of course what an outsider would identify as a riskier investment stance the crowd members see as very safe, almost a sure thing. Crowd members give little thought to the consequences of being wrong. Such a discussion would not be sanctioned by the crowd, and doubters would be cast to the crowd's fringes or expelled.

I have found a crowd's intolerance of contrary views to be its single most important identifying characteristic. This intolerance shows itself in the form of ridicule and abuse of any skeptical consideration of its theme. I have written an investment blog (www.carlfutia.blogspot.com) for several years. I try to take the viewpoint of a contrarian trader. When the comments on my blog are the most numerous and abusive I know that a market turn is imminent.

Crowd intolerance of contrary views can manifest itself in other, more dramatic ways in the world of asset management by mutual funds, pension funds, and hedge funds. Money managers who do not join the crowd run a significant risk of being fired or put out of business. The same fate can befall any investment guru who dares cross the crowd. Both these sorts of things happened in dramatic fashion during the late stages of the 1994–2000 stock market bubble.

Founder Julian Robertson closed the investment firm Tiger Management in March 2000, right at the top of the stock market bubble. He did extraordinarily well for his investors, earning an average annual return net of fees of 25 percent during 20 years. But the bubble year of 1999 was his undoing as his fund dropped 19 percent while the S&P 500 rose 21 percent. His investment method couldn't account for the bubble crowd's massive buying power. His poor performance in 1999 would have caused his investors to abandon him in droves had he not shut down his firm when he did. So one of the most talented hedge fund managers of his generation was forced out of business by the actions of the bubble crowd, whom he had chosen to ignore.

If you have a taste for irony, you will find the saga of Stanley Druckenmiller even more intriguing. Druckenmiller ran a good part of George Soros's hedge fund, the Quantum Fund, from 1988 through 2000. He was and is an enormously talented investor. But like so many experienced investors, he did not participate in the late 1990s technology boom, believing that it would come to no good end. This reluctance began to hurt the Quantum Fund as its investors questioned the wisdom of staying out of the technology sector.

During the summer of 1999 Druckenmiller had an epiphany about the tech sector while he was attending an investment conference. Upon his return he put the Quantum Fund into many of the technology stocks that were rising dramatically during the latter half of 1999, the terminal stage of the NASDAQ Composite index's 400 percent rally from its 1998 low point. The Quantum Fund's performance during the latter half of 1999 was outstanding. Sadly, Druckenmiller's tech portfolio was buried by the dramatic sell-off during March–May 2000, which was eventually to bring the NASDAQ down 80 percent from its 2000 high. This setback led to Druckenmiller's departure from the Quantum Fund and to Soros's temporary shutdown of the fund's speculative activity.

The stories of these two talented investors, Robertson and Druckenmiller, illustrate well the fate of money managers who don't align themselves with dominant investment crowds. The crowd will abandon even the most talented manager if he is not committed to the crowd's investment theme. Every manager knows this, and all understand the risk of being put out of business for failing to toe the party line in their portfolios. This of course reinforces the influence of any investment crowd. The irony of Stanley Druckenmiller's experience is that he bent to the crowd's pressure at precisely the wrong time. The resulting portfolio whipsaw severed his relationship with the Quantum Fund.

The story of Gail Dudack and the TV show *Wall $treet Week* also illustrates the power of an investment crowd to harm the careers of those who oppose it. Dudack was chief market strategist during the 1990s at the brokerage firm S.G. Warburg. Like so many experienced market watchers, Dudack recognized the stock market bubble for what it was, and in late 1997 she announced her bearish views to her clients. She was also a regular guest on *Wall $treet Week with Louis Rukeyser*, a very successful weekly TV stock market show produced for the public broadcasting affiliates. By November 1999 her bearish views had so irritated Louis Rukeyser, the show's popular host, that he removed Dudack from his list of regular guests and from her slot in his Elves Index, a joint market assessment of the technical analysts who appeared on his show.

Rukeyser was in the business of attracting viewers, and as everyone in the entertainment business agrees, the way to do this is to give people what they want. By 1999 the bubble crowds had grown so intolerant of contrary views that Rukeyser felt compelled to throw Dudack under the bus.

Here we have before us the experiences of two prominent hedge fund investors and one prominent market strategist. All three fell before the intolerant onslaught of the bubble crowd during the brief period from November 1999 through May 2000. It is not a coincidence that all the stock market averages reached their highs in January–March 2000.

It is not surprising that the intolerance of investment crowds can affect financial journalists as well. In 1995 and 1996 Allan Sloan, a financial columnist at *Newsweek*, wrote several columns expressing his skepticism about the accounting methods of America Online (AOL), a company that pioneered the commercialization of Internet connectivity. AOL's stock had soared since its initial public offering in 1992, and Sloan believed it to be grossly overvalued. Needless to say, his skeptical views were not welcomed by the investment crowd, who believed in AOL. He eventually stopped writing about AOL, which, with exquisite timing, reached a merger agreement with Time Warner in the spring of 2000. Why did he stop? Maggie Mahar quotes Sloan in her fascinating book *Bull!* (HarperCollins, 2004), which chronicles the bubble:

> *I knew I was right, but whenever I published one of those stories, everyone would carry on. . . . Finally I just gave up. I shouldn't have, but I did. There are only a limited number of swings you can take—eventually you look like a crank.*

The social and financial pressure an investment crowd can exert on disbelievers cannot be overestimated. While much of a crowd's growth occurs as the result of an information cascade, the continuous strengthening of a crowd's mental unity through constant affirmation, repetition, and dramatic price changes in the crowd's asset makes this unity a powerful tool of persuasion. It magnifies the crowd's impact and importance and puts pressure on even the skeptics to join.

SUGGESTIBILITY, VOLATILITY, AND DISINTEGRATION

As the mental unity of an investment crowd grows adherents to its investment theme become homogeneous in their thinking. When this happens the crowd develops an important characteristic that mature crowds share with herds of animals. Its members become very suggestible, and are apt to take action or modify their beliefs when presented with a strong image of something they desire or fear. Suggestibility opposes logical persuasion, but, as we have seen, every crowd member so strongly believes in the rationalizations offered by the crowd that no logical persuasion is necessary. Consequently, images presented to the crowd by its leaders or the media will be acted upon immediately by members of the crowd without further questioning.

This is the essence of herd behavior. The members of a herd find safety in numbers but only so long as the herd stays together in a group and acts together as well. An investment crowd holds together only so long as the price of its asset(s) moves in the direction expected by the crowd. But this can happen only if crowd members respond almost instantly to the appropriate images and their implied suggestions.

A fascinating example of the suggestibility of stock market crowds developed during the late stages of the stock market bubble in the late 1990s. Companies with ".com" in their names were priced at a premium by the market, and several were motivate to change their corporate names for this reason. Of course, no value per se resides in a mere name, but the *image* of a dot-com company was strongly associated with stock market profits. This made every such stock a favorite of the bubble crowds of the late 1990s. Similar things happen in every stock market boom and illustrate the important role that images play in investment crowds.

Once an investment crowd becomes herdlike in its behavior, the price of its asset becomes much more volatile. Where once daily price movements up or down seemed normal in magnitude, one instead sees daily price fluctuations in much wider bands. The market seems to soar or tumble with little rhyme or reason, and every tidbit of news, relevant or not, has an exaggerated effect.

A dramatic increase in price volatility is one of the signs that an investment crowd has reached maturity and that the information cascade supporting the crowd has become very fragile. With members of the crowd at their most suggestible, willing to accept both hopeful and fearful images at face value, every new bit of information has an exaggerated impact on the crowd and on the market price. Because price has become so volatile, the messages crowd members think they see in price changes will have ever more powerful effects on their willingness to stick with the crowd's theme. Any negative news, even if not associated directly with the crowd's theme, can bring down its information cascade because it may trigger significant selling or buying of the crowd's asset, perhaps by investors outside the crowd. The crowd's suggestible state guarantees that such price movements are highly likely to snowball as members of the crowd successively take flight.

While dramatic increases in price volatility are signs of a mature investment crowd, the increased fragility of its information cascade also means that the disintegration of the cascade is almost impossible to predict ahead of time. In subsequent chapters we will take a closer look at the problem of identifying the imminent disintegration of investment crowds, a problem that every contrarian trader must be able to solve.

CHAPTER 6

The Historical Context for Market Mistakes

Exhausted investment themes • clues that an investment crowd is mature • look for the market mistake • market mistakes in the context of the market's history • only need a guesstimate • look at market's price history and then at media content • this method focuses directly on the market mistake, not on fair value itself • price history more useful than estimates of earnings • regularity in emotional behavior of crowds • data sources for historical prices • beginners' mistakes • how to identify a stock market bubble • examples of 1929, 1966, and 2000 • how to identify undervaluation in the stock market • examples of undervaluation • the peak oil bubble

MATURE INVESTMENT THEMES AND MARKET CROWDS

Every contrarian trader must learn how to identify the point at which an investment theme has exhausted itself. At this juncture the information cascade has done its work and the market commitments of the investment crowd have grown about as large as is likely based on historical precedents. The associated market crowd has reached maturity and is nearing the disintegration associated with old age. The crowd has forced the market to make a valuation mistake. Price stands well above or below fair value. Soon economic forces and sharp-eyed value investors will begin the process of correcting the market's mistake. Once this process begins, the crowd will disintegrate and price will return rapidly to fair value, sometimes continuing well past that point to produce another valuation mistake in the opposite direction. This return to fair value is the investment opportunity that a contrarian trader seeks to anticipate and exploit. For this reason the contrarian trader must be always vigilant, always on the lookout for mature investment themes and investment crowds.

Are there any clues that can warn us that a market might be the hands of a mature investment crowd? Since mature crowds force markets to make mistakes, to trade well above or below fair value, it makes sense to try to identify these market mistakes directly. *I believe that every market mistake can be identified by putting it into the context of the market's historical price fluctuations.* I will explain the kind of computations needed to identify this context.

Of course any such method will at best yield only approximate answers. But this is not a problem for the contrarian trader. His assessments of whether the market is over- or undervalued will be only one input to his decision process. He only needs these guesstimates about possible over- or undervaluation to get him into the right valuation ballpark, to indicate the possibility that a mature market crowd may be causing a valuation mistake.

In this chapter I want to show you how to identify situations in which a market may be trading significantly above or below fair value. The novel aspect of the methods I explain is that they use only the market's price history to estimate the current position of fair value. No information about past dividends or profits or estimates of their prospective levels is needed. In a sense we will be extracting from the market's price history information about how fair value changes over time, as well as information about the size of typical market mistakes. Using this information, we will compute a rough estimate of the current fair value price.

Locating price relative to fair value is only the first step in the process of spotting a potential contrarian trade. In subsequent chapters I will show you how to combine this valuation information with an analysis of media content. The stories appearing in the electronic and print media give you a way to observe information cascades as they proceed and to assess the strength of associated market crowds. It is the combination of a potential valuation mistake together with solid, affirmative evidence that this mistake is caused by a mature market crowd that is the key to a profitable contrarian trade.

MISTAKES VERSUS FAIR VALUE

In Chapter 5 I explained why the disintegration of a bullish investment crowd usually results in the birth of bearish one, and vice versa. The cycle of alternating bullish and bearish crowds is a universal feature of financial markets. This cycle of birth and death is responsible for the mistakes markets make—for prices being alternately too high and then too low relative to fair value.

But what is fair value? We have already seen that economists compute the fair value price of an asset by discounting to the present the estimates of the asset's future cash payouts (dividends in the case of common stocks). Sadly, this wonderful theoretical concept is not very useful as a yardstick for the contrarian trader. I have found it more useful to try to identify market mistakes directly instead of focusing my attention on estimates of fair value. In fact, I think this can be done by studying a market's historical price behavior. Why might this be so? The market prices we observe result from the confluence of two kinds of investment activity. The first arises from a rational calculation of value based on purely economic and statistical considerations. The second arises from the psychological and emotional character of investment crowds and information cascades. I think the latter shows far more regularity than the former. Moreover, this regularity in psychological and emotional behavior is very difficult to exploit, because the typical investor is a part of this phenomenon, not apart from it. So we would expect to see such regularity showing more persistence instead of being destroyed by the few traders capable of exploiting it.

The method I have adopted uses historical price data to identify situations in which the market is trading significantly above or below fair value. It does this by tabulating the extent and duration of a market's typical swings from high to low and low to high. My working hypothesis is that at historical high points the market was overvalued and at historical low points it was undervalued. I expect to see consistency in the duration and the extent of the swings from undervalued to overvalued conditions and back again. Such consistency I regard as an empirical fact about the psychological life cycle of crowds. As such, it should be quite independent of the specific economic environment of the time.

Because this method rests on empirical estimates of the effects of crowd psychology on markets, it can be expected to work only if a market has enough participants to support the formation of large investment crowds, especially crowds of people who are not normally attentive to financial markets. For this reason this approach works best with the stock market averages, the bond markets, and some commodity markets (those that attract public attention). It is much less useful in estimating when the price of an individual stock is high or low relative to fair value.

MARKET DATA SOURCES

Before going further I think it is useful to identify some sources for the market data that you will need to do the calculations I will describe. These sources have changed a lot during the 40 years I have been participating in the financial markets. Years ago you had to collect this data from newspapers, or, if you were lucky, you might have been able to purchase some of it already tabulated from some obscure source you happened to hear about. But nowadays computers and the Internet have made the price data aspect of contrarian trading so much easier. The Internet has become a tremendously useful data repository for the contrarian trader. Having computational power at hand on your desktop is a tremendous laborsaving device when analyzing this data.

At present there is no single comprehensive data source for the information you will need, but as computing power and communication resources expand I expect this to change over the next 10 years. Whenever I need data I don't already own I often can locate a source by using Google or some other search engine. Here are three online data sources that I have found very valuable. They will no doubt be either outdated or defunct in a few years. No matter. I am sure you will still be able to use online search tools (like Google) to identify new data sources.

The first one is Yahoo! Finance (http://finance.yahoo.com). This data is comprehensive and free! Once you have identified a stock or stock market index, Yahoo! offers access to daily, weekly, or monthly historical data, which can be downloaded as an Excel spreadsheet. Excel itself has charting capabilities that you can use for a preliminary data analysis.

There are a number of sites that offer downloadable data for stocks, stock market indexes, currencies, and commodities on a subscription or one-time-purchase basis. Here are two of the most widely used: Commodity Systems Inc. (www.csidata.com) and MetaStock (www.equis.com).

THE DEADLY MISTAKE

The goal of every contrarian trader is to beat the market—to earn an investment return that exceeds the return earned by the buy-and-hold strategy. (Sophisticates might want to make appropriate adjustments for portfolio risk when making this comparison.) There is only one kind of mistake a contrarian trader can make that will prevent him from matching or exceeding the buy-and-hold return: being out of or even short the market when it rising. (Being fully invested when the market is falling does no harm to his performance relative to buy-and-hold.)

Sadly, it is precisely this mistake that novice contrarian traders are most prone to make. Why? I think there are two reasons. First, periods of market overvaluation tend to be of longer duration than periods of undervaluation, so there is simply a lot more opportunity to make this kind or error. Second, there is much more variability in the size of the mistake a market can make in the direction of overvaluation. These two factors work together to make the task of identifying periods of overvaluation much more difficult and much more risky than the task of identifying periods of undervaluation. Combine the technical difficulty of identifying periods of overvaluation with the novice's eagerness to show the world how clever he is, and you have a reliable recipe for disaster.

I am convinced that the difficulty of identifying periods of market overvaluation means that the contrarian trader, especially the novice, should focus his efforts on identifying and exploiting periods of market undervaluation. I'll have more to say about this matter in Chapter 11, in which I discuss "The Grand Strategy of Contrarian Trading." In the meantime, I think the way to proceed is to adopt an asymmetrical approach to this problem by developing criteria for identifying overvaluation that are more stringent than those for identifying undervaluation.

WHEN IS THE STOCK MARKET (EXTREMELY) OVERVALUED?

I take it as axiomatic that the contrarian trader wants to avoid being caught in the stock market debacles of the sort that followed the bubbles of the 1920s and the 1990s. These were two of the three distinct instances of extreme stock market overvaluation during the past 100 years. The associated stock market tops occurred in 1929, 1966, and 2000. Notice that these market tops were separated by 37 and 34 years, almost one and a half generations in each case. This sort of extreme overvaluation does not occur very frequently, perhaps once or at most twice in the lifetime of a contrarian trader. In these three cases the subsequent drop in the inflation-adjusted Dow Jones Industrial Average amounted to 87 percent to the 1932 low, 62 percent to the 1974 low, and 42 percent to the 2002 low. The 2007 high in the Dow was substantially above its 2000 peak but according to my analysis (see chapters 14 and 15) was not associated with a stock market bubble. Nonetheless, from its 2007 high to its 2008 low the Dow dropped an inflation-adjusted 51 percent. Being able to sidestep declines of this magnitude should be a goal of every contrarian trader. But how might this be done? Are there any common features in the price fluctuations preceding these important stock market tops that might have warned of gross overvaluation?

Here is the way I try to answer this sort of question. Each of the first three market tops ended a bull market that had not been interrupted by any decline of as much as 30 percent in nominal terms or by any decline that lasted as much as eight months from high to low. These were the bull markets of 1921–1929, of 1949–1966, and of 1987–2000. In inflation-adjusted terms, prices advanced 496 percent, 334 percent, and 346 percent respectively during these bull markets. These advances lasted 8, 17, and 13 years respectively. Moreover, only the first of these three bull markets began from the preceding crash low. The start of the 1949–1966 bull market occurred after 17 years had elapsed from the 1932 low, while the 1987–2000 bull market started 13 years after the 1974 low.

Let's see if we can combine these observations to make some rough-and-ready guesses about the top of the next bubble. One possibility is that the low we are now seeing develop in 2008 will be historically analogous to 1921. I think it far more likely that the 2008 low will play this role than will the 2002 low. Why? As we will see later, the bearish crowds of 2008 are very powerful, indeed much more well-developed than were the bearish crowds of 2002. I don't think we would see such strong bearish information cascades occur in the midst of a bull market leading to a bubble top. So let's suppose that 2008 is analogous to 1921. In this case we would expect a top to develop around 2016 after an advance of at least 250 percent in real terms from the 2008 low, which I will take as 7,552 in the Dow Industrials. Assuming inflation of 3 percent per year for the next eight years, the bubble top would occur near 33,000 in the Dow around 2016.

Why did I use 250 percent instead of the larger numbers associated with the three previous bubble bull markets? I wanted to be conservative, yet stay in the same ballpark. Half of the biggest advance is 248 percent, and this is not too much less that the other two. But feel free to do your own guesstimating!

Why 2016? Well, the obvious answer is that if 2008 is like 1921, then since the 1921–1929 bull market lasted eight years this one should, too. But actually I would be very surprised if the next bubble top occurred so soon after the 2000 top. I think it more likely that if a bubble bull market is actually starting in 2008, then it will probably last between 13 and 17 years, putting the top sometime during the years 2021 to 2025. This would be long enough after the 2000 top for a new generation of investors to grow up and make the same mistakes their parents and grandparents made during the bubble of the 1990s.

If 2008 is not the start of a bubble bull market, then the top of the next bubble will be pushed out further in time and much higher in price. The next bubble bull market would then have to start some number of years after 2008 and from a price level higher than the 2008 low. Once you think you have seen the starting point of the bubble bull market, you can use the precedents cited earlier to guesstimate the level and timing of its ultimate top.

I have just illustrated how a contrarian trader can identify situations of extreme overvaluation in the stock market. But such bubble tops are infrequent events. There are many less dramatic bull market tops occurring in the intervals between major bubble tops. These less dramatic bull market tops are seen on average every four or five years. Can the method I have just illustrated be adapted so as to help identify these situations of less extreme overvaluation? I believe it can. In fact, I'll tell you about two simple rules of thumb I use to do this. But first a warning: I think only an expert, experienced contrarian trader should attempt to identify these less extreme periods of overvaluation. For the reasons I cited earlier, the costs of making a mistake—of anticipating a top when none occurs—can be very substantial. I don't think the effort is worthwhile for a newcomer to contrarian trading.

That being said, here are my two rules of thumb for identifying moderate periods of overvaluation. First, a typical bull market in the U.S. stock market averages about 24 months from low to high. Second, a typical bull market carries the averages upward about 65 percent from low to high. These are two useful facts, but of course the real difficulty lies is determining whether any particular bull market will be typical. I'm afraid I will have to leave this as the subject of another book.

WHEN IS THE STOCK MARKET UNDERVALUED?

I think that the typical contrarian trader would do well to specialize in identifying and exploiting periods of market undervaluation. Periods of undervaluation tend to be of much shorter duration than periods of overvaluation. Moreover, bearish market crowds tend to be more vocal, emotional, shorter lived, and easier to identify that bullish crowds. Finally, the relentless upward path of economic progress in free market economies stacks the deck in favor of trying to exploit undervalued situations. The secular upward trend works to mitigate any mistakes the contrarian trader may make in his effort to identify periods of undervaluation and the associated bearish crowds.

How frequently do the stock market averages in the United States become undervalued? The answer depends on just how big a valuation mistake we are talking about.

The really big undervaluation mistakes in the U.S. stock markets occurred in 1932 and 1982. I say this because the 1932 low associated with the Great Depression ended a drop in stock prices of 85 percent in real terms from the 1929 high. The 1982 low ended a drop of about 74 percent in real terms from the 1966 high. You might wonder about the value of Tobin's q ratio at these lows (see Chapter 5 for a discussion of Tobin's q ratio). At both of these lows the q ratio was 0.5 or below and thus indicated that the stock market was 50 percent undervalued relative to the replacement value of the real assets owned by the companies in the market average.

Was either the 2002 low or the 2008 low a comparable valuation mistake? I don't think so, and here are my reasons. First, the drop in the inflation-adjusted Dow was just 42 percent from the 2000 high and 51 percent from the 2007 high. These numbers are relatively high in a historical context, but neither is high enough in my judgment to make them comparable to the 1932 and 1982 situations. Second, at the 2002 low the q ratio was 1.5 and at the 2008 low the q ratio stood near 1.0. Neither reading is comparable to the levels of 0.5 seen in 1932 and 1982. (See Chapter 16 for more discussion of stock market valuations at the 2008 low.) I think the combination of these two facts means that at the 2002 and 2008 lows, the stock market was not nearly as undervalued as it had been at the 1932 and 1982 lows.

We see then that valuation mistakes of the 1932 and 1982 variety may occur only once every 50 years, so the next one may not be due until 2032. Obviously, the contrarian trader has to look for less extreme examples of undervaluation.

For more than 100 years the U.S. stock market has established bear market low points on average every four years, with perhaps 70 percent of these successive low points being separated by an interval of three to five years. Thus during a typical investing lifetime of 40 years an individual would on average encounter about 10 of these opportunities. I like to think of bear markets as falling into three categories. A short bear market would typically drop the stock market averages 20 to 25 percent and last about eight or nine months from high to low. A normal bear market would drop the averages about 35 percent and last about 18 months from high to low. An extended bear market would drop the averages about 45 percent or more and last 30 months from high to low.

Extended bear markets are rare. The 2000–2002 drop in prices was an extended bear market lasting 31 to 33 months, depending on which average you use as a yardstick. The Dow dropped 39 percent (no inflation adjustment) during that time, while the S&P 500 dropped 50 percent. The bear market that began in 1937 didn't end until 1942, a span of 61 months during which the Dow dropped 52 percent. The preceding extended bear market was the 1929–1932 event, during which the Dow fell 89 percent in nominal terms in a 34-month period.

Normal bear markets were also rather unusual events during the twentieth century. The 1981–1982 drop in the Dow lasted 16 months but carried the average down only 25 percent. The 1976–1978 bear market dropped the Dow 28 percent over an 18-month period. The 1973–1974 bear market dropped the Dow 46 percent over a 21-month period. The 1968–1970 bear market saw the Dow drop 36 percent over 17 months. Notice that all of these bear markets occurred during the adjustment period in which the stock market moved from an extremely overvalued condition in 1966 to an extremely undervalued one in 1982.

The most common bear market—and the one I think contrarian traders should become skilled in exploiting—is the short bear market that lasts about eight or nine months and drops prices about 20 to 25 percent. Short bull markets are a phenomenon associated with extended stock market advances, such as those of 1921–1929, 1942–1966, and 1982–2000. I'll have a lot more to say about how these short bull markets can be exploited when I describe "The Grand Strategy of Contrarian Trading" in Chapter 11. Here let me cite some typical instances of short bear markets.

There was an unusually brief bear market associated with the Long Term Capital Management crisis of 1998. Then the Dow dropped 22 percent in barely two months. Another unusually brief bear market was associated with preparations for the first Gulf War of 1991. From a high in July 1990, the Dow dropped 23 percent in about two and a half months. A third unusually brief bear market occurred in 1987 for no obvious reason. Then the Dow dropped 37 percent in three and a half months, with most of the decline occurring on a single day, October 19, 1987.

Notice that these were three consecutive short bear markets, and each was of very subnormal duration compared with the eight- to nine-month average for the species. Perhaps this was a clue that a bubble bull market was under way during 1987–2000. A similar situation developed during the bubble bull market of 1921–1929, which was interrupted by subnormal bear markets in 1923 and 1926. This may prove to be a clue that a bubble bull market is under way the next time we see such a phenomenon develop.

Short bear markets were prevalent during the 1942–1966 stock market advance. There was a short bear market in 1946, which dropped the Dow 25 percent in five months. Another occurred in 1956–1957. It lasted 18 months (with 99 percent of the decline occurring during the final three months) and dropped the Dow 20 percent. The short bear market of 1960 dropped the Dow 18 percent in nine months, while the short bear market of 1962 dropped that average 29 percent in six months. Finally, the 1966 short bear market carried the Dow down 27 percent in eight months.

What do these statistics tell us? Every time the stock market averages drop 20 to 25 percent from a high and three to five years have elapsed since the preceding bear market low point, we must suspect that the market has entered a zone of undervaluation. This is the time to look closely for evidence that a bearish market crowd has become mature and is about to begin its process of disintegration. I'll have much more to say about how to do this in subsequent chapters.

THE PEAK OIL BUBBLE

Just so you won't think that the tabulation method I have illustrated for the stock market averages can't be applied elsewhere, let's take a look at a completely different market, that for crude oil. In July 2008 crude oil sold at $147 per barrel. (This is being written in August 2008.) I think a very mature investment crowd has grown around the theme of peak oil and is about to start its process of disintegration. Recall that believers in the peak oil theme assert that worldwide production of crude oil soon will or already has reached the highest level it will ever attain, and supplies of petroleum will soon start contracting. The implication is that crude oil prices have nowhere to go but up.

Let's take a look at what a tabulation of the historical data on oil prices can tell us. Before the first Arab oil embargo in 1973, crude sold for $2.35 per barrel. By 1981 it had risen to a high of $39 before declining. In 1998 it reached a low price of $11 and, as mentioned, it traded at $147 in July 2008. Here is the way I look at this price history.

In eight years from 1973 to 1981 crude oil rose 710 percent in inflation-adjusted terms. From 1981 to 1998, an interval of 17 years, it fell 84 percent in inflation-adjusted terms. In 10 years from 1998 to 2008 crude oil advanced 910 percent in inflation-adjusted terms. Note that the duration of this 910 percent advance exceeds the duration of the 1973–1981 advance by only two years. The inflation-adjusted price rises are comparable also: 910 percent versus 710 percent. This is a good reason to think oil was very overvalued at $147, and, as I have mentioned, a very vocal, bullish investment crowd has formed around the peak oil theme.

The prognosis is that crude oil is about to begin a drop in its inflation-adjusted price that may well last 17 years. The 1981–1998 drop carried the price down 84 percent. If inflation averages 3 percent over the next 17 years, then an inflation-adjusted drop of 84 percent from the $147 level would put the price of crude at $38 in 2025. Remember that all of these numbers are adjusted for an expected level of inflation that I have guessed will be 3 percent per year for the next 17 years. You will have to update this guess with actual inflation numbers to get updated versions of these price projections.

CHAPTER 7

How Crowds Communicate

The information conveyed by information cascades • two types of information • beliefs and stories that make up the investment theme • the role of the media • the confirming action of market prices • 1994–2000 bubble as an example • the potent brew of emotional persuasion • the role of the mass media • telling people what they want to hear • media amplification • monitor the media midwives • what media sources to use • print media • Internet media • blogs • television and talk radio • flipping and the real estate bubble • Jay Leno • tomorrow's media will be different from today's • be flexible and alert to changes • monitoring the markets • data sources I use • here, too, things will change • the value of historical accounts

WHAT DO INFORMATION CASCADES TELL INVESTORS?

In the first part of this book we developed a theory of investment crowds. Investment crowds are responsible for the many mistakes markets make. Crowds are an inevitable feature of our social environment. They arise naturally from our desire to form social bonds and make use of the information about our world that is transmitted via these human connections.

To recognize an investment crowd, one has to understand the communication processes that enable the investment crowd to form and the nature of the information these processes convey. Remember that an investment crowd arises from an information cascade. We want to learn how to recognize a cascade in action and to identify the sort of information it conveys. If we can do this, we have a good chance of being able to identify an ongoing cascade and to watch the associated crowd as it grows and eventually forces a market mistake.

The information transmitted in a cascade is of two types. First are the specific beliefs and facts conveyed by the founding members of the crowd to potential new members. This is the stuff of the crowd's investment theme. It is a logically coherent story but one intended to trigger an emotional response rather than scientific agreement. Typically, this first sort of information is transmitted through the electronic and print media, although person-to-person contact often plays a role as well. This transmission mechanism is open to public view. The transparent nature of the media gives us the opportunity to watch the information cascade develop simply by keeping track of the number and intensity of the messages.

However, information that merely elaborates on an investment theme would not by itself be persuasive were it not accompanied by a second, more dramatic piece of persuasion: a big change in the market price in the direction predicted by the theme that has enriched a small but visible group of investors (or made them a lot poorer!). Indeed, it is the prospect of getting rich or the fear of getting poor that creates the emotional power the investment theme needs to attract a crowd of investors.

To illustrate this last point, let's recall the dot-com bubble of 1994–2000. Does anyone imagine that investment themes like the new economy and the transforming power of the Internet would have been taken seriously if the stocks of America Online (AOL), Yahoo!, and other dot-coms hadn't first staged impressive advances, if a steady stream of initial public offerings hadn't made their lucky buyers rich? No, I don't think so, either. But once investors saw how much money they might have made had they picked up these themes early enough, they were hooked. The logic of the investment theme was simply icing on the cake, a convenient justification for joining the crowd.

We see then that economic and business information and forecasts, the dreams and fears of investors, and the movements of prices in the financial markets all have important roles to play in the creation of an investment crowd. They all are part of a potent brew of persuasion that manifests itself in an information cascade. But a dramatic change in the price of some asset always comes first. This is the prime mover and seed of the information cascade that will ultimately create an investment crowd. Only after the fact is the price change ever explained by appeal to economic and business developments. Even then, these explanations are only dry, unemotional facts. By themselves they will not persuade an individual who has no time or skill for scientific analysis. To do their work, these explanations are leavened with emotional appeals to greed, to fear, and to the natural human desire to get ahead of one's fellows. Then and only then will the information cascade gather momentum and create a new investment crowd.

THE ROLE OF THE MASS MEDIA

There would be no investment crowds in the modern world without the print and electronic media. Indeed there is a fascinating symbiotic relationship between the media and investment crowds. When people get rich or poor because of a big change in the price of some asset or commodity, the media have a story to tell and one they can sell. Remember that the media business is all about telling people what they want to hear so that advertisers will be willing to pay to reach an attentive audience. Stories like this attract readers and thus advertisers. But then an interesting thing happens. Because the media business is very competitive, the same story is picked up by other media outlets and in this way spreads far and wide. These human stories of success or failure become widely known. Success breeds imitators while failures encourage others to share their stories of distress. This process in turn generates even more stories of the same sort, and these stories in their turn encourage more imitators. The entire process amplifies the effects of the original story. What begins as a whisper, barely audible even to the careful listener, eventually becomes a cacophony of communication among the media and its newborn offspring, the investment crowd.

This is indeed a fortunate situation for the contrarian trader. Because the print and electronic media are midwives to the birth of investment crowds, we have the opportunity to watch crowds develop from toddlers to mature adults just by monitoring media content. The particular methods I use to interpret the significance of this content will be the subjects of subsequent chapters. For now I want to discuss the media sources I monitor to help me identify information cascades in operation.

As I write this in 2008, the print media are still the most important lines of communication for the information cascades that build investment crowds. I check the *New York Times* and the *Chicago Tribune* every morning for interesting stories about the economy, finance, and business. Front page stories are especially noteworthy. Any major metropolitan newspaper can be used in the same way. In fact, if you read a local, small market paper you will occasionally find stories on these topics that have a more personal, local flavor and that can be just as significant as a similar one in a major newspaper.

After daily newspapers, the next most important means of monitoring information cascades are weekly and monthly newsmagazines. Those of general interest like *Time* and *Newsweek* are the most important ones to watch, because they generally do not devote much space to economic and business subjects. When they do, especially if the story appears on the cover, you have a significant and unusual situation, which tells you that the associated investment crowd is probably a very important and substantial one.

Other general interest and politically oriented magazines can also be used in this way. Over the years I have used stories from *U.S. News & World Report*, the *New Yorker*, *New York* magazine, the *New Republic*, and *Harper's* (to name just a few). Any magazine of significant circulation can be used for this purpose. In fact, for this reason I periodically visit my local big-box bookstore (in my case Barnes & Noble) because it has a large magazine section. I check out the cover stories for all the magazines displayed, even the ones I don't normally read. I do this whenever I think an information cascade has reached critical mass. It is amazing how easily cascades can be identified using just this simple device.

So far I have left out business-oriented magazines like *Fortune, BusinessWeek*, and the *Economist*. These can be very valuable, too, especially when a cover story is devoted to a recent market event. But you must keep in mind that these sources generally have many cover stories devoted to the economy and business, so such covers don't carry the same weight and significance as do the covers of *Time* or *Newsweek*.

You have no doubt noticed that I have left the *Wall Street Journal* off my list of print media sources. There is a good reason for this. The *WSJ*'s primary focus is on business and finance. Consequently it is difficult to identify the importance of a story from its positioning on the newspaper's front page. The only *WSJ* stories I pay attention to are those describing in some detail the workings of an investment crowd that I have already identified from other sources. I use the *WSJ* as a corroborating source, not a primary one.

Over the past 10 years, an important competitor to the print media has arisen. I call these the Internet media because they are delivered primarily through the Web browser you use to access online resources. Every one of the print media nowadays has an electronic edition that can be accessed over the Internet. The Web content published by the print media changes from hour to hour and from day to day, so it is more difficult to track and record. The same is true of content that appears on sites like MarketWatch or Bloomberg. The basic thing to keep in mind is that the changeability of this content makes it relevant to very short-term (days, not weeks) crowd behavior and thus is of limited use for gauging information cascades. However, one can get a sense of what these sites regard as news over periods of months just by paying daily attention to them. For example, stock market industry groups come into and fall out of favor and so are mentioned more or less frequently over a period of months. The same is true of individual stocks or commodities. Remember that the Internet media want to keep people's interest and therefore highlight stories they think will interest the biggest segment of the public. So their editorial choices tell you something about their editors' perceptions of the markets that hold the most interest for their readers.

I also follow many blogs devoted to investing, finance, and economics. I won't name them here, simply because my list changes frequently—the lifetime of a typical blog is only a couple of years (or even less). However, general interest blogs like Instapundit as well as blogs with a strong political point of view can be very useful reading. You can be sure that any economic or financial market that attracts intense public interest will find mention on these blogs, together with links to other relevant Internet material. Keeping up with the content of a diversified list of blogs is an essential activity for the contrarian trader.

There are other electronic media that are important but not distributed on the Internet (at least not yet). These are network and cable television, talk radio, and the movies. Here, too, the basic rule that the media are profit-seeking entities that have to cater to people's interests and prejudices serves the contrarian trader well. Generally, programming specials can tell you a lot about what people hope for or fear. Even more significant are new TV series that appear just as an associated crowd is about to begin its disintegration process. The most recent example of this sort occurred in 2005–2006 with the appearance of several cable shows devoted to house flipping (i.e., buying a house, fixing it up, and then selling it for a profit, all within a couple of months). The first episodes of these shows marked almost the exact top of the real estate market and preceded the subprime market debacle of 2007–2008. As I write this (July 2008), a new reality series has appeared on cable TV. It's called *Black Gold* and depicts the day-to-day activities of the roughnecks who man the oil rigs on three separate West Texas drilling projects. For future reference, note that the price of crude oil is currently $143 per barrel.

Another illustration of how TV shows can give useful information to the contrarian trader occurred in July 2002, just as the S&P 500 index was approaching its bear market low at 768 (its low that month was 771). I am a fan of the *Tonight Show with Jay Leno*. For the first time in my memory Leno started telling jokes about the stock market crash and the economic recession (which had in fact ended in late 2001) in his monologues that month. At the time I found this strong corroborating evidence that the bear market crowd of 2002 was about to disintegrate and that the stock market's low was at hand.

A WORD ABOUT PERSONAL FLEXIBILITY AND THE FUTURE OF MEDIA

I am writing this chapter in July 2008, but I hope that this book will be of interest to future generations of investors as well. The phenomenon of investment crowds is a timeless one. One can expect the nature of mass media and their means of delivery to evolve in unpredictable and surprising ways over the years ahead. I don't doubt that my future readers will find the preceding discussion antiquated in its specific details.

However, the general principles by which one identifies information cascades are timeless. To apply them, one needs to monitor the specific forms of mass communication of one's era. The forms and technology used by media will evolve, so a contrarian trader must be constantly involved in a media watch and be flexible and willing to adjust his procedures as needed. Some media will grow in popularity, whereas others will decline. It is the contrarian trader's job to keep abreast of this evolutionary process, of the constantly changing nature of modes of mass communication. It will be the content of these media that enables the contrarian trader to identify ideas and themes that drive information cascades.

MONITORING THE MARKETS

While the mass media play an essential role in helping the contrarian trader identify information cascades and the investment crowds they create, these media are not the only grist the trader can or should use in his trading mill. A contrarian trader must have extensive knowledge of the historical behavior of financial markets. He must be able to put the markets being pushed by investment crowds into a quantitative context. Ideally, he wants to be able to estimate how big a mistake a market may be making and to get some sense of when or whether the associated investment crowd is still growing stronger or is instead on its last legs.

This is not easy to do for even the most skilled contrarian trader. But it is impossible to do at all without a substantial body of historical market data. In subsequent chapters I'll discuss specific ways of using this historical data to monitor the status of an investment crowd. In this chapter I want to confine my attention to sources of data and to the kind of data one wants to monitor and use.

At the moment the single most useful source for historical stock market data is the free Yahoo! Finance web site, from which one can download data in spreadsheet format. As the years pass this source will grow in value. But remember that the Internet and information storage technologies are evolving rapidly. So 10 years from now the situation may change and Yahoo! may no longer be a good data source. It is the job of the contrarian trader to stay abreast of informational resources so that when he needs historical information he knows where to look.

Another good source of historical information in chart-based format currently is the online Chart Store web site. For an annual subscription fee one can view historical charts of stock market averages, interest rates, foreign markets, currencies, and commodities.

A third source for chart-based stock market data that I use at the present time is StockCharts.com, another subscription-based web site; it has a vast number of charts kept up to date in various user-controlled formats.

The only thing I am sure about is that 10 years from now I will probably be using different sources for my historical market data than I use now. The financial world is constantly evolving and with it the nature of the information resources one must use to keep abreast of events. It is the job of a contrarian trader to know where he can obtain relevant information even as the world changes around him.

STUDYING THE HISTORY OF BUBBLES AND CRASHES

There is another source of information that can help the contrarian trader place current information cascades and investment crowds in their proper historical context. These are the historical accounts of past market bubbles and crashes. These historical accounts can be entertaining, but they always provide food for thought and opportunities for critical analysis as well. Later in Chapter 16 I shall suggest a number of books that I have found useful and interesting for this purpose. No doubt many more will appear as time passes. History is always being written and often revised in the light of new information.

When I got my start in the stock market in 1965 the great crash of 1929 had occurred 36 years earlier. It seemed to me then as distant as the time of the Roman Empire. I like to think that even as a novice I was influenced by the experiences of other speculators, which I had learned about from reading historical market accounts. As I write these words, the market events of the intervening 43 years have also been recorded for posterity by many authors. To today's novice contrarian trader these events no doubt seem to be ancient history, too. But my personal experience as a market participant during the past 43 years informs everything I do as a contrarian trader. It is essential for every contrarian trader to build his technique upon a body of experience, even if at the beginning of his career it is only secondhand. The only access the novice has to the experience of these market events is through these historical accounts. Make use of them.

CHAPTER 8

Constructing Your Media Diary

Skill of a contrarian trader • from deduction to action • media diary aids analysis and strengthens trader's belief in his deductions • a trading tool and a training tool • your diary will be your anchor to windward • how my diary made a difference in 2002 • a wonderful learning tool • put your diary in a notebook • cut and paste • what media content is relevant • excerpts from my diary in 2005 • excerpts from my diary in 2006 • magazine covers • examples from 2006

GAINING THE EDGE

A contrarian trader's edge arises from two unusual skills. The first is his ability to consistently identify investment crowds and their investment themes. The second is his capacity for making rational deductions from these observations and translating these deductions into buying or selling for his portfolio in the markets. It is relatively easy to acquire the first skill. But it is the second that is the more difficult and yet the more essential one. It is his ability to translate observation and knowledge into profitable investment actions that distinguishes the contrarian trader from the run-of-the-mill devil's advocate or naysayer.

Your media diary plays an essential role in helping you develop both these skills. It will be a contrarian trading tool as well as a contrarian training tool. It will contain all the material you need to identify investment crowds, their investment themes, and the emotional state of the crowd. More important, by studying your diary in the light of subsequent market action, you will gain confidence in your deductions and will strengthen your ability to act contrary to the theme of the crowd at the right time. Your diary will be your anchor to windward on the sea of finance against its constant turbulence of boom and bust.

Let me remind you again that it is very, very, *very* hard to be a contrarian trader. If you are to succeed, you will need the help of a well-maintained, up-to-date media diary. It will help you resist the siren songs of the media, which are the principal means of communication for investment crowds. It will teach you to float above the panic that develops during plunging markets and the euphoria during soaring ones. It will help you to shrug off the scorn and derision of crowd members who discover you are betting against them. The rest of the world will think you are at best rash and at worst stupid; and on those occasions when your trades don't work out, the "I told you so's" will be deafening and very hard to endure. But your media diary will be there to offer objective evidence that you made the reasoned choice despite any unfavorable result. The emotional world of any contrarian trader is a turbulent one, and emotional turbulence is the enemy of clear thinking. It will be your media diary that will help you to navigate these turbulent emotional waters successfully.

How will your media diary do all this? How will it enable you to acquire the emotional balance needed for the high-wire performance of contrarian trading? The answer is surprising simple: Your media diary will objectify the emotional content of media messages and market movements by freezing them in time. In this way they can be reexamined when the immediate emotional stresses of the moment have passed. By doing this you will be able to see clearly the correlations between the content of the media when a crowd is enthusiastic and subsequent market performance. These historical observations based on firsthand, real-time recording of media content will develop your ability to identify the emotional extremes of crowd behavior and strengthen your willingness to invest opposite the crowd's theme at such times. The media content preserved in your diary will help you remember how you *felt* at the time. Only by learning how the media make you *feel* when a contrarian investment opportunity is at hand can you learn to act contrary to the media messages that urge the crowd onward to its doom and disintegration.

Your media diary will play another essential role as well. It will be your principal tool for identifying investment themes and the associated investment crowds. Your media diary will record the media messages that play a central role in motivating investment crowds. These messages are the principal means of communication among investment crowd members. Media content is the driving engine of information cascades. By studying this content and comparing it to analogous historical situations, you will be able to assess just where an investment crowd stands in its life cycle. These deductions in turn will help you implement "The Grand Strategy of Contrarian Trading" (see Chapter 11).

I have kept a media diary for more than 20 years. It has proved itself invaluable for identifying investment crowds. It has time and again helped me select the right moment to take a contrarian stance in the market. It has taught me to have confidence in my own judgment and to resist the seductive call of investment crowds. My diary is my single most important contrarian tool. If you want to become a contrarian trader, you must start your media diary now. In this chapter I explain how I maintain my media diary and what material goes into it. This is the most important chapter of this book.

HOW MY DIARY MADE A DIFFERENCE IN 2002

Before we get into the details of building and maintaining a media diary, I'd like to tell you a true story that underlines the value of such a diary, even for a novice trader. This story shows what a valuable educational tool your media diary can be.

Back in March 2000 the stock market had reached the peak of the 1994–2000 bubble. The S&P 500 traded as high as 1,553 and eventually dropped almost 50 percent to a low at 768 in October 2002. The home of the dot-com and telecommunication stocks, the NASDAQ Composite index, reached a high of 5,132 in March 2000 and dropped almost 80 percent to a low of 1,108 in October 2002.

In January 2000 it was obvious to me and to many others that a stock market bubble had inflated. The only question was how big a mistake the market would make before the bubble popped. This is just about the hardest judgment any contrarian trader has to make. If you get it wrong, the damage to your net worth can be serious. I knew that the typical bull market in the stock market averages lasts about two years. The preceding bear market low had occurred in October 1998 with the S&P at 923. Combining these two facts, I guessed that the bubble would continue to inflate until roughly October 2000.

Over a three-week period from March 24 to April 17, 2000, the S&P dropped about 14 percent, from 1,553 to 1,333. The NASDAQ Composite dropped a stomach-churning 25 percent during the same three weeks. Since I expected the market to move above the 1,553 level later in the year, this seemed to me an opportunity to put cash reserves to work with the prospect of earning 15 percent over the subsequent six months.

My media diary emphasized this opportunity, too. On Saturday, April 15, the *New York Times* ran its page 1 headline: "Stock Market in Steep Drop as Worried Investors Flee; Nasdaq Has Its Worst Week." The same day our local paper, the *Morristown Daily Record*, headlined: "Wall Street Wreck." I should say that both averages reached their low points early Monday morning, April 17, and continued upward for four and a half months. The S&P did not make a new high but did rally to 1,530 by August 31. A week later I was telling my clients to sell in anticipation of a drop below 1,300.

Anyhow, although I am the investment strategist in our family, I always consult my wife before we change the allocation in our retirement portfolios. In this particular instance we were having dinner with our three children at a local pizza place on Friday, April 14. Over pizza I suggested to her that we put cash to work in the stock market because the severe drop of the past three weeks had presented an unusual opportunity. But she felt very uncomfortable about doing this, citing the severity of the drop; she suggested a wait-and-see stance instead. I knew that this was tantamount to passing up the opportunity entirely, but for various reasons I chose not to argue the issue.

A few weeks later my wife and I were discussing this lost opportunity. She explained that the headlines at the time were very scary and made it hard to act, so I took her down to my office and showed her my media diary. We looked at the two headlines cited earlier, which I had clipped out and pasted into my diary. Then I reviewed with her the previous five or six buying opportunities in the stock market and showed her the headlines and other media content that appeared as the buying opportunities presented themselves. Of course in every case the time to buy was when the headlines were scariest.

Fast-forward to late July 2002. The S&P 500 index had that month dropped to its lowest level in more than four years. Alan Greenspan, chairman of the Federal Reserve, blamed a corporate culture blighted by "infectious greed" for the breakdown in investor confidence. On NBC's *Tonight Show* Jay Leno regaled his audience with jokes about crashing stock prices and a swooning economy.

The July 29 issue of *Time* magazine had a cover story asking: "Will You *Ever* Be Able to *Retire?*—With *Stocks Plummeting* and Corporations in Disarray, Americans' Financial Futures Are in Peril." (Emphasis is in the original.)

For the previous week's issue of *Barron's* Ben Stein and Phil Demuth wrote an article entitled "A Long Way Down." They predicted that stock prices still had a long way to fall because corporate earnings statements could not be believed.

On July 20 I was up at 6:30 in the morning and opened our front door to retrieve the Saturday editions of the *New York Times* and the *Chicago*

Tribune. I was spreading the newspapers out on our breakfast table when my wife walked into our kitchen. We sat down together, me with my coffee and her with a bowl of Special K. I like to start with the *New York Times* but she prefers to read the *Chicago Tribune* first.

Here was the *New York Times* headline that morning: "Market Continues Four-Month Rout; Dow Plunges 390." The headline of a story by Floyd Norris right next to this headline read: "Adding to Loss of Investments, a Loss of Faith."

"Yikes!" I thought. My wife read the *Tribune* headline to me: "Dow Dives to a Four-Year Low. Sell-Off Deepens: People Are Really Feeling Pain Now."

We were both silent for a minute or so. She was obviously digesting the headlines and I wondered how she would react. Finally she looked across the table at me and said, "I guess it's time to buy?"

"Yes," I replied.

On Monday morning, July 22, we bought index funds for our retirement accounts with the Dow at 8,019 and the S&P 500 at 846. During the subsequent five years these averages advanced more that 75 percent from our purchase price.

Here was a situation in which a complete novice was able to make a very shrewd investment decision. My wife had observed firsthand in my media diary the correlation between scary market headlines and buying opportunities. From this she was able to draw the obvious and correct conclusion. Without a media diary that faithfully captured the emotional state of the crowd and preserved it for future examination, this sort of learning experience would not have been possible.

GET READY TO CUT AND PASTE

To start your media diary, the first thing to do is buy some five-subject spiral notebooks plus some manila folders to use for keeping files of multipage stories and magazine covers. You will also need a good pair of scissors and lots of Scotch tape. Take one of the notebooks and put a title on the front cover; I like to write *Diary* together with the date of the first entry. When the notebook has been filled up, I add the date of the last entry to the cover and then put the entire notebook on my bookshelf for future reference alongside my older diary notebooks.

What sort of media content deserves to be preserved in your media diary? The answer to this question is simple, but perhaps a little surprising. Remember that market movements always generate news stories that encourage the belief that prices will continue to move in the same direction. People want explanations for market events, and this demand for explanation is something the news media strive to satisfy. Therefore, you want to look for stories reinforcing the optimistic or pessimistic moods that arise from rising or falling asset prices. These are the stories that will reinforce the beliefs of the investment crowds you have identified. The most important of these are the ones that directly convey some obvious emotion (i.e., push the emotional buttons of some investment crowd). Such stories might promote fear or optimism; it doesn't matter which. These displays of emotion generally show up in emotionally tinged words or expressions, or descriptions of investor behavior. Pictures often can be used as emotional messengers, so don't forget to watch for them, too.

We'll see that when enough such stories appear in a relatively short interval of time, especially if they are likely to trigger emotional responses from investors, the trend that the story seems to encourage will instead probably reverse. You will principally be interested in media content likely to catch the attention of the casual reader, people who, like yourself, are pressed for time and can't examine stories in any detail. It is the casual reader who is most likely to be affected by the emotional tone of media content. Moreover, it is the casual reader whom news editors want to attract to boost sales. The things that attract the attention of casual readers are headlines, story headers, and magazine covers. When I find a story that has such a headline or header, I might read the first two or three paragraphs to try to gauge its emotional tone, but rarely will I read more than that.

Be especially alert for stories that editors think are important enough to put on a newspaper's front page or that are otherwise highlighted by their position in the paper or by the emotional content of their header or of a picture appearing with the story. As a general rule, a prominent placement on the front page signals two things: First, the editors think their readers will find the story of great interest, and this gives you a read on just where the editors think the crowd's attention is currently focused. Second, the prominent placement attracts the attention of more people, and thus is a more powerful reinforcement of the crowd's mood and beliefs. Here I should add that the editorial page can also be a very good source of material for your media diary. Most newspapers rarely comment on market movements in editorials, so when they do you can be pretty sure that an investment crowd is on the verge of disintegration. The articles that appear on op-ed pages can also be valuable in this regard.

You will want to be as systematic as possible in checking for market-related stories in all the sources I cited in the preceding chapter. Here is my own daily routine for surveying media content.

I start each morning by taking a look at the *New York Times* and the *Chicago Tribune* over breakfast. I am principally interested in stories that appear on the front page of either newspaper, but sometimes there will be a story on the front page of the business section or even a story inside the paper somewhere that attracts my interest. When I find such a story, I make sure to tear out those pages and add them to my stack of articles to paste into my spiral notebook.

I'll clip any story that is likely to catch the casual reader's attention because of its headline or header, or even because of a picture that appears along with the story. The story's subject is usually some aspect of the economy, business, or the behavior of the stock, bond, or commodity markets. But sometimes you will find a story that focuses on an investment crowd you have identified, explains its motivations, and gives an indication of its emotional state. I put this sort of story in my diary, too. I want to emphasize once more that that you are looking for media content that tends to reinforce the beliefs of the investment crowds you are following. Your goal is to be able to efficiently separate the content that will play an important role in reflecting and reinforcing crowd beliefs from the content that is just part of the daily and weekly media noise the financial markets generate.

I'd be less than honest at this point if I didn't tell you that experience with keeping a media diary matters here. As time passes and your diary lengthens, you will get better at selecting the stories that are really helpful for assessing the state of an investment crowd and at ignoring the ones that are of only marginal use. Knowing just which stories are important partly comes from firsthand knowledge of what goes on in markets on a day-by-day basis. It also arises from my knowledge of where market prices stand relative to recent and historical ranges and extremes. This skill has taken many years to develop but proves invaluable time and again. You can develop it, too, with practice. (That is why you should start your media diary now.)

When I first started keeping a media diary, I tended to clip far too many stories. I thought that the diary would permit some sort of statistical analysis of media content. I soon learned that this was not only impractical but wrongheaded. The media diary's real value lies in the experience of reading the headlines and the articles in your diary against the backdrop of market behavior at the time. By doing this you get a sense of the mood of the crowd that you can get in no other way. More important, you acquire a feel for the intensity of an investment crowd's emotional reaction to market and economic events. This intensity of feeling and belief is something only my media diary can convey to me. It can be judged in no other way. This is one reason that statistical, survey-based approaches to contrarian trading tend to have little value. They don't give you the ability to assess the intensity of an investment crowd's beliefs, fears, and hopes.

Once I have clipped what I need from the daily newspapers, I go down to my office and check a number of news web sites together with several market-oriented and a few general-interest blogs. I don't often put material from these sources in my media diary. Only once or twice a week on average do I find a story or opinion piece that I feel gives useful information about one of the investment crowds I am tracking. Recently I have started to save screen shots of headlines of web sites (like MarketWatch) that are devoted solely to financial markets. I am sure that as time passes and electronic sources become increasingly important parts of the media industry I'll devote more time to capturing and recording their messages to investment crowds, too.

Once I've checked my Internet sources, I glance at the magazines that may have arrived in the mail. I don't subscribe to every magazine that might have useful content. Instead I check each magazine's web site for the latest issue. It is usually easy to see just by looking at its cover whether there is any content related to investment crowds in the magazine.

When I find a cover story that is market related, I tear off the cover and staple it to the inside pages of the associated story. If I don't already subscribe to the magazine, I try to buy a copy from my local bookstore. If this isn't possible, I return to the magazine's web site and print out a copy of the story along with an image of any associated cover. These magazine stories I file in a folder labeled "cover stories." I have another folder containing stories of contrarian interest that aren't cover stories and are too long to put in my spiral notebook media diary.

EXCERPTS FROM MY MEDIA DIARY: NOVEMBER 2005

I'd like to give you a more detailed illustration of what my diary actually looks like so that you can get a better sense of the kinds of stories it contains. My object now is not to explain in any detail how the diary can help you to make investment decisions. Instead my immediate goal is to give examples of stories I see as important, examples of materials I like to preserve in my diary, and examples of the sort of market consequences this information can lead you to anticipate.

I have just pulled down from my shelf of media diaries the one containing content that appeared between October 25, 2005, and September 18, 2007, a period of about 23 months. Generally I find that anywhere from 18 to 30 months of material will fill up a single five-subject spiral notebook. Exactly how many months of material it will take depends on the nature of the markets at the time. Quiet markets generate less media commentary than do volatile ones or ones setting records of one sort or another.

The first entry in this diary was a story that appeared on November 4 in the business section of the *New York Times* (henceforth abbreviated *NYT*). It was headed "Bears Have Their Day" and discussed the fact that 2005 had been a good year for hedge funds specializing in short selling. I clipped this article because I knew that whenever the short sellers are prominent in the newspaper it is time to buy stocks. This was no exception. The S&P 500 rose from about 1,220 when this story appeared to about 1,450 on the last day recorded in this diary.

The next clipping was a *Wall Street Journal* story on November 8 headed "Foreign Stocks Get New Push." The story tells of Wall Street firms raising their allocation levels to foreign stocks to record levels. Foreign stocks make money for investors primarily when the dollar falls, so I interpreted this story as a bet against the then rising trend of the dollar. It was definitely *not* a story that reinforced the bullish trend in the dollar at the time. In fact, about a month later the dollar started a 30-month, 24 percent drop and thus made these Wall Street firms look like geniuses. I should say that I did not see this big drop in the dollar coming, largely because of stories like this one that did not indicate the presence yet of a significant bullish dollar crowd.

The November 14 issue of *Newsweek* provided my next diary entry. It was Robert J. Samuelson's column entitled "Worry While You Spend," which had a great interlinear subhead: "What explains the gap between Americans' glum mood and their free-spending ways?" I clipped this story because it reinforced my view that no bullish stock market crowd had developed despite a three-year rally from the 2002 low, which had already carried the S&P 500 from 768 to 1,220. I found this remarkable, but I should emphasize that the absence of a crowd tells you nothing in and of itself about prospective market direction. (See the previous paragraph about the dollar for emphasis of this fact.)

My next entry was a story dated November 4 that appeared on the MarketWatch web site. Note that it was pasted into my diary out of proper chronological sequence. This sort of thing happens, especially with Web or magazine content, and I don't worry too much about it. But I am careful always to note the source of every clipping and the date of its appearance.

This MarketWatch story was a column by Mark Hulbert, who edits the *Hulbert Financial Digest*, a newsletter that tracks the recommendations and market performance of financial newsletters. I have found Hulbert's columns very informative at times because he himself is a devotee of the contrarian art. Moreover, he has at his disposal hard data about opinions, which would be very difficult for any individual to duplicate. In this particular column Hulbert tells the reader that the bond market timing newsletters he tracks at the *Hulbert Financial Digest* have as a group never been more bearish on bond prices. He offers statistical evidence to back up this observation. I should note that according to my records the bond market made a low point on November 4 and then rallied for two consecutive months. However, after the rally bond prices eventually dropped below their November 4 low. Nonetheless, Hulbert's contrarian warning was a very valuable piece of information for a contrarian trader, and the subsequent market rally was normal for the kind of evidence that Hulbert offered in his column.

Along the same lines was a *Wall Street Journal* story dated November 17, which was pasted into my diary just after the Hulbert column. It was headed "A Message in the Bond Market." It warned that the yield curve was about to invert and said this was bearish for bond market investors. The story reinforced my view at the time that bond prices would rally at least for a couple of months.

The next story pasted into my diary was a brief column that appeared in the business section of the *New York Times* and was headed "Rapid Rise: Google Passes $400 a Share." I saved this not because I thought it had immediate market significance but because I wanted to keep the story of the Google crowd current in my diary. I had been following it for 15 months, ever since Google's initial public offering (IPO) at $85 per share in August 2004. The reason for my early interest was a very unusual circumstance surrounding this IPO. At the time, the investment crowd focused on Google was a bearish one, not the bullish crowd one normally expects to see at the time of an IPO. This was so unusual that I noted it and brought it to the attention of my clients. I began commenting on Google in the web log I started in 2005 (you can find it by googling my name). My basic theme was that until the bearish crowd in Google morphed into a bullish one, Google's stock price would probably rise far more than anyone expected. In April 2005 with the stock trading at $224 I cited a $500 target, but this proved to be way too conservative. By November 2007 Google had reached $747.

The November 28 issues of *BusinessWeek* and *Fortune* gave me my next two diary entries. The *BusinessWeek* story was headed "This Spree Could Spur a Stock Surge." It described how the boom in private equity purchases of public companies was adding fuel to the stock market advance from its 2002 lows. I believed this to be an accurate assessment of one of the reasons for the bull market in stocks, and I clipped the article because I wanted to keep tracking this story until its end—which probably would be associated with an important stock market top (it was, in 2007). The *Fortune* story was of a different sort. It was entitled "Investors Are In for a Shock" and subtitled "Financial assets are richly priced." The article is accompanied by a cartoon of an investor who has climbed a staircase but, like Wile E. Coyote, has continued past the end of the staircase and now hovers in midair (prior to a crash). I love to paste stories that are accompanied by interesting photographs, cartoons, or charts into my diary. They always have more emotional intensity than media content without any particular visual interest. This particular story asserted that the returns on financial assets are likely to be far worse than people expect. I should point out that the bull market in stocks had two more years to run at the time this story appeared. I clipped the column as evidence that a bullish stock market crowd had not yet formed.

EXCERPTS FROM MY MEDIA DIARY: JUNE 2006

I put only eight stories in my diary during the month of November 2005. It was a slow month but an otherwise typical one. The markets were generally stable or rising at the time. You will find that most months won't provide diary material dramatic enough to call for any investment actions. Just the opposite is true for months associated with stock market drops. The pages of my media diary fill rapidly at such times. One of these months was June 2006.

On May 5, 2006, the S&P 500 index closed at 1,325. It fell the rest of the month and reached a low close of 1,223 on June 13. This was a relatively quick 8 percent drop in prices, normal for a bull market. From the June 13 low the index would rally to a high close of 1,575 in October 2007, an advance of 29 percent. Here is what I recorded in my media diary during June 2006.

The first story of the month was another column by Mark Hulbert. It had nothing to do with the stock market. Instead Hulbert's focus was on gold, which had reached a high of $725 early in May along with the stock market and had since dropped about $100 per ounce. I should note that the actual low of this drop occurred on June 14 with gold selling at about $550. Hulbert noted in this column that gold timing newsletters had by late May moved from a very bullish stance to a position of being on average completely out of the gold market. He interpreted this bullishly. As I have said, I like to keep a record of Hulbert's views because he tries to take a contrarian view of the markets and often offers useful facts to back them up.

The next diary entry was a column by Daniel Gross from the *New York Times* business section of June 4. In it he noted the strong performance of the U.S. economy during the first quarter of 2006 and contrasted this with consumers' rather pessimistic expectations of the future. I thought this was significant, again because it suggested there was no important bullish crowd then active in the stock market.

On June 6 the *Wall Street Journal* headlined its personal section with a story headed "Cash Becomes a Hot Investment." The story said that stock market volatility and rising interest rates were prompting investors to shift into money market funds and certificates of deposit (CDs). I interpreted this as a bullish omen for both the stock and bond markets. I have already explained what followed for the S&P 500 index. The bond market rallied for six months from its June 2006 lows.

That same day I clipped a *Wall Street Journal* story by E. S. Browning that was headed "Dow Falls 1.77% as Fed Chief Adds to Investor Jitters." This merited inclusion in my diary because of the use of the word *jitters*, an indicator that fears were building among stock market investors.

Next among the June 2006 diary entries were two out-of-sequence entries of content from the Internet. Both appeared on June 5. The first was a MarketWatch column by Peter Brimelow, which reported the gold bug Harry Schultz's prediction that gold was headed for $3,000 per ounce. The second item was a column by Michael Barone, political commentator. I underlined the most important sentence of his piece: "Yet Americans are in a sour mood, a mood that may be explained by the lack of a sense of history." This clipping was only a small contribution to the story of a general disconnect between actual economic conditions and Americans' views of the future. I didn't see this as a situation encouraging the development of a bullish stock market crowd.

"Foreign Markets Extend Decline as Rate Fears Curb Risk Appetite" was the headline of a front page, below-the-fold story in the *Wall Street Journal* on June 9 that I clipped for my diary. The phrase *rate fears* I felt had bullish implications for the stock market and for interest rates. My attention is attracted to stories that contain phrases indicating strong emotions of one sort or another.

From the June 12 edition of *Barron's* I clipped part of the "Up and Down Wall Street" column, which that week was written by Michael Santoli. In it he made two observations that put him in both bullish short-term (right) and bearish long-term (wrong) camps. I underlined in red these sentences:

[A]nxiety levels, measured both statistically and anecdotally, seem to have risen more than the 5% to 6% decline from recent stock-index highs would warrant.

and then:

[T]here's an emerging sense of foreboding auguring a less-generous [market] environment.

On June 13 I clipped an item from Bill Cara's blog. It showed a picture of a black bear and was accompanied by this comment:

As traders are now glued to their screens in hopes of seeing some evidence that today and tomorrow's U.S. inflation data will permit the funds rate to fall, this is the picture they are getting.

The *Wall Street Journal* had a front page story on June 14, the day after the low was made in the S&P 500, which was headed: "Tumbling Markets May Be Reflection of Strong Growth—Investors Struggle to Adapt to Demise of Easy Money; Dow Gives Up 2006 Gains." That same day the *Wall Street Journal*'s markets section was headlined: "Interest-Rate Fears Drive World-Wide Slide." The next day the *New York Times* had a front page story, placed right next to the headline story, which was headed: "A Modest Rise Still Amplifies Inflation Fears—Lessons of 70's Prompt Strong Warnings."

On June 16, on its front page, the *New York Times* published a line chart of the Dow Jones Industrial Average recording the drop from its May 10 top. The caption of the graph said: "Relief, at Least for Now." But in the text of the caption one finds: "But the increased volatility in the markets suggested that their troubles may not be over." The graph was interesting not just because of this text but because it showed a picture of a market in the process of dropping. Images like this one are very good reflections of emotional states and serve also to amplify these emotions, in this case fear.

The *Chicago Tribune* of June 16 was headlined, in reference to Ben Bernanke, chairman of the Federal Reserve: "When Big Ben Speaks . . . the Market Reacts." The headline was accompanied by an intraday chart of the Dow for the previous day, which showed the start of a rally when Bernanke started to deliver a speech in Chicago.

At this point you have probably noticed that the frequency of stories that I believed pushed emotional buttons increased around the time of the market low on June 13. This is typical of the media content associated with low points in the stock market. The stronger the display of emotion via story frequency and intensity, the more important and long-lasting will be the low. Highs, by contrast, tend to occur against a more diffuse background, sometimes accompanied by an absence of strong emotion of any kind. We discuss this in more detail in Chapter 9.

The June 19 issue of *Barron's* was interesting for several reasons. First, the inveterate stock market bear, Alan Abelson, noted in his column that the latest Investors Intelligence survey of market letters showed more bearish sentiment than at any time since the bear market low of October 2002. He observed that this meant that some sort of bounce (rally) was inevitable. But then he went on to dispute the longer-term implications of these numbers: "[W]e suspect that the glimpse of reality that unhinged the markets will become the increasingly prevailing view in the months ahead." In other words, Abelson dismissed the longer-term significance of the large bearish contingent in the survey, arguing instead that, aside from a short-term bounce, the bears would be right this time. In my experience there is nothing as bullish as a bearish view that explicitly dismisses the significance of widespread bearish sentiment.

In that same issue, *Barron's* had two stories that were also relevant for the stock market. The first was the midyear roundtable of market seers offering their predictions for the second half of 2006. The story was headed: "High Anxiety." Wow! Seldom does one come across an emotion-laden headline like this one.

The second story was about a fellow named Robert A. Haugen. Haugen's thesis was that increasing stock market volatility was inevitable and would set the stage for depression or worse. He recommended shutting the stock market for two days a week to calm things down. This *Barron's* story illustrates a general principle. Journalists may not reveal their biases to you directly, but they often will do so indirectly though their choice of story material. Moreover, this very choice of subject matter reveals their perception of readers' interests and concerns. In this instance the choice of Haugen as the subject for this story was essentially an attempt to appeal to the current fears of *Barron's* readers and to offer an implicit bearish prediction of the future.

The June 18 Sunday edition of the *New York Times* had a column by Mark Hulbert in which he also catered to the then-current bearish sentiment. In its first paragraph he says: "Bad news, stock investors: the market is likely to underperform garden-variety money market funds through the end of next year."

There are a handful of other stories I put into my diary later that month, but they all reinforce the theme, which I think you can see clearly by now. As the market reached its June 13 low in 2006, more and more stories appeared encouraging readers to think prices would go still lower.

This example also illustrates an important media diary principle: Look for media messages that tend to reinforce the view that recent market movements will continue. These are the messages that fuel information cascades and that will enable you to assess the strength of investment crowds.

INTERPRETING MAGAZINE COVERS

An important part of my media diary is my collection of magazine covers. I keep these in chronological order in separate file folders labeled by year of appearance. I described the magazines I monitor regularly in the previous chapter, but any weekly or monthly magazine can be the source of a cover that speaks to an investment crowd.

I first learned the value of using magazine covers in contrarian trading from Paul Macrae Montgomery. In the early 1970s Paul observed that when *Time* magazine had a cover story about a prominent business personality, about the stock market, or about some other finance-related matter, one could often infer that an important move in the markets was imminent, a move that was likely to be in the direction opposite to what the cover suggested. Optimistic covers led to unexpected drops in prices, while pessimistic covers had the opposite effect.

The theory behind this phenomenon is a simple one. If a business- or stock market–related story makes it onto a *Time* cover, this means that it has already caught the popular imagination and is the theme of a large investment crowd. This is true precisely because *Time* covers rarely concern business topics. When they do they must reflect opinion that has been accepted by the general population of investors. In such circumstances the investment crowd has little capacity for growth, and the time for its disintegration is probably at hand.

In the next chapter I'll have more to say about general guidelines for using magazine cover stories to identify investment crowds. For now I'd just like to explain a few criteria you can use to determine whether a cover story is important enough to put into your diary.

First, you want the cover story to focus on a specific financial market or a specific stock. This is important because investment crowds organize themselves around specific markets. The cover itself might highlight a person who is closely associated with the market, for example the company's CEO or the chairman of the Federal Reserve. You want to look for covers offering implicit predictions for the direction of the market or some emotional response to the market's recent behavior, the more definitive the better.

Covers that talk about the condition of the whole economy generally do not give useful information about investment crowds. I save these sorts of covers as indicators of general mood but don't use them to assess the status of investment crowds. In contrast, covers that speak of the levels of interest rates or inflation can be useful in identifying bond market investment crowds.

The most important feature of an important cover story is its emotional content. The more the cover appeals to fear or to greed, the stronger its implication for the imminent demise of an investment crowd. To illustrate how I select covers for my media diary, let's look at the cover stories I saved from the year 2006.

The first cover story was from *Time* magazine's January 30 issue. The cover showed Bill Ford of Ford Motor Company and asked: "Would You Buy a New Car from This Man?" The cover caption suggested Ford had big ideas for saving his company and the auto industry. The significance of this cover story was hard to judge. It appeared after a 50 percent drop in the price of Ford stock from $16 to $8 over the preceding two years. One would expect such a cover to express bearish sentiments. But instead it seemed to offer hope to investors that the worst might be past. One should note that the price of Ford stock was essentially unchanged during the subsequent two years.

The next cover story of interest also concerned the auto industry and appeared in *Fortune*'s February 20 issue. Unlike the warm red, yellow, and green colors of the *Time* cover, this cover appeared with a depressing black background with a blue GM logo. The cover was headed: "The Tragedy of General Motors." The cover caption read: "It is the instinctive wish of most businesspeople that General Motors not go bankrupt. . . . And yet the evidence points, with increasing certitude, to bankruptcy." GM stock had dropped from $45 to $17 over the preceding two years, a much bigger percentage drop than Ford's. Moreover, this GM cover was starkly bearish in tone. As such, it was a strong indication that the bear crowd had grown large and complacent about GM. The price of GM went from $17 to $42 over the subsequent 20 months.

The February 12 cover of *Barron's* featured Google's logo Photo-shopped to read "Gurgle." The logo was shown sinking beneath the water in a washbasin or tub, the implication being that Google was going down the drain. At the time, Google's stock had dropped about 100 points from its early 2006 high of $475 and would drop a bit further to a March low of $331. But over the subsequent 20 months the price of Google's stock would advance from $331 to $747.

It is interesting to note that a week later *Time* magazine also had a Google cover story. This story was headed: "Can We Trust Google with Our Secrets?" This magazine cover told me little about the Google bullish investment crowd. It was not very specific and didn't imply any particular direction for Google's stock, even though it did have some emotional content, as revealed by the use of the word *trust*.

The next cover of interest to me during 2006 was the cover of *Barron's* May 1 issue. It depicted a bull reclining comfortably against two pillows with a big smile on his face. The story was headed: "Dow 12,000." The Dow Jones Industrial Average reached a high at 11,700 just a week later and then dropped sharply to 10,700 during the market break, which ended in June 2006. This story was an unusual example of a bullish cover that precisely timed a scary short-term drop in the stock market.

The May 27–June 2 issue of the *Economist* showed a brown bear on its hind legs peeking out from behind a tree. It was headed: "Which Way Is Wall Street?" This was a specific prediction of declining stock prices. A bull or a bear that appears on a magazine cover after the market has risen or dropped a substantial amount is usually a sign that the price movement is about to reverse. The low in the S&P occurred at 1,223 on June 13, and the average reached the 1,575 level 16 months later.

I remember being particularly impressed by the cover story of the *New York Times Magazine*'s June 11 issue. It showed a black background against which a hairy, giant "debt monster" was pursuing little people who were running from it in blind terror. The cover caption was classic: "America's Scariest Addiction Is Getting Even Scarier." The color scheme and the double use of the adjectives *scariest* and *scarier* showed strong emotional content. Appearing as it did after a monthlong drop in the stock market, it strengthened and amplified the emotions of the bearish crowd that had developed by then.

Next we come to two cover stories that illustrate that one cannot blindly take a market position opposite to that implied by a magazine cover. These stories appeared in the July 24 and November 6 issues of *Barron's*. The July 24 cover said "Time to Buy," and this advice was right on the mark. The November 6 cover was headed: "Next Stop 13,000?" The appearance of the question mark weakened the significance of this story, but nonetheless the Dow made it up to the 13,700 level the following year before any substantial reaction set in.

The important thing to keep in mind about cover stories is that they are significant only if they are specific in their implications and if they reinforce the belief that current market trends will continue.

CHAPTER 9

Important Investment Themes

Investment themes • long-lived versus short-lived themes • first the market moves • then comes the rationale • categories of themes • new era themes • things are always different this time • the abandonment of traditional valuation standards • war and political crises • bearish crowds are common • war crowds form and disintegrate quickly • in the United States buy the outbreak of shooting • sell peace • financial crises • generally very brief • most intense bearish crowd forms just before resolution • the subprime crisis • individual companies and industries • Google • commodity booms • oil at $147 and gold at $1,000 • interest rates and the bond market • predicting a 25-year drop in interest rates in 1982 • using your media diary to track investment themes

TELLING THE MARKET'S STORY

Your media diary contains need-to-know information about developing investment themes. Remember that investment crowds develop around investment themes. An investment theme is a rationale for market behavior. It tells the market's story by explaining why prices have changed so dramatically and by offering, at least implicitly, a prediction for their direction in the immediate future. The explanatory nature of an investment theme is important here. It is this apparently logical explanation of the past that sustains the associated information cascade. This is the identifying feature of any investment theme around which an investment crowd will develop.

In Chapter 5 I discussed some of the investment themes that were associated with the stock market bubble of 1994–2000 and with the subsequent bear market of 2001–2002. These were very important investment themes—the associated crowds were big and long-lived. The bubble crowds' life cycles each extended over several years, while the bear market crowd's life span was about 24 months. But investment themes and their crowds can be short-lived as well. This is especially true of the bearishly themed stock market crowds. On average, bearish crowds disintegrate sooner than bullish crowds. Moreover, one often finds a very short-lived bearish crowd developing in response to some external event, which is blamed for a relatively brief drop in the averages, say one lasting a few weeks and amounting to 5 percent or a little more. In Chapter 8 we saw an example of such a crowd forming during June 2006. At that time the external event was a rise in interest rates, which was blamed for generating fears that the Federal Reserve would pursue a tighter monetary policy.

When you use your diary material to identify an investment theme, keep in mind the basic sequence of events accompanying the development of any investment crowd. First comes a dramatic rise or fall in the market averages or in the price of an individual stock or industry group. This generates media content, which notes this price change and offers an explanation for it. These media explanations will increase in number, frequency, and emotional intensity as long as the associated price trend continues. This is the evidence you look for to tell you that an information cascade is under way. Your job as a contrarian trader is to assess the current strength of the crowd and to use available historical precedents to make an educated guess about where the crowd is in its life cycle.

In principle, an investment theme may tell any plausible story or even offer a completely novel explanation for a change in market prices. Even so, I have found that most investment themes fall into a small number of categories. It's useful to know what these categories are and to be familiar with a number of historical examples of each. Background knowledge like this makes real-time identification of investment themes an easier task.

NEW ERAS

Every generation or so, the stock market in the United States experiences a multiyear advance in prices that multiplies the market averages several times and is not interrupted by any significant, sustained downward move. These advances enrich the typical investor and always encourage the development of one or more bullish investment crowds. The classic examples are the 1921–1929 bull market, during which the Dow Jones Industrial

Average rose from 60 to 380, and the 1994–2000 bull market, during which the same average advanced from 3,800 to 11,750. An equally dramatic example is the 1949–1966 bull market, during which the Dow rose from 169 to 1,000.

As these sustained advances in stock prices proceed, one invariably finds a particular kind of investment theme emerging, a theme I like to call the "new era" theme. People notice that stock prices have been advancing steadily and have already risen higher than normal in a typical economic expansion. Investors want to know *why* this is happening. The media are happy to meet this demand for answers. The usual explanation is that there are new industries or technological or financial innovations that are driving the economy to previously unseen heights of prosperity. In the 1920s the boom was in radio (the new technology of that decade) and the automobile industry. Installment credit was the financial innovation of the time, and it multiplied the purchasing power of the era's consumers. The new era of the 1960s was associated with the computer, electronic, and airline industries. The principal financial innovation of the time was a macroeconomic one—Keynesian economics had triumphed in the economics profession, and many believed that its prescriptions had made recessions a thing of the past. There were two other innovations of note. The first was the concept of the industrial conglomerate—a merger of firms in different industries, which supposedly allowed shrewd management to extend its reach and effects, and which diversified the risks of industry-specific business performance. The second innovation was the concept of the high-capitalization, perpetual growth stock, neatly encapsulated in the Nifty Fifty growth stocks, which predominated institutional portfolios in the early 1970s. During the dot-com years of 1994–2000 the new technology was the Internet and the personal computer. When the globalization of markets (which new communications technology permitted) was added to the stew, the new economy theme made its appearance.

The key identifying phrase of new era thinking is "things are different this time." Stay alert for this sort of assertion when you are culling material for your media diary. Many people will recognize that the stock prices are overvalued by historical yardsticks. But investors must be persuaded that this will not lead to the typical historical consequence, a crash in prices and a return to normal valuation levels. Otherwise, why would they continue to buy stocks? During a new era boom in stock prices, look for media content urging investors to abandon traditional stock market valuation standards. They will invariably be told that paying only for earnings or dividends is the old way of thinking, now out of date and typical of those people who just don't get the significance of new financial or industrial innovations. The stock market bubble of the late 1990s offered classic examples of the "things are different this time" theme. In fact, I think this theme was carried to the second order of silliness. The first order of silliness consists in justifying stock prices by revenue growth instead of by earnings or dividend growth. But in the second-order realm one looks not to revenues but to the share of potential customers, the so-called *eyeball count* to justify extraordinarily high valuations. Put another way, investors were assured that although these new Internet retailers and information services lost money on each customer they gained, they would make up for this by increasing the number of customers they served!

EFFECT OF WAR AND INTERNATIONAL POLITICAL CRISES ON THE STOCK MARKET

War or the threat of war always energizes the investment community and focuses the attention of a large part of the general population on media messages. Investment crowds form quickly in such circumstances and often disintegrate just as quickly, so the contrarian trader has to be alert for these rapid changes in beliefs and expectations.

As a rule, the threat of war and especially the start of shooting creates buying opportunities for investors who live in the country destined to be victorious. The prospect of war almost always encourages the growth of a big bearish crowd. The crowd focuses on the consequent loss of human life, the destruction of economic infrastructure, and the general uncertainty about the outcome of war, and expects stock prices to drop as a result. The thought of an imminent war depresses people. But once war is declared, this bearish crowd begins to disintegrate as soon as there is reason to expect ultimate victory. The resulting rise in stock prices eventually causes the development of a bullish, victory crowd. The advent of peace then usually marks the start of the disintegration of the bullish investment crowd that developed as victory became more and more certain. One sees this sequence of events in the U.S. stock market time and time again.

The prospect of the Civil War dropped prices 35 percent on the New York Stock Exchange from the time Abraham Lincoln was nominated in 1860 until the shooting started at Fort Sumter in April 1861. From the Fort Sumter low point prices then rose 300 percent, reaching their peak when Lincoln appointed Ulysses S. Grant as the commander of all Northern armies in March 1864.

The sinking of the battleship *Maine* in Havana's harbor in February 1898 triggered war fears that sent the stock market averages downward by 15 percent until the United States declared war on Spain two months later. Prices then turned around and rose 27 percent until August, when hostilities halted.

The start of the European war in July 1914 closed the New York Stock Exchange because it was feared that the start of shooting would trigger a financial panic. When the exchange reopened in December, prices immediately began to advance and the subsequent bull market carried the Dow Jones Industrials from 53 to 110 just after Woodrow Wilson's reelection in 1916. Here again the prospect of entry by the United States into war was a bearish development, and prices dropped from 110 to 90 by the time the country declared war on April 6, 1917. However, unlike previous instances, prices continued downward for eight more months after the declaration of war to reach a low point at the 65 level in December 1917. From that point the Dow advanced 35 percent until the Armistice in November 1918.

On December 7, 1941, Japan attacked the U.S. fleet at Pearl Harbor. The United States declared war on Japan on December 8 with the Dow trading at 112. The stock market dropped another 18 percent to 92 in April 1942, just prior to the turn toward victory in the Pacific at the battle of Midway in early June 1942. The Dow subsequently continued upward to the 212 level in May 1946, nine months after the surrender of Japan and a full year after the surrender of Germany.

The Korean War began on June 25, 1950, and the Dow dropped from 224 to 197 over the next three weeks. U.S. ground troops entered Korea on July 1. The 197 low in the Dow has not been seen since.

The Cuban missile crisis occurred in October 1962. In June of that year the Dow ended a 25 percent drop from a high at 734 in December 1961. The June low at 535 was not broken at any time during the missile crisis. The first inkling of Soviet missiles in Cuba reached the U.S. intelligence services in August 1962 with the Dow at 620. The market dropped to a low at 549 on October 24 as the crisis developed. A peaceful resolution was reached on October 28.

The Vietnam War was a different kind of conflict because it had no definite beginning through a declaration of war or start of hostilities. However, it did have a definite end for the United States with the Paris Peace Accords, which were signed on January 27, 1973. The Dow reached a record high close at 1,051 on January 13, 1973, and over the subsequent 23 months dropped nearly 50 percent to a low at 577 in December 1974.

The Watergate scandal forced the resignation of Richard M. Nixon from the presidency of the United States on August 9, 1974. As noted before, the Dow reached its low four months later, and that December low was at essentially the same level as an earlier low on October 10.

The first Gulf War began for the United States in January 1991. Saddam Hussein's Iraq had invaded Kuwait in early August 1990. From its July high in 1990 at the 3,000 level, the Dow dropped to a low at 2,363 on

October 11, 1990. Prices never went lower than that even as the United States continued to prepare for war. It was widely expected at the time that the start of shooting would send prices below their October low at 2,363. I appeared on CNBC several times that fall and in early January, and asserted the contrary view that the stock market was about to begin a huge rally. The United States commenced air operations against Iraq on January 15, 1991, with the Dow closing the previous day at 2,482. Over the next six weeks the Dow advanced 20 percent. The Dow has never since been as low at 2,482.

The United States was attacked by terrorists on September 11, 2001. The Dow ended the previous day at 9,605 and the stock market was closed for several days after the attack, reopening on September 17. The Dow continued its drop, reaching a low at 8,235 on September 21. From there the Dow rallied to 10,635 on March 19, 2002.

The second Gulf War began with the invasion of Iraq by U.S. forces on March 20, 2003. The run-up to the war was a confusing time politically in the United States and internationally as opposing political forces debated the merits and dangers of such an invasion. The Dow Industrials reached a low at 7,425 on March 11, and then moved upward to 14,164 on October 9, 2007. Subsequently the average dropped 24 percent by July 2008. It will be interesting to see whether history will record the second Gulf War as being won during the last half of 2007 following the defeat of Al-Qaeda in Iraq. If so, this would be yet another case in which victory or the assurance of victory marked an important top in stock prices.

This historical review should convince you that the threat and the reality of war exert a strong influence of the public's emotions. The emotional turbulence associated with war encourages the rapid development and disintegration of investment crowds, and these crowds force markets into valuation mistakes. The frequent market mistakes arising from wartime conditions offer very important opportunities to the contrarian trader.

FINANCIAL CRISES CREATE CROWDS

Financial crises that attract wide public attention are usually associated with the collapse or near collapse of some domestic or foreign financial institution or of the credit of some sovereign nation. Most financial crises are of relatively short duration, and as a rule they generate bearish investment crowds. I'd like to briefly review a number of such crises that have occurred during the past 35 years. Note how frequently crises are associated with stock market buying opportunities. This happens because the news of the crisis spreads rapidly in the media, as does the fear such news generates. In a matter of days or weeks the associated information cascade has persuaded everyone who can be persuaded to join the bearish crowd. The crisis reaches its climax with some sort of government intervention—a guarantee or rescue—and the bearish crowd begins to disintegrate.

There have been a number of financial crises over the past thirty-five years. On June 21, 1970, the Penn Central Corporation defaulted on its commercial paper obligations and declared bankruptcy. This briefly threw the U.S. commercial paper market into turmoil. One should note, however, that a 17-month-long bear market in stock prices had ended just four weeks earlier with the Dow closing at a low of 631 on May 26. It is also interesting to note that the June 1 edition of *Time* magazine featured Federal Reserve chairman Arthur Burns on its cover and was captioned: "Is This Slump Necessary?—Facing an Economy on the Brink." The Dow proceeded to advance to 1,051 on January 11, 1973.

The 1974 low in stock prices developed two months after the resignation of Richard Nixon from the presidency. This was a political crisis, but a weak economy was the subject of *Time* cover stories on September 9 and October 14. The failure of the Franklin National Bank occurred on October 8, and the low point of the S&P 500 index at 62.28 occurred on October 10. The S&P 500 has never since traded as low.

On August 12, 1982, Mexico's finance minister informed the U.S. Federal Reserve that Mexico would default on certain short-term debt obligations and that its foreign exchange markets would close the following day. A month earlier the Penn Square Bank had failed in Oklahoma. The Dow Jones Industrial Average reached a low at 777 on August 12, 1982, after dropping from a high at 1,024 in April 1981. The 777 low kicked off a bull market that over the next 25 years carried the Dow to 14,164.

The July–October period of 1998 saw a brief but sharp 20 percent drop in the U.S. stock market averages. On August 17 the Russian government devalued the ruble and defaulted on debt obligations. The resulting turmoil in world debt markets brought a U.S. hedge fund, Long Term Capital Management (LTCM), to the brink of insolvency. Judging the firm too big to fail, the U.S. Federal Reserve organized a takeover of the LTCM portfolio on September 23. One should note that the Dow reached its closing low near 7,530 on August 31 and its intraday low for the year the next day. The Dow then advanced to 11,750 by January 2000.

The last financial crisis I'd like to review is the subprime crisis of 2008. I'll have more to say about this in a later chapter. For now, suffice it to say that the crisis was born of the worldwide housing bubble, which peaked in the United States in 2005. That spectacular advance in housing prices was fueled partly by easy credit and partly by mortgage loans made to borrowers of subprime quality, borrowers who often had insufficient assets or income. This was only possible because mortgage loans were securitized, bundled together into packages that were in turn sliced and diced into new securities, so-called tranches. The subprime loans were hidden from view behind the complicated mathematical formulas that determined the payouts investors got from each tranche. These formulas depended on financial variables with which no one had any statistical experience, so investor payouts were impossible to predict. Instead, buyers of mortgage securities relied on the ratings that firms like Moody's Investors Service and Standard & Poor's provided for these bonds. Here of course we have a case of the blind being led by the blind. In any event, when large numbers of subprime borrowers began to default on their mortgages, the prices on certain tranches of mortgage securities fell spectacularly. (In late July 2008 Merrill Lynch effectively wrote down mortgage securities with face value of $36 billion by 95 percent!) Even worse, no one in the financial community could be sure which banks or brokerage firms carried such securities (now known as toxic waste) on their books. This effectively froze markets for certain kinds of securities and loans, and the resulting constriction of credit threatened to plunge the United States and the rest of the world into a serious recession or depression.

The stock market consequences of the subprime crisis have not yet been completely recorded as I write this (in November 2008). There have been at least three major government-sponsored rescues of financial institutions so far. The first occurred in mid-March 2008 when the brokerage firm of Bear Stearns collapsed and was purchased by JPMorgan Chase. The second occurred in mid-July when mortgage intermediaries Fannie Mae and Freddie Mac were rescued by a Federal Reserve credit guarantee and by a congressional housing rescue package. The third was the rescue on September 16 of the insurance giant, American International Group. But of even more importance was the government decision in mid-September to allow the bankruptcy of the Lehman Brothers investment bank.

The financial crisis associated with the panic of 2008 was a significant exception to the historical rule that such crises tend to be brief. Instead of lasting a matter of weeks, just a few months, the panic of 2008 extended through most of the year, and as this is being written in late 2008, it shows no signs yet of abatement. Even so, I think that history will record that the September–November 2008 period, the time when the crisis was most intense and when panic was in the air, was a terrific buying opportunity in the U.S. stock market.

NEW INDUSTRIES AND COMPANIES

This category is almost self-explanatory. Technological progress and business innovations are constant facts of life in the capitalist economy's

Schumpeterian world of creative destruction. New industries arise and new business firms emerge to bring these innovations to market.

Railroads were the speculative darlings of the late 1800s, but industrial firms began to take the reins from the railroads in the early 1900s, a change signaled by the formation of the Standard Oil holding company in 1899 and of U.S. Steel in 1903. During the subsequent two decades the automobile industry grew spectacularly. Led by Ford and General Motors, it changed the economic landscape for business and consumers forever. Radio was the big technological innovation of the 1920s and RCA was the speculative leader of the U.S. stock market of 1929.

Fast-forwarding to the 1960s, we find the computer industry's first incarnation in the form of IBM, the biggest manufacturer of mainframe computers at the time. The passenger jet led to a rise in airline travel during the same period, and airline stocks were among the growth stocks of the time. In 1980 the birth of the biotechnology industry was heralded by the initial public offering (IPO) of Genentech, a biotechnology firm started in 1976. The biotechnology sector is still rapidly growing today. The 1980s also saw the computer industry's second incarnation with the advent of the personal computer (PC), brought to market by IBM in 1981. Computer software became a growth industry at the same time when Microsoft captured the rights for producing the IBM PC's operating system.

The 1990s witnessed the popularization of the Internet and the rapid development of telecommunications technology in the form of the mobile phone and fiber-optic cable networks. New companies like America Online, Dell Computer, Lucent Technologies, and WorldCom led the stock market upward during those years.

One of the most interesting new companies of the first decade of the new millennium is Google, whose search engine technology dominates the market today and has been used as a device for selling online advertising. Google had its IPO in August 2004 at $85. Three years later Google stock had risen to $747 but it then fell to a low of $247 during the panic of 2008. An interesting thing about Google is that there was a very well-developed *bearish* crowd at the time of its IPO. This was unprecedented in my experience and let me to take a very bullish stance on Google at the time. You can read the story of Google's IPO in Chapter 14.

The investment themes associated with new companies and emerging industries are usually bullish themes and project virtually unlimited growth ahead for the company or industry. But the contrarian trader should be careful about being too skeptical about such themes when he first sees them emerge. The fact is that in a big, ever more global economy any new technology or innovation has a lot of potential for growth. Of course no tree grows to the sky, but as we will see in subsequent chapters, the contrarian trader is often wise to join the bullish crowds of these individual companies and industries temporarily. The trick is to stay alert for the spread of the bullish contagion to less attractive and compelling related situations. Once late-coming competitors arrive on the scene, it is usually time for the contrarian trader to leave the bullish crowd and consider taking a different investment position opposite the crowd's theme.

COMMODITY BOOMS

Every so often the price of some industrial or agricultural commodity rises dramatically, sometimes to new historical highs, in response to some change in demand or supply conditions. Occasionally several commodities do this simultaneously—a situation that often is associated with economy-wide inflation. Big moves in commodity prices often spill over into the stocks of companies associated in one way or another with the commodity. These companies may be producers, providers of services or equipment to producers, banks that finance producers, and so on.

The 1972–1974 period saw a dramatic rise in agricultural prices for wheat, corn, soybeans, and related products. Gold went from $35 per ounce to $200 by the end of 1974. In October 1973 the first Arab oil embargo occurred, and by 1974 the price of crude oil had increased fourfold to $13 per barrel. A second though less pronounced advance in commodity prices occurred during 1979–1980 and was associated with the second oil crisis, which saw the per-barrel price of crude oil rise from $13 to $39. The year 1980 also saw a peak U.S. inflation rate of 13 percent, the highest level of the preceding 30 years and a level not seen since. Accompanying this general inflation was an upward move in gold prices from $100 per ounce in 1975 to $850 in January 1980.

By 1998 the price of crude oil had dropped to $11 and in 1999 gold had declined to the $250 level. From there commodity prices started to move upward, partly in response to growth in emerging economies like India and China and partly in response to liquidity supplied by central banks to cushion the deflation of the stock market bubble during the bear market of 2000–2002. By 2008 agricultural prices had moved well above the high levels last seen in 1973–1974. Gold had moved above $1,000 and crude oil in July 2008 traded at $147.

These spectacular moves in commodity prices have encouraged the development of investment crowds in oil, gold, and various agricultural commodities. My reading of the historical record leads me to believe that we have seen by far the biggest part of the run-up in commodity prices. (This is being written in August 2008.) Over the coming years these markets will remain very volatile even as prices should move downward to more sustainable levels. These adjustments will see the birth and disintegration of many investment crowds in related markets and should provide a wealth of opportunities for the contrarian trader.

INTEREST RATE MOVEMENTS AND THE BOND MARKET

During the past 30 years the development of new financial instruments, principally the money market fund and adjustable rate mortgages, has brought the behavior of interest rates and of the bond market to the attention of the general public. This means that the contrarian trader can often identify investment crowds in the bond market, especially after a long move in interest rates upward or downward has occurred.

One contrarian indicator of the stock market boom that properly began in 1982 was the popularity then of money market funds, which were regarded as fail-safe vehicles for assuring a prosperous retirement. In 1982 people had come to believe that annual returns of 10 percent or more on money market accounts were the norm and not the exception. Simultaneously a huge bearish crowd had formed in the bond market. Its theme was that high inflation was a perpetual feature of the economic landscape and that holding long-term bonds was an invitation to capital loss. Long-term bond prices had reached their historical low points in September 1981 and long-term interest rates their corresponding historical highs.

The bearish investment crowd in the bond market was so adamant in its views that in late 1982 I was prompted to publish a bond market prediction. In it I asserted that the 1981 highs in long-term interest rates would not be exceeded for many years to come. I predicted that bond prices would advance and long-term interest rates would fall for 25 to 30 years. In September 1981 the 30-year Treasury bond yielded 15.30 percent, and when I published my prediction the yield was around 11.00 percent. By late 2008 the yield had dropped to 3 percent, the lowest seen in more than fifty years. I think the bullish bond market crowd is about to begin its disintegration. If I am right about this I don't think we will again see treasury bond yields this low during the next thirty years.

USING YOUR MEDIA DIARY TO TRACK INVESTMENT THEMES

If you faithfully maintain your media diary, it will be a treasure trove of information about the latest popular investment themes. I suggest you try to use the categories I have discussed in this chapter to organize the themes you find in your diary. One way to do this would be write in next to each diary entry the name of the category or the specific theme you think that particular piece of media content reinforces. You may also want to keep a separate index of themes. In such an index you would keep a separate page for each theme you have identified and are following. On this page write in chronological order the date and a very brief description of every diary entry that reinforces the theme. The advantage of this approach is that it will reveal at a glance just how much attention each theme is getting from the media, and this will help you to judge the size and importance of the associated investment crowd. You will also find this information helpful in determining the intensity of the crowd's beliefs, and this sort of information is very helpful in determining just where the crowd is in its life cycle.

CHAPTER 10

Interpreting Your Diary: Market Semiotics

Market crowds and information cascades • the role of the mass media • your media diary • semiotics, the study of signs • reading between the lines • role of the price chart • Paul Montgomery and magazine cover stories • Time magazine's cover story marks the end of the bear market • read the newspaper • the importance of headlines • front page stories and editorials • crystallizing events • weighing the evidence • more semiotics

MEDIA AND INFORMATION CASCADES

Market crowds are built by information cascades. The way to detect a strong or growing market crowd is to observe directly its associated information cascade. The amazing thing is that the contrarian trader can do this simply by monitoring the content of the mass media. The information communicated in a cascade does not flow principally through private, person-to-person channels. Instead, the mass media act as the hub of a global communications network that facilitates the communication that sustains an information cascade. Individuals communicate with this media hub (and indirectly with each other) every time they read a newspaper or magazine or connect with the Internet to check the content of their favorite web sites.

Why is this so? Remember that the media are in a never-ending competitive struggle for readership and for the attendant advertising revenues. To attract readers, the media must provide information and other content that people will find topical, relevant, and interesting. The media are in the business of telling their readers what they want to hear. To survive in this very competitive environment, the media must have very sensitive antennae tuned to the interests and concerns of their audiences.

From this it follows that the media act as wonderfully reflective mirrors to public opinion. But they play another important role as well. In the process of mirroring public opinion they amplify and focus it by bringing this opinion to the attention of others who don't yet share the consensus view. In other words, the media not only report on the progress of an information cascade, they amplify and strengthen the cascade itself.

YOUR MEDIA DIARY: A LIVING HISTORY OF INFORMATION CASCADES

Your media diary will serve you as a real-time history of information cascades. Just follow the guidelines I set out for you in Chapters 7 and 8. Be sure to keep your diary up-to-date. As you put new entries into your diary, try to associate each one with a specific investment theme. Note the theme of each diary entry in the diary itself or, if you prefer, keep a separate index of themes and the dates and content of the associated diary entries. I think you will find that most of your diary entries will be associated with the types of themes I discussed in Chapter 9.

If you follow these procedures, your media diary will become a living history of ongoing information cascades in the financial markets. But your diary entries will need further interpretation if they are to help you judge the current strength and stage of development of the associated market crowds. This art of interpretation I like to call market semiotics.

SEMIOTICS: THE STUDY OF SIGNS

What are signs? Probably the first examples of signs that come to mind are the signs we encounter daily when navigating the road to work or when finding our way around an unfamiliar building. These signs often display information in the form of text and/or familiar symbols. Sometimes the symbol is just a color (as with a traffic light) or an arrow pointing in some direction. In general, a sign is something that stands in for or represents something else.

Let's consider the traffic light example a little more carefully. Why is the color red associated with the command "stop"? This might simply be a convention that has developed over many years. Any other color could have been associated with the command to stop as well. However, one might also suspect that there are physiological reasons for the association of the stop command with the color red. Perhaps the color red is more likely to stand out among the colors typically encountered in nature or in human environments and thus is more likely to attract a person's immediate attention. In any case, the color red has acquired an association with the command "stop" or the warning "danger," even when it appears in completely different contexts—a magazine headline, for example. The color red can now be interpreted as something that stands for the command to stop. But it also has become something more—it has become a sign or the alert for danger.

Semiotics is the study of signs, of things that stand in for or represent other things. Most signs typically have many layers of meaning. The first is the layer holding the obvious content or the intended message of the sign. But there are often deeper, hidden layers of meaning that arise from the sign's use in other contexts.

Let's take a newspaper headline as an example. Suppose we open the morning paper and see a headline that reads, in big block letters, "Stock Market Crash." What are the layers of meaning of this sign? It *is* a sign, after all—it is not the stock market itself! The first layer of meaning is contained in the obvious content of the message: The stock market has dropped. A second layer of meaning is conveyed by the use of the word *crash*. This word has a very dramatic and unpleasant connotation associated with physical destruction and death. Yet a third layer of meaning arises from the fact that this sign takes the form of a headline. It is the first thing most readers will notice. The newspaper editors must believe this event is important and that it has attracted the attention of their readers and of the general public. Moreover, they must think that even the casual reader's interest will be piqued by the headline. A final layer of meaning is conveyed by the fact that the headline is set in big block lettering. This signifies that the message is even more important than usual and moreover often is associated with the presence of some danger.

So we have peeled away at least four different layers of meaning in our hypothetical newspaper headline "Stock Market Crash." You might say that we have read between the lines of this piece of media content. I like to think of semiotics as the art of reading between the lines, of extracting meaning from the form, context, placement, and associations of a media message as well as from its superficial content.

Why might it be useful to learn the semiotic art of reading between the lines? Our goal as contrarian traders is to identify market crowds that are near the point of disintegration. It is at this point that the crowd displays extreme mental unity. This unity is associated with a homogeneous and heightened emotional state of the crowd's members. Now, most media content purports to convey just the facts. But we need to identify the strength of the emotions hiding behind the facts. It is the strength of these emotions that identifies the point where a market crowd is liable to begin its disintegration.

Here is where the semiotician's skill at interpreting signs and reading between the lines plays a crucial role, for the emotions of a crowd are rarely seen in the substance of the news. Instead they show up, as it were, between the lines, in the deeper layers of meaning conveyed by the content's media placement, the form of the content, associated colors and pictures, or choice of descriptive vocabulary, among other clues.

THE MOST IMPORTANT SIGN: THE PRICE CHART

Let's start with an obvious observation. In life, the "up" direction is a happy one and the "down" direction is a sad one. We want more, not less, of anything we consider good or desirable. The same is true of markets. A stock or stock market average that is advancing in price is making investors happy, but one that is dropping in price is bringing pain to the same investors.

The first sign we look for to help identify a bullish but aging investment crowd is a price chart that shows a dramatic upward trend in prices; the longer and more substantial the advance in prices, the more likely it is that a bullish crowd is nearing its demise. How can we give quantitative meaning to the words *longer* and *more substantial*? In Chapter 6 I offered a method for tabulating a market's historical swings. This method will enable you to identify the approximate time-price zone in which a market is likely to be making a valuation mistake. In all cases, high points will be associated with charts showing prices that have been going up for some appreciable amount of time.

Without a bullish-looking price chart, no bullish investment crowd can form. It is the appearance of the price chart—the fact that prices have been advancing significantly and for an appreciable amount of time—that buttresses the logic of the information cascade and entices people to join an investment crowd.

Naturally, exactly the same considerations apply to bearish-looking price charts and bearish investment crowds.

These observations may seem obvious, but I cannot overemphasize their importance. The market's price chart and the associated historical price tabulations are the starting point of any contrarian analysis you do.

Remember that there can be no bear market unless there is first a bull market, and no bull market unless there is first a bear market.

Newcomers to the art of contrarian trading are often confused by the fact that in any market at any point in time there are always some bullish and some bearish voices to be heard, each with its own plausible arguments and rationales. This is only to be expected. After all, if a market is an active one, there must be plenty of buyers *and* sellers participating every day. There are always lots of bears and bulls at hand. The art of contrarian trading requires that you learn how to identify the side of the market that is operating as a crowd, unified in its market rationales and emotions. It is only human nature that this side of the market will be the one associated with the most recent, strong, and durable trend in the market price: upward for a bullish crowd and downward for a bearish one.

If you keep the semiotic significance of the price chart in mind, you will avoid two very common errors novice contrarian traders make.

The novice's first mistake is to cherry-pick media content that disagrees with his own market view. On this basis the novice can often persuade himself that his market view is a contrarian view, even if his market view in fact makes him part of a growing investment crowd. You are much less likely to make this kind of error if you keep in mind the kind of market chart that is typically associated with a bullish or with a bearish investment crowd. The chart is essentially an objective piece of information, at least when seen from a broad-brush, semiotic point of view.

The novice's second mistake is to seize upon a prominent bullish story that appears very early in a bull market or a very prominent bearish story that appears early in a bear market and conclude that the new trend is about to reverse.

The most spectacular instance of this in my memory occurred in August 1982, just as the Dow Industrials began the bull market that would carry this average from 777 to 11,750 by the year 2000. An August 1982 issue of *Barron's* weekly had a picture of a rip-snorting bull on its cover. Certain bearish market prognosticators of the time, Joe Granville in particular, interpreted this cover as a sure indicator of an imminent market drop. How wrong they were! And a look at the chart of the Dow would have shown that this contrarian interpretation of the Barron's cover story was wrong-headed. The Dow had been dropping for well over a year and had been turning upward for only three weeks!

A second, almost as interesting example of this phenomenon occurred in April 2000, just a month after the very top of the stock market bubble on March 24, 2000. The April 24, 2000, issue of *Newsweek* asked: "Is the Bull Market Really Over?" For reasons evident from other details of the cover, *Newsweek* was begging for the answer *yes*. And it *was* over!

So cover stories are not always wrong. Sometimes they are eerily prescient. This sort of novice error can be avoided by remembering that a bullish market crowd forms only when the market chart is obviously showing a strong and durable upward trend and the market tabulations described in Chapter 6 warn of potential overvaluation. When the *Barron's* cover appeared in 1982, the market charts of the stock averages showed either a bearish or a flat longer-run trend. There had not been time enough and prices had not rallied far enough for a bull market crowd to form. So the experienced contrarian trader had no reason to draw bearish inferences from the *Barron's* cover. When the *Newsweek* cover appeared, the market chart was still pointing upward. So no bearish crowd could yet have formed, and thus there was no reason for the contrarian traders to draw (long-run) bullish inferences from this cover.

MAGAZINE COVER STORIES

The pioneer in cover story interpretation is Paul Macrae Montgomery. In the 1970s Montgomery originally developed his theory of contrary opinion analysis using the archive of *Time* magazine cover stories. Since then he has expanded upon this very original idea and developed it into a practical theory of the psychological and emotional sources of market fluctuations. I have learned a lot from Paul, and many of my ideas have been inspired by his work.

Next to the semiotic interpretation of the market chart, the most convincing piece of evidence that a market crowd is a mature one is an unusual magazine cover story associated with the crowd's investment theme. The meaning of the term *unusual* in this context depends on the source of the media content. For example, it is unusual for *Time, Newsweek*, or other general interest weekly or monthly magazines to publish a cover story associate with a financial market. So such cover stories are especially indicative of a mature market crowd. However, *Business Week* and *Fortune* both specialize in business and financial news, so financial cover stories in these magazines are not so unusual. The *Economist* is more of a general interest magazine than it used to be, but it still emphasizes a business and financial view of world news.

Note that a magazine cover story might not concern the market directly, but rather an individual closely associated with it, for example the CEO of an industry that has been a bull market leader.

An important example of this phenomenon occurred when *Time* made Jeff Bezos, founder of Amazon.com, it man of the year in December 1999. Bezos personified the new economy theme of the stock market bubble that peaked in March 2000. When interest rates are the focus of a market crowd, the appearance of the chairman of the U.S. Federal Reserve on the cover of *Time* or *Newsweek* would have special significance. In March 1982 *Time* magazine featured the then Fed chairman, Paul Volcker, on its cover with the caption "Interest Rate Anguish." The bond market was scraping bottom at the time, and long-term interest rates were close to their historical highs (reached on September 30, 1981). That cover marked the start of the disintegration of the bearish bond market crowd. The result was a bull market in bonds and a drop in long-term interest rates that lasted 25 years.

Magazine covers can be a treasure trove of semiotic information about market crowds. Here is an illustration. My favorite *Time* cover of recent years is its July 29, 2002, cover. This issue hit the newsstands almost on the exact day that the S&P 500 traded at 771. This average then rallied to 965 before dropping to an early October low at 768. The cover itself showed a grandmother on roller skates working as a carhop at a fast-food drive-in. The cover asked: "Will You *Ever* Be Able to *Retire*?" The subtitle read: "With *Stocks Plummeting* and Corporations in Disarray, Americans' Financial Futures Are in Peril." (Emphasis is in the original.)

Here is my semiotic analysis of this cover. First, the chart of the market averages was pointing downward. Stock prices had been dropping for almost two and a half years and had fallen nearly 50 percent from their highs. The NASDAQ Composite had fallen nearly 80 percent. My tabular analysis indicated that the market was probably making a mistake of undervaluation, so it was very likely that a strong bearish crowd was at work.

This *Time* cover provided incontrovertible evidence that there was indeed a bearish crowd and that it was in all likelihood a mature one. The cover had several layers of meaning. First, it affirmed that stocks had been plummeting, something that anyone could see from his brokerage statements or from the chart of the averages. It also affirmed that corporations were in disarray because of widespread accounting fraud and pension plan underfunding due to the stock market drop. So this cover was associated with two prominent investment themes: the plunging stock market theme and the corrupt corporation theme.

The cover pushed several emotional buttons as well. This is a very important aspect of market semiotics. Market crowds have strong emotional attachments to their investment themes. It is this emotional attachment that gives the crowd its mental unity. So when analyzing media content *always* pay special attention to the emotional aspects of the message. In the case of this *Time* cover we notice the use of the word *plummeting* to describe stock prices. Americans' financial futures are in *peril*. Corporations are in *disarray*. All three words have unusually negative emotional associations and connote a situation that is out of control, a time ripe for panic. The cover also plays to the fear all retired or soon-to-retire people have for their financial futures. Will they be able to live out their lives without being reduced to poverty? The cover asks: "Will You *Ever* Be Able to *Retire?*" It suggests that this is not a good time to retire and that the plummeting stock market has made it likely you will have to work menial jobs for a good part of your retirement to survive. This appeal to a generalized fear for your future is a second and very important emotional button that this cover pushes. To top this all off, the central character depicted on the cover was granny, a helpless victim of corporate greed and Wall Street malfeasance.

The emotional messages that are this cover's subtext convinced me at the time that this bearish stock market crowd was forcing a mistake of undervaluation. I believed then that a new bull market was just around the corner. The S&P 500 index doubled during the ensuing five years.

NEWSPAPER HEADLINES

The major metropolitan newspapers are published seven days a week and 52 weeks a year. Every issue contains a lead headline on the front page. Rarely do such headlines concern a financial market. When they do, the contrarian trader sits up and takes notice. Such a headline is convincing evidence of a market crowd at work and of a contrarian trading opportunity at hand.

How does one uncover the emotional content of a headline? The first and most obvious aspect of any headline is its prominence on page 1. Some headlines are confined to the right-hand side of the newspaper and appear only at the top of the associated story. Other headlines are spread across the top of page 1 and are for this reason of much more emotional significance. The emotional content of a headline is also emphasized by the type size in which it is printed. Big, bold, block lettering has much more emotional impact than smaller lettering. A headline can also be emphasized by a photograph or a chart appearing near it. The value of this sort of clue cannot be underestimated.

The emotional content of a headline can also be found in the choice of words appearing in its text. Words associated with fear, uncertainty, and other negative emotions speak for themselves and should be noted. Words denoting exuberance, confidence, hope, joy, and the like are also significant, though far less common in newspaper headlines. Here are a few recent examples that illustrate the application of these principles.

The headline for the January 17, 2008, issue of the *New York Times* read: "Fed Chief's Reassurance Fails to Halt Stock Plunge." Let's put this headline in the context of a market chart. The S&P 500 index had reached a high at 1,576 on October 9, 2007, and had dropped as low as 1,364 the previous day, January 16, 2008, for a drop of about 14 percent in three months. According to the market tabulations I discussed in Chapter 6, this was not yet a situation associated with an important long-term undervaluation mistake. So the contrarian trader would not have taken this headline as evidence of a mature bear market crowd at work in the stock market.

A similar conclusion arises from a semiotic look at the headline. First, the headline was spread over only the first two columns of the newspaper and its type size was not at all unusual for the typical headline. There was some significant emotional content, as can be seen by the use of the word *plunge* and by a photograph appearing right underneath the story of the Fed chairman as he appeared on TV. The photograph was captioned: "Ben S. Bernanke's face loomed over the Chicago Board of Trade." The use of the word *loomed* in this context evoked the image of a ghostly, larger-than-life superbeing speaking to his subjects. I note also that the headline states Bernanke's *reassurance failed* (my emphasis), and this undermines one's confidence in the benevolent powers of this superbeing.

Not even a week later, a more dramatic headline appeared. The January 22, 2008, issue of the *New York Times* was headlined: "World Markets Plunge on Fears of U.S. Slowdown." It is instructive to compare this headline to the January 17 headline. The January 22 headline was spread across four columns instead of just two. It appeared in larger type. Right underneath the headline were three *color* photographs. The first and largest showed an image of a chart of the Nikkei 225 index for the Japanese stock market. It depicted yellow bars on a blue background and showed the average dropping steadily lower. The other two photographs were smaller and showed people around the world reacting to the plunge. The fact that there were photographs associated with the headline emphasized its emotional content, and the fact that the photographs were in color doubled this emphasis.

The next day, January 23, saw another *New York Times* headline concerning the stock market. This one was in even bigger and bolder type than the previous day's, although it was spread over only two columns. However, it appeared alongside several graphs, and the entire story was spread across the entire front page. These details all indicated a more powerful emotional state for a bearish stock market crowd than was indicated by the previous day's headline. The January 23 headline read: "Fed, in Surprise, Sets Big Rate Cut to Ease Markets."

By January 23 the S&P 500 had dropped 20 percent from its top on October 9, 2007. This put it on the fringe of potential undervaluation according to the price tabulations of Chapter 6, although the drop had lasted only three months, rather a short time for a significant bearish market crowd to form. So the contrarian trader might anticipate a relatively short-term bullish trading opportunity here. At the very least he would not be tempted to join the bear crowd by selling stocks at this juncture.

FRONT PAGE STORIES AND EDITORIALS

Headlines convey very significant information about market crowds to the contrarian trader. But sometime a market-related story appears on the front page of a newspaper without being the headline. Such stories provide additional evidence for the existence and strength of a market crowd, so I make a point of putting them into my market diary, too. The semiotic principles of interpretation are the same as for headlines. The additional bit of information that can be useful concerns the story's placement on the front page: Being close to the top of the page (above the fold is the most significant placement) and positioned to the far left or far right of page 1 increases the weight one should give to the story.

Another source of evidence for market crowds at work can often be found on the first page of the paper's business section. Headlines here, especially if accompanied by photographs, are important material for your diary. However, they do not carry the same weight they would have if they appeared as the headline on the paper's front page.

Very occasionally a general interest newspaper will print an editorial discussing the situation in some financial market. Because this is so unusual I am careful to paste such editorials into my media diary and use them to assess the strength of market crowds.

CRYSTALLIZING EVENTS

Very often it will happen that an investment crowd's views will be reinforced and apparently vindicated by some event external to the market itself. The outbreak of war, the signing of a peace treaty, the failure of banks or other financial institutions, corporate bankruptcies, and currency devaluations are all examples of such events. I like to think of these events as things that crystallize investor sentiment. They harden beliefs that until then may have been only weakly articulated and defined. As such, crystallizing events are generally associated with the imminent disintegration of an investment crowd. I discussed a number of examples of crystallizing events in Chapter 9. Be alert for them as signs that a valuation mistake is being made.

Along the same lines, one should pay special attention to situations in which the media hold out individuals as exemplars of market or business success or failure. During the late 1990s, at the height of the stock market bubble, there was a constant stream of media stories describing in great detail the wealth and lifestyles of the newly minted Silicon Valley millionaires. In 2002, during the depths of the bear market that followed the bubble collapse, most of the bullish analysts who helped inflate the bubble and many of the corporate leaders of collapsed enterprises were pilloried in the media. This was a symptom of stock market undervaluation.

THE WEIGHT OF THE EVIDENCE

So far I have discussed various methods and approaches for analyzing media content. I have taken the view that this content consists of signs with many layers of meaning. The job of a contrarian trader is to peel away these layers of meaning, always looking for the emotional significance of every sign.

How much media and semiotic evidence must there be before the contrarian trader can be confident that he has identified a market crowd on the verge of disintegration? Is there some mathematical formula or guideline that can be applied to this process to make it more objective, to enable one to weigh the media evidence in some objective manner?

I don't believe there is any simple criterion or formula that can provide reliable answers to these questions. Over the years I have grown more and more skilled at weighing the semiotic evidence only because I have faithfully kept up my media diary. This has given me the opportunity to make comparisons among similar historical market junctures and the intensity and frequency of the media content associated with them. So I think the best way to develop the semiotic skills you need for identifying market crowds is to practice. Real-time practice can be reinforced by reading accounts of past bubbles and bear market low points. Such historical information will give you a sense of the conditions and the nature of public opinion associated with mature investment crowds.

One might naturally believe that the bigger the valuation mistake, the more pages of one's market diary one will find devoted to the communications of the associated market crowd. But there are times when a big valuation mistake is being made by a market crowd even though only a few (but important) media stories appear to confirm it. This was the case at the bottom of the bear market in 2002. There was certainly a general bearish malaise at the time, but only the *Time* magazine cover story in July of that year and a *Newsweek* August cover story pointed specifically to the market low. So a contrarian trader must be careful not to expect a blizzard of cover stories and/or newspaper headlines to announce the imminent demise of an investment crowd. Sometimes just a few pieces of evidence will do the job, and the volume of evidence is not necessarily correlated with the significance of the opportunity. This is one important reason why contrarian trading is at least as much art as it is science. And an artist's skills require constant practice to develop and maintain.

MORE ON MARKET SEMIOTICS

You should not take the guidelines I have offered in this chapter as the last word on the interpretation of your market diary. As the contrarian trader gains experience, his creativity begins to inform his work. Over the years I've made a number of observations about the signs associated with market crowds. Here are two examples that have helped me and may well help you in the future.

Consider first the publishing industry. It can provide the contrarian trader with useful clues about the existence of market crowds. I remember back in the late 1970s and early 1980s when bookstores had only one or two shelves devoted to the stock market or investing. By contrast, at the peak of the stock market bubble in 2000 Barnes & Noble had easily 20 or more shelves devoted to the subject of investing. Even more telling, there were very many titles on subjects like day trading or technical analysis that were not even of interest 20 years earlier. As one might expect, during the eight years subsequent to the 2000 bubble top, the shelf space devoted to books related to the stock market has shrunk dramatically. This is a very good indicator of declining public interest in the stock market.

Along the same lines, one can keep track of new book titles that appear on the subject of investing and related financial matters. At least three books predicting Dow levels ranging from 30,000 to 100,000 were published right at the top of the 1994–2000 stock market bubble, and this was a definitive indication of a mature bull market crowd. (The top of the Dow in 2000 was 11,750, and the top in 2007 was 14,164.) I suspect a similar phenomenon is occurring as I write this in the fall of 2008. A number of books have recently been published or are forthcoming that discuss the subprime meltdown in the financial markets over the past year. I think this means that a powerful bearish stock market crowd has developed. If so, this is a tremendous buying opportunity in the U.S. stock market.

Another interesting sign is a very subtle one, but nonetheless it is of great importance. An information cascade attracts new members to a market crowd by offering a rationale or logical explanation for past and future market performance. The cascade here is acting in a persuasive role, encouraging investors to accept the crowd's interpretation of events instead of their own. But a point is eventually reached in the life of every crowd when these rationales become premises instead of explanations. The time for logical argument has passed. In other words, what was once offered as an explanation for a rising market, say, at some point becomes accepted as a fact, not a theory. As such it no longer needs justification or supporting argument. At this juncture the crowd's beliefs have become the axioms upon which all of its discussion and actions are based. The crowd here achieves its mental and emotional unity. Its disintegration lies not far ahead.

It is possible to detect this transition by observing carefully the balance that media content maintains between an effort to justify the crowd's beliefs and the best way to take advantage of the beliefs' investment implications. In the late stages of a crowd's life cycle, virtually all of the content will be devoted to methods for exploiting the market's projected movements, not to explanations of why these movements should occur at all.

CHAPTER 11

The Grand Strategy of Contrarian Trading

Becoming a contrarian trader • learn by doing • start small • a word to young readers • put yourself in the line of fire • my experience as a postcard trader • investment vehicles for contrarian trading • the advent of the exchange-traded fund (ETF) • investment goals • no need to be perfect • an example from the boom and bust 1990–2002 • tax issues • CTS #1: don't speculate • why this is really a contrarian strategy • CTS #2: avoid big mistakes • inoculate yourself against crowd contagion • CTS #3: Contrarian Rebalancing • underweight when a bullish crowd develops • overweight when a bearish crowd develops • an example • best strategy to follow for the typical aspiring contrarian trader • suggestions for more aggressive contrarian trading strategies • an aggressive stock market strategy • look at bonds, commodities, stock market sectors, and individual stocks • it's harder to track the crowd in such situations • the bandwagon strategy • the danger of trying the short side of a market • the odds favor the stock market bulls in the long run

CONTRARIAN INVESTMENT PLANNING

In this chapter I want to show you how to take the ideas we have developed in the preceding 10 chapters and incorporate them into a contrarian investment plan.

Every contrarian trader begins as a novice. As a novice, the best approach is to start your media diary and to spend time constructing market

123

tabulations of the sort I explained in Chapter 6. You should also think about the types of investment strategies I describe in this chapter and choose one that suits the time you can devote to your investments. I have found that learning by doing is the most effective way to acquire the skills of a successful trader or investor. Making decisions when there is real money at stake is the essence of the experience and the only way to find out whether your emotional makeup is suitable to the contrarian approach to markets.

With this in mind, I suggest that you begin your learning-by-doing phase by starting small. Devote only a small part of your investment portfolio to a single contrarian trading strategy. After a two- or three-year testing period, compare your contrarian trading results to your other investment results. If the contrarian results are visibly superior, earmark more of your portfolio to your contrarian trading strategy.

A word to my younger readers: At this moment you may have little or no savings that can be devoted to investments of any kind, let alone to contrarian trading. But there is still a learning by doing opportunity for you to develop your contrarian trading skills. In addition to your media diary, keep a notebook in which to record specific buy and sell decisions without making actual trades. This is called *paper* trading or investing.

It is even better if you have a friend to whom you can e-mail your investment decisions in real time, just as you would buy or sell in an electronic market. Ask your friend to keep a file of your e-mail "orders." This is the closest you can come to the actual experience of risking real money on your decisions, and it is far better than paper trading, where only you know if you have cheated.

When I was starting out as a contrarian trader in college, I mailed a postcard every few weeks to a very experienced and successful money manager who happened to be a family friend. On this postcard I would give buying and selling instructions based on the market average. The experiment lasted only a year, but it was an invaluable experience. Something was at stake: my own credibility and pride, something as valuable to me as money (of which at the time I had none!). Because I had something at risk when I made my decisions and mailed the postcards, I experienced something very similar to risking real money against an uncertain prospect. If you can do this, even if no actual money is at stake, you will acquire a treasure trove of experience in interpreting your market diary and identifying potential market mistakes. You will also learn a lot about your suitability for contrarian trading. Later, when you have saved enough to begin an investment program, your skills and experience as a contrarian trader will have been developed to the point where they will make a visible, positive contribution to your investment results. So don't pass up this opportunity to build your investment skills now. Prepare them for use when you have money to invest!

CONTRARIAN TRADER'S INVESTMENT PORTFOLIO

What kind of assets are suitable vehicles for a contrarian trader's investment plan? The key thing to remember is that his principal tool is his media diary. It follows that the contrarian trader should focus on markets that receive the frequent attention of the print and electronic media. This means that a typical contrarian trader will focus principally on stock market and bond market investments.

But opportunities in other markets sometimes arise. Occasionally there will be a lot of media attention on the currency markets, particularly on the U.S. dollar. Sometimes agricultural commodities make it to the front pages of newspapers and the covers of general interest magazines. Over the past three or four years the crude oil market has attracted worldwide attention. During the same period precious metals like gold and silver have experienced information cascades that have built big investment crowds in these markets. In my opinion, these currency and commodity market opportunities are generally best left to the very experienced contrarian trader. These markets usually move very quickly, and investments in them are typically highly leveraged. Not only can they be dangerous, but contrarian trading opportunities in these markets arise only sporadically. The typical contrarian trader's attention is best focused on stocks and bonds, the biggest markets in the United States.

Financial innovations over the past 20 years have been a boon to the contrarian trader. Up until the 1970s the only way to take advantage of contrarian trading opportunities in the stock or bond market averages was to buy a portfolio of individual stock or bonds. Not only did this involve high transaction costs, but it made it difficult for an investor of average means to construct a portfolio that was sufficiently diversified to reliably track the market averages. Mutual funds were generally not appropriate for this purpose because of their high management fees coupled with so-called load charges. These expenses made them unsuitable for anything other than the buy-and-hold investment strategy.

In recent years this financial landscape has been completely transformed, to the delight of the contrarian trader and of the average investor as well. Indexed mutual funds whose sole objective is to replicate the performance of the stock or bond market averages have grown popular. They are available to the investing public at low cost in terms of their management and transaction fees.

Of even greater importance to the contrarian trader has been the emergence of exchange-traded funds (ETFs). It is my view that these are ideal vehicles for contrarian trading. An ETF is an investment trust whose shares are listed for trading on an organized stock exchange like the American

Stock Exchange and the New York Stock Exchange. The trust holds a portfolio of shares designed to track some specific market average and stands ready to exchange the shares in the trust for portfolios of individual stocks that make up that average. This exchange provision means that arbitrage between the ETF shares and the market portfolio it tracks is possible and will keep the price of the ETF shares in proper alignment with its chosen market average.

By far the most actively traded ETF at this writing is the S&P 500 "Spider" ETF, so-called because it tracks Standard & Poor's Depositary Receipts (SPDRs); its ticker symbol is SPY. There are other actively traded ETFs that track other U.S. market averages, as well as some that track subsectors of the U.S. stock market such as the financial sector, energy sector, or precious metals. There are also ETFs that track various sectors of the bond market. An even bigger innovation has been the development of inverse ETFs, which rise in price when a specific market average falls and vice versa. However, I urge you to be cautious when buying inverse ETF's in the hopes of taking advantage of a fall in some market. Because of the way inverse portfolios are constructed and managed, inverse ETF's may fail to move inversely to their index exactly. Worse, in extreme circumstances they may even wind up moving in the same direction as the index instead of inversely to it!

THE INVESTMENT GOAL OF THE CONTRARIAN TRADER

The contrarian trader's goal is to beat the market. But what does this mean in practical terms? For most people, beating the market means outperforming the buy-and-hold investment policy. (If you are an expert in portfolio analysis, you will probably want to qualify this last statement by adjusting for portfolio risk.) I want to emphasize that one need not sell near the exact top of a bull market or buy near the exact bottom of a bear market to beat the buy-and-hold strategy. You need only do your buying and selling in the general vicinity of these tops and bottoms. Here is an example that illustrates this point.

Let's imagine a hypothetical contrarian trader whose noncash investments are all in an S&P 500 index fund. During the first part of the 1990s let's suppose he was fully invested. The stock market showed no real evidence of a bullish investment crowd until 1996 at the earliest. Imagine that, for whatever reason, this contrarian trader concluded in 1997 that there was a mature bullish stock market crowd that was about to disintegrate.

He therefore sold his entire portfolio at an average of 950 in the S&P. I should say that a contrarian trader who followed the Contrarian Rebalancing strategy described later in the chapter would not have sold until early 2001, and then near the S&P 1,250 level. Here I want to illustrate the experience of a trader with only average or below-average skills.

At what level in the S&P might this trader have restored his original long position? I think there was a very good contrarian buy opportunity in the S&P 1,000 to 1,050 range in October 1998. But let's suppose our hypothetical trader passed this opportunity up for some reason. (Again, an experienced contrarian trader would have seized the 1998 buying opportunity with both hands.) Instead, let's suppose that this trader waited until he saw the July 2002 *Time* magazine cover (which I discussed in the preceding chapter) before deciding to reinvest his portfolio in the stock market. Let's suppose furthermore that he did this at an average of 900. (In fact, my wife, a complete novice, did this at the 820 level at that time.)

The net result of our hypothetical trader's decisions was a sale in 1997 at 950 and a purchase in 2002 at 900. Now, the yield on money market instruments exceeded the yield on the S&P by an average of 250 basis points per year during this five-year period. (A basis point is one one-hundredth of a percentage point, so 250 basis points is 2.50 percent.) So a tax-deferred portfolio sold at 950 in 1997 and then invested in a money market fund until 2002 would have grown to a value equivalent to the 1,074 level in the S&P and in 2002 would have been reinvested at the 900 level. This represents a gain of 19 percent relative to the buy-and-hold strategy during that time, or about 350 basis points per year. Moreover, this was achieved by taking no market risk during those five years. In contrast, the buy-and-hold strategy during those five years was fully invested throughout a bubble of historical proportions and its ensuing collapse. I should point out that any professional money manager who beats the buy-and-hold strategy by 300 basis points per year is a hero on Wall Street.

In my opinion our hypothetical contrarian trader exhibited only average or even below-average skills over the 1990–2002 time frame. Yet he did visibly better than the market during the dangerous and very difficult bear market period of 2000–2002 and over the entire 13 year period as well. He did not sell anywhere near an important top. His buying was more skillfully done, but still was nothing to brag about.

This example illustrates that to achieve market-beating results it is not necessary to be anywhere near perfection in the timing of your buy and sell activity. The main thing is to have enough portfolio liquidity available to take advantage of bearish market crowds when they form. They are much easier to identify than bullish crowds and are usually very near to disintegration once they can be identified.

A WARNING ABOUT CAPITAL GAINS TAXES

The active contrarian strategies described in this chapter will subject the investor to capital gains taxes when employed in a taxable investment account. These taxes may affect the contrarian trader's performance relative to the baseline buy-and-hold strategy. This issue demands careful consideration before one adopts a contrarian trading strategy in a taxable account. In fact, for this reason only expert contrarians should use such strategies in a taxable account. Generally, contrarian trading strategies are more suited for use in tax-deferred retirement accounts.

CONTRARIAN TRADING STRATEGY #1: DON'T SPECULATE

You may have found the first few chapters of this book so persuasive that you have decided that contrarian trading is not for you. If so, you have already achieved more than many aspiring investors do in a lifetime. Congratulations on your self-knowledge! It will save you from many personally and financially painful experiences in the world of investing.

Contrarian Trading Strategy #1 (or CTS #1 for short) is: *Don't speculate.* Instead choose an allocation for your investment portfolio among indexed mutual funds or ETFs that mirror the stock market averages, the bond market, and money market instruments. A simple example would be a 60-30-10 allocation among Spiders, a bond market index fund, and a money market fund. Each year, at the same time of year, take a look at your portfolio to see if market movements during the past year have changed your portfolio's allocation away from its desired 60-30-10 allocation. Then do whatever buying or selling is necessary to bring your portfolio back to 60-30-10. If you do this systematically, year after year, your investment results will be better than those of the typical professional money manager!

You may wonder why I call this a contrarian trading strategy. *Trading* it certainly is not. But it is a *contrarian* strategy in the truest sense of the word. How many investors do you know who follow it? Not many, I'm sure. Why? Because to follow it you first must recognize that you do *not* have a speculator's edge over other investors. Good for you! Now you can spend more time with your family, pursue your other interests, and not be bothered at all by the ups and downs in market prices and public psychology.

CONTRARIAN TRADING STRATEGY #2: DON'T INVEST WITH THE CROWD

This is a somewhat more active approach than CTS #1 but is still in the spirit of winning by avoiding mistakes. It is an essentially defensive strategy. Contrarian Trading Strategy #2 is: *Don't invest with the crowd.* If you can avoid becoming part of big investment crowds you will also avoid the financial losses attendant to a crowd's disintegration and collapse. Not only this; you will also avoid the foolish decisions investors caught in such collapses often make that compound their mistakes (like keeping their money in money market funds thereafter, or throwing good money after bad).

In this contrarian trading strategy, your media diary acts as an inoculation against the information cascades that build investment crowds. You will know that a cascade is under way and see that the market is in the process of making a valuation error. Armed with this knowledge, you will not be tempted to increase you portfolio allocation to the crowd's investment theme, especially when the siren song of the crowd is strongest. In this way you can avoid big losses in your portfolio when the crowd inevitably disintegrates. At the same time you pursue whatever investment strategy you prefer, even if it is not an explicitly contrarian one. To be a winner in the game of investment, it is essential to avoid big mistakes. Follow CTS #2 and you will achieve that goal.

CONTRARIAN TRADING STRATEGY #3: CONTRARIAN REBALANCING

The strategy of *Contrarian Rebalancing* aims to sidestep the market collapses that attend the disintegration of bullish investment crowds. It also tries to be overweighted in a market that is undervalued and in the grips of a bearish crowd. This is the strategy I think most aspiring contrarian traders should use. I think of it as a very conservative strategy, and I discuss more aggressive contrarian trading strategies later in this chapter. I think that this strategy works best when the contrarian trader has chosen to limit his investment universe to ETFs or indexed mutual funds that mirror the stock and bond market averages. So let's suppose he adopts a baseline (normal) allocation of 60 percent stocks, 30 percent bonds, and 10 percent cash, the same allocation as was used to illustrate CTS #1. (There is nothing special about these allocation percentages. They are, however, the average allocations of investors as a group.) Here's how CTS #3 works in the stock market. During a bull market, any above-normal allocation to the stock market should be cut back to normal levels once the averages have risen about 65 percent from the low of the preceding bear market. However, this should be done only if the advance has also lasted at least 20 months. I think the S&P 500 is the best market index to use for these calculations.

When should the stock market allocation be cut to below-normal levels? The worst mistake a contrarian trader can make is to be underinvested in stocks during an extended bull market. Such markets are times when the baseline buy-and-hold strategy performs best. To avoid this mistake, the Contrarian Rebalancing strategy dictates that a below-normal stock market allocation can be adopted only in the following circumstances. First, the S&P has advanced at least 65 percent from its preceding bear market low. Second, the contrarian trader must be able to identify a bullish stock market crowd from the material in his media diary. Finally, and most importantly, the 200-day moving average of the S&P 500 must fall 1 percent from whatever high it has reached during the bull market. (This moving average is calculated by adding up the latest 200 daily closes in the S&P and then dividing the total by 200, an easy task in a spreadsheet.) This last requirement will keep the contrarian trader invested in stocks during those rare times when a stock market bubble sends prices upward more than anyone can anticipate.

How does CTS #3 tell the contrarian trader to act during a bear market? If the bear market results from the disintegration of a bullish stock market crowd that was visible toward the end of the preceding bull market, the contrarian trader would have cut back his stock market allocation to below normal once the 200-day moving average of the S&P dropped 1 percent from its high point. In all other circumstances the contrarian trader would sit through a bear market maintaining a normal stock market allocation. In either case, once the S&P has dropped 20 percent from its preceding high point and a bearish stock market crowd has developed, the contrarian trader looks for an opportunity to increase his stock market allocation to above-normal levels. This he does once he observes the 200-day moving average of the S&P 500 advance 1 percent from whatever low it makes after the drop of at least 20 percent that has encouraged the growth of a bearish stock market crowd.

THE AGGRESSIVE CONTRARIAN

In contrast to his conservative cousin, the aggressive contrarian trader will generally make two or more changes to his stock market allocation each year. The aggressive contrarian allocation strategy I describe now is a long-only strategy and involves no short sales or purchases of inverse exchange-traded funds (ETFs). There is a simple reason for this: Every trader can benefit from specializing in one specific trading strategy and in using a small universe of trading certain instruments. In the case at hand I am suggesting that most aggressive contrarians should focus on increasing or decreasing their stock market allocations with the goal of beating the results of the buy-and-hold strategy. The stock market part of their investment portfolio should be invested in ETFs like the Diamonds or Spiders (which track the Dow and the S&P respectively) that mirror the performance of the major market averages. Such a long-only strategy will lose money when the averages are in bear markets. But the psychological demands it makes on an individual are much more modest that those made by a strategy that allows short sales, too.

Every contrarian trader should keep in mind that his investment goal is to beat the market—that is, to do better than the performance of the benchmark buy-and-hold strategy. Sadly, I find that many investors believe it is more important to be *right* in their guesses about the prospective direction of movements in the market averages. Nothing could be further from the truth. In fact, philosophers would call such an attitude a *category mistake.* Right and wrong are concepts that have no place in evaluating investment performance. The only concepts that matter are profit and loss, especially when measured relative to some appropriate benchmark. The contrarian trader is emphatically *not* in the business of detecting high points or low points in the stock market averages. He is concerned only with uncovering market mistakes in a timely way and in making portfolio adjustments that will exploit such mistakes. Over time he will be able to measure his success or failure by comparing his portfolio's performance to that of the buy-and-hold strategy.

A LONG-ONLY STRATEGY FOR THE AGGRESSIVE CONTRARIAN TRADER

The basic idea underlying this long-only strategy for an aggressive contrarian is simplicity itself. Look for a bearish information cascade and assume an above-normal allocation to the stock market when one is spotted. Reduce this allocation to normal or to below-normal levels after the market has advanced a historically typical amount from the low point associated with the bearish information cascade.

Bearish information cascades in the context of bull markets tend to be shorter in time and associated with more modest drops in the averages than are bearish cascades the context of bear markets. To take advantage of this, the aggressive contrarian trader must have some way of distinguishing between bull markets and bear markets in the averages. A mechanical method for doing this using changes in the direction of the 200-day moving average of the S&P 500 has already been discussed. Here is another, more sensitive mechanical method for identifying bull and bear markets. Watch the relationship between the S&P 500 index and its 200-day moving average. When the S&P 500 drops 5 percent below its moving average after a bull market of normal extent and duration, the aggressive contrarian can be pretty sure a bear market is under way. If the average moves 5 percent above its 200-day moving average after a bear market of normal extent, one can be confident a bull market is under way. I should point out here that I think that for bear markets in general it is better to be concerned only with the extent of the bear market (the percentage drop from the preceding bull market high), because the time duration of bear markets varies wildly.

Now for the details of this long-only strategy: In a bull market the aggressive contrarian trader wants to be on the lookout for bearish information cascades. Often these will show up as newspaper headlines about falling stock prices. Sometimes one finds only page 1 stories, not headlines. Depending on the tenor of the times, one might find bearish magazine stock market covers as well. One must remember that bearish cascades in a bull market tend to be very brief, lasting a matter of days or at most a few weeks.

But a bearish information cascade is not by itself enough evidence to justify increasing your stock market allocation. In addition, you want to see the S&P 500 closing below its 50-day moving average (just add up the past 50 daily closes and divide by 50—easy to do in a spreadsheet). The S&P should also be relatively close to its rising 200-day moving average, say within 1 percent if above it or less than 5 percent below it. Sometimes it is also helpful to compare the extent of the recent short-term drop in the S&P to the extent of previous drops in the context of the same bull market, since these short-term drops tend to be the same size. If these additional criteria are met, then it will be time to increase stock market allocation to above-normal levels.

Having increased his stock market allocation to above normal during a bull market, the aggressive contrarian now is on the lookout for the opportunity to move the allocation back to normal levels. (I don't think there is ever any justification for moving to below-normal allocations in a bull market.) Generally this will come when the S&P has advanced to a new bull market high. Here it is often useful to look at the percentage gains made in previous upswings in the same bull market, for they often turn out to be comparable. The time to move stock market allocations back to normal levels often comes when the current upswing has equaled the average percentage gain of previous upswings.

In a bear market this approach has to be modified a bit. The typical stock market allocation for the aggressive contrarian is then a below-normal one. A below-normal allocation can be temporarily increased during the bear market, but only in special circumstances.

First, a bearish information cascade must be visible in your media diary. It is important to note that bearish information cascades last longer in a bear market than they do in bull market. One must give the market enough time to drop from a short-term high to a new low point for the bear market to reinforce the bearish state of affairs in investors' minds. As a rule I want to see a drop of about two months in duration in the S&P to new bear market lows before I act on any indication of a bearish cascade. Then, if the S&P is also trading at least 10 percent below its 200-day moving average, it is generally time to increase stock market exposure. To time the subsequent reduction in stock market exposure, watch the 50-day moving average of the S&P. When the S&P moves 1 percent *above* its 50-day moving average, it is time to return your stock market allocation to below-normal or to normal levels.

Of course, like all strategies that objectively try to distinguish between bull and bear markets, this one will always be late. In other words, it will identify a bull market only after the low of the preceding bear market has occurred, and a bear market only after the high of the preceding bull market has occurred. Missing the start of a bear market is generally not too much of a problem, because in most bear markets the worst percentage declines develop toward the end. But missing the start of a bull market can be a very expensive mistake. It is in the early stages of a new bull market that the buy-and-hold strategy makes its biggest percentage gains, and the aggressive contrarian trader generally does not want to wait for the bull market signal from the 200-day moving average before adopting a bull market policy.

I handle this dilemma by using my tabulations of the duration and extent of preceding bear markets and by paying careful attention to the relative intensity of bearish information cascades during bear markets. If the most intense bearish cascade (as measured by the number, frequency, and semiotic content of media stories) occurs after a bear market has dropped the averages a typical amount, I am willing to bet that the bear market is complete and that the next up leg will be the first of a new bull market. Once I have an above-normal stock market allocation because think that the first leg of a new bull market is under way, I then wait for the S&P to rally for at least six months and 25 percent from its bear market low. At that juncture I start watching the 50-day moving average. As soon as it drops 0.5 percent from a high point, I reduce my above-average allocation back to normal levels.

The novelty and power of this aggressive stock market strategy arise from coordinating bearish information cascades with the position of the S&P 500 relative to the appropriate moving averages. Historical tabulations of previous market swings play an important role, too, especially near the end of bear markets.

MORE AGGRESSIVE CONTRARIAN TRADING STRATEGIES

This is the realm of the expert, experienced contrarian trader. The ideas I am about to discuss can be very dangerous to your financial health unless you already have several years of experience with contrarian methods and have been able to beat the market significantly during that time.

First, one may apply these contrarian methods to smaller markets. It is often possible to take advantage of market crowds that form in bonds, in commodity markets (crude oil, gold, silver, soybeans, etc.), or in individual stocks or industry groups. The problem one faces here is that these markets generally attract much less public interest than does the stock market as a whole. Consequently, it is more difficult to observe the communication process and the information cascade that builds the associated investment crowd. Doing this often requires participation in industry associations, subscriptions to special-interest publications, attendance at investment and industry-sponsored seminars and events, and the like. This makes much greater demands upon a contrarian trader's time and commitment.

Even so, there are very significant contrarian opportunities open in these market segments. The reason for this is the advent of ETFs intended to replicate the performance of these markets. These instruments make it possible for the experienced contrarian trader to take advantage of swings in interest rates, commodity markets, and individual stock market sectors (e.g., finance, housing, banks, technology) efficiently, with low trading costs and good diversification. Therefore, trying to identify mature market crowds in these markets can be well worth the time and effort required.

Here is another idea, a different twist on the usual contrarian trading approach. I like to call this the *bandwagon strategy*. Bullish market crowds generally take at least a year, or more often several years, to develop and mature. This contrasts with the typical bearish crowd, whose lifetime is measured in months. Since bullish crowds take so long to develop, the contrarian trader can often beat the market by detecting the communication process that is building the bullish crowd soon after it starts. At this juncture the market is probably still trading near fair value. The bullish crowd is still far from being mature. The trick at this point is to join the bullish crowd temporarily by adopting the crowd's investment theme and buying the asset that attracts the crowd's interest. By doing this the contrarian trader is trying to participate in a market move that will bring the price from fair value up into the rarefied air of extreme overvaluation. These bull markets in individual sectors, stocks, or commodities often show great percentage gains over fair value and can make a very significant contribution to a contrarian trader's investment results.

It goes without saying that this bandwagon strategy can be dangerous. The contrarian trader might forget his methods and become a permanent member of the chosen investment crowd. If he allows this to happen, his investment portfolio will suffer for it, and this is why only an expert should attempt this sort of strategy.

So far I have said nothing about methods for taking advantage of the disintegration of a bullish market crowd and the accompanying big drop in the price of the associated asset. There is a good reason for my reticence here, because taking the short side of any market, either shorting stocks directly or by buying an inverse ETF, is a dangerous tactic. Bullish market crowds tend to last longer, are harder to identify, and may carry prices to levels of overvaluation that no one can imagine. In the U.S. stock market, indeed in the stock market of any free-market economy, the long-run odds always favor the bulls. For these reasons taking the bearish side by buying an inverse ETF, for instance, means bucking the long-run odds, which favor the bulls. Doing this successfully requires a very high level of skill and market knowledge. Moreover, a long-short strategy typically yields much more volatile investment results than does a long-only strategy. Even when generally positive, investment returns that jump around a lot put a great deal of emotional stress on an investor, and this usually leads to bad decisions. It is not something I recommend to the novice contrarian trader.

CHAPTER 12

The Great Bull Market of 1982–2000

Gloom in 1982 • amazing stock market gains during the next 18 years • the 1987 crash • bull market crowd before the crash • Contrarian Rebalancing during the 1987 crash • the same strategy during the 1929–1932 crash • the savings and loan crisis • the 1990 bear market crowd • I'm on CNBC • the conservative contrarian increases his stock market allocation • no joy during a big rally • the bubble starts to inflate • irrational exuberance in 1996 • the conservative contrarian stays with stocks for four more years • the aggressive contrarian during the bull market • 1987 revisited • my experience during the crash • bullish at the 1990 low • the 1998 collapse of Long Term Capital Management • bearish information cascade • the aggressive contrarian goes long • the bubble's grand finale

PROLOGUE

During the summer days of August 1982, stock market prospects appeared gloomy. Three years earlier, in its August 13, 1979, issue, *BusinessWeek* magazine published its "The Death of Equities" cover story. Now *BusinessWeek* seemed prescient. Stock prices were nearly 10 percent lower in August 1982 than they had been at the time of the *BusinessWeek* cover story. No one imagined then that the greatest bull market in history was about to begin. On August 12 the Dow closed at 776.92. That same day the S&P 500 index closed at 102.42. During the subsequent 17 and a half years the Dow would rise an astounding average of 16.42 percent annually

137

until it reached its towering high close at 11,722.98 on January 14, 2000. The S&P would do even better, advancing an average of 16.63 percent each year until it reached its high close of 1,527.46 on March 24, 2000.

But these two averages were tortoises compared to the hare of the NASDAQ Composite index. On Friday the 13th in August 1982 this index closed at 159. On March 10, 2000, it stood at 5,048. The NASDAQ had gained an unprecedented average of 21.73 percent annually over a period of almost 18 years to reach its bubble top in the new millennium.

This chapter chronicles most of this great bull market from the perspective of the contrarian trader. We pick up the action in 1987 at the time of that year's stock market crash. Our story of this great stock market bubble culminates during the 19-month period from August 1998 through March 2000, which saw the index of the bubble stocks, the NASDAQ Composite, rocket up 235 percent from 1,499 to 5,408.

Stock market bubbles occur perhaps once every 30 years on average. During the twentieth century we saw peaks of minor bubbles in the U.S. stock market in 1906 and 1973. Major bubbles developed in 1929 and 1999. Bubbles like these will happen again. We might expect the next one around the year 2030 if it develops on schedule. It seems that a generation must pass and its mistakes be forgotten before the seeds of another stock market bubble can be sown.

THE 1987 CRASH

Among the more dramatic events of the 1982–2000 bull market was the market crash of 1987. On October 19 of that year both the Dow and the S&P 500 fell about 20 percent, a one-day drop greater than any other in the history of the U.S. stock market. This panic decline was the biggest part of a very brief bear market. In the S&P 500 (the index I recommend for use by contrarian traders) the 1987 top occurred at 336.77 on August 25 and the closing low at 223.92 on December 4, a drop of 34 percent. In the Dow the corresponding numbers are a high of 2,722 on August 25 and a low of 1,739 on October 19, a drop of 36 percent.

Investors were very fearful after the crash, and this showed in the newspaper headlines and magazine covers at the time. In its October 20 edition the *New York Times* headlined in big, bold, black letters: "Stocks Plunge 508 Points, a Drop of 22.6%; 604 Million Volume Nearly Doubles Record; Who Gets Hurt?" In its November 2 edition (on the newsstands October 26) *Time* magazine published an all-text cover in black and white on a red background, the colors of fear. The headline read: "The Crash: After a Wild Week on Wall Street the World Is Different." Of course, the world really hadn't changed at all; only investors' perceptions of it had changed. *Newsweek* magazine chimed in with the cover of its November 2 issue. It depicted a line chart in red showing a drop in prices and an inset photograph of worried investors. It was headlined: "After the Crash."

In this headline and these covers we see the bearish information cascade triggered by the crash itself and the search for the explanation of such an extraordinary one-day drop. There was an almost instantaneous change in sentiment, and a bearish stock market crowd developed quickly. Such a rapid and dramatic shift in sentiment over only a few days is a very unusual phenomenon. How would a conservative contrarian trader employing the Contrarian Rebalancing strategy responded to the crash?

In mid-1987 there seemed little doubt that a substantial bullish stock market crowd had developed during the preceding three years. I had just begun keeping a media dairy that year, and the documentary evidence it contains pointing to a bullish information cascade is sketchy. But I do remember that five years of steadily rising prices had lifted the gloom that had prevailed in August 1982. By August 1987 the dividend yields of the Dow and the S&P had dropped to historically low levels. Price-earnings ratios on the averages were above 20, at the time a historically high level (but one that would be spectacularly exceeded 13 years later). Market commentators publicly worried about a possible stock market bubble.

During the earlier stages of the 1982–1987 advance the Contrarian Rebalancing strategy called for an above-normal stock market allocation. But once the S&P 500 reached the 250 level in 1986 and had risen 65 percent from its July 1984 low at 148, the conservative contrarian trader would have reduced his stock market exposure to normal levels because the bull market had entered a zone of potential overvaluation based on historical tabulations. Once he observed the generally bullish commentary in the media during the first half of 1987 and the historically high price-earnings ratio and low dividend yield on the S&P, he would have concluded that a bullish stock market crowd had formed. At that point he would be looking for a drop of 1 percent in the 200-day moving average of the S&P 500 as a signal to reduce his stock market exposure to below-normal levels.

The 200-day moving average turned down by 1 percent from its high by November 20, 1987, when the S&P itself closed at 242. This occurred *after* the intraday bear market low for this average, which occurred on October 20 at the 216 level. The conservative contrarian trader would have by then noted the bearish information cascade cited earlier. Moreover, at the October low the averages had dropped about 35 percent from their 1987 highs, a drop of normal extent when a bull market crowd disintegrates. What to do on November 20?

The answer is simple. Follow the rules of the Contrarian Rebalancing strategy! Even though a steep, 35 percent drop had already occurred and a bearish crowd was visible, the fact that the 200 day moving average had turned downward by 1 percent meant that the stock market allocation had to be reduced to below-normal levels. But remember that this is done only because bullish crowd was visible at the preceding stock market top. If no bullish crowd had been visible, the Contrarian Rebalancing strategy would have dictated that a normal stock market allocation be maintained during any subsequent drop.

Having reduced his stock market exposure to below-normal levels at the S&P 242 level on November 20, 1987, what would be the conservative contrarian trader's next move? He had observed a drop of at least 20 percent in the averages and a bearish stock market crowd. The Contrarian Rebalancing strategy then requires a move to an above-normal stock market allocation once the 200-day moving average turns up by 1 percent. This happened on September 9, 1988, with the S&P closing at 267 that day. On that part of his portfolio representing the difference between a normal and below-normal stock market allocation, the conservative contrarian trader fell behind buy-and-hold investors during that nine-and-a-half-month period by about 10 percentage points (or 1,000 basis points).

INTERLUDE: THE 1929–1932 CRASH AND BEAR MARKET

The inexperienced contrarian is probably already beginning to doubt the efficiency of the Contrarian Rebalancing strategy. After all, didn't buy-and-hold investors do better during the 1987 crash? Yes, they did. But any market strategy must be judged on its performance over the years, not by its performance during any one market episode.

There is an even more important point to be made here. The Contrarian Rebalancing strategy is very cautious in moving to an above-average stock market allocation once a bear market has begun. There is good reason for this. Sometimes a market crisis develops into an economic crisis as well. In such circumstances one finds a sequence of distinct bearish information cascades, each leading to progressively lower lows in the stock market and potentially dropping the averages a very substantial amount from their highs. The classic example of this phenomenon occurred after the Crash of 1929. During the 1929–1932 bear market the Dow Jones Industrial Average fell from 381 to 40, a 90 percent drop over 34 months. There were repeated bursts of pessimism, each triggered by new signs of a deteriorating economic situation: record high unemployment, bank failures, and so on. This sequence of bearish information cascades began in late 1930 when the Dow was still above the 200 level and continued through the bank holiday of March 1933.

This was a situation when the tactic of using the 200-day moving average as an indicator would have dramatically improved performance relative to the buy-and-hold strategy. In 1929 the 200-day moving average of the Dow had fallen 1 percent from its high by October 28 when the Dow closed at 261. A reduction in stock market exposure to below-normal levels was then warranted. This moving average continued to drop steadily for more than three years afterward. It finally turned upward by 1 percent from its low on March 31, 1933, about two weeks after the end of the 1933 bank holiday. On March 31, 1933, the Dow closed at 55. Then and only then would the conservative contrarian trader have been justified in moving his below-normal stock market exposure to above-normal levels.

THE S&L CRISIS, THE 1987–1990 BULL MARKET, AND THE 1990 BEAR MARKET CROWD

A number of legislative changes during the 1980s lengthened the list of permissible real estate investments by savings and loan (S&L) associations and commercial banks. These changes also made it easier to finance loan portfolios by paying higher yields on a wider variety of deposits. The result was a boom in lending on commercial real estate. Sadly, many of the resulting loans were unsound or fraudulent and these led to the collapse of many savings and loans and commercial banks. The situation became so dangerous to the economy's health that in August 1989 the U.S. Congress passed the Financial Institutions Reform, Recovery, and Enforcement Act of 1989. One of its provisions established the Resolution Trust Corporation, which was to purchase and then dispose of failed thrift institutions taken over by regulators after January 1, 1989.

The continuing stream of S&L and bank collapses during 1988–1990 was a backdrop that discouraged the development a bullish stock market crowd. Memories of the 1987 crash were strong as well, and these also put a damper on bullish sentiment.

The conservative contrarian trader who followed the Contrarian Rebalancing strategy would have assumed an above-normal stock market allocation on September 9, 1988, when the S&P 500 closed at 267. In July 1990 the S&P had reached 368.95 while the Dow hit 2,964, gains of 65 percent and 71 percent respectively from their crash low points in 1987. Since more than two years had passed since those lows, the conservative contrarian would then have reduced his stock market exposure to normal levels. Since no bullish information cascade was yet visible in his media diary, he would not be contemplating any further reduction in stock market exposure even if the 200-day moving average of the S&P 500 were to subsequently decline by 1 percent.

On August 3, 1990, the world awoke to the news that Iraq had invaded Kuwait and was massing troops on the border with Saudi Arabia, the source of much of the world's crude oil supply. The stock market averages had already begun to drop in late July, and this news accelerated the decline. The first stock market headline appeared in the *New York Times* on August 24: "U.S. Stocks Plunge on Heavy Selling over Crisis in Gulf." By then the S&P had already dropped to 307.06 from its high close of 369.95, a decline of nearly 17 percent. This wasn't quite the 20 percent minimum drop for a bear market, but the latter percentage was reached on the nose on October 11, 1990, when the S&P closed at 295.46, its bear market low close.

During the period between August and October the media were worrying about possible war in the Gulf and its economic and human consequences. More than this, there were additional worries about rising unemployment, a possible recession brought on by the real estate bust, and a Federal Reserve policy of restraint intended to bring down uncomfortably high inflation rates of over 6 percent.

Evidence for this bearish information cascade was not hard to find in magazine cover stories. First up was *BusinessWeek*, which asked on the cover of its August 13 issue: "Are We in Recession?" The cover of the October 1 issue of *Newsweek* featured: "The Real Estate BUST." The October 15 issue of *Time* magazine, appearing just days before the low in the stock market, showed a photograph of a man hanging from a clock hand high above a busy city street. The cover caption read: "High Anxiety—Looming Recession, Government Paralysis, and the Threat of War Are Giving Americans a Case of the Jitters." Not to be outdone, the *New Republic*'s October 29 issue showed a cartoon picturing an abyss and captioned: "Oil prices are doubling. Foreigners don't want to lend us any more money. The real estate market is in the toilet. The banking system is tottering. Rising unemployment and stagflation are just around the corner. And the government can't think of a damn thing to do about it. Uh, oh." Bringing up the rear was *New York* magazine. Its November 19 issue showed on its cover a 1930s-era photograph of a young man dressed in a three-piece suit and shouldering a box of apples with a sign that said: "Unemployed—buy apples—5 cents each." The cover caption? "Hard Times."

Even a novice contrarian would have recognized this bearish information cascade. By mid-October a very bearish stock market crowd had formed. It was universally believed that war with Iraq would send the stock market much lower, and that the banking crisis would not be resolved anytime soon.

At that time I made a number of television appearances on the then very young financial network, CNBC. I was relentlessly bullish about the stock market and about the bond market in every TV interview I gave. I predicted that the S&P would rise from its 295 low to over 400 over the next couple of years. I also predicted that long-term bond yields would drop from the 9 percent level then to 6 percent during the same time frame. Both predictions were on the money. I offered a number of technical reasons for these views, but my confidence in them arose from my recognition of the depth of the prevailing bearish sentiment and the strength of the convictions of the bearish market crowd. Mine was a very lonely market stance. The CNBC staff referred to me as "the bullish market technician" to distinguish me from their other guests!

Through all these events the Contrarian Rebalancing strategy dictated holding a normal stock market allocation. Since the averages had dropped 20 percent from high to low and since a very obvious bearish stock market crowd had formed, the conservative contrarian would be looking for a turn upward in the 200-day moving average of the S&P to tell him to increase his stock market allocation. On March 26, 1991, this moving average did turn up by 1 percent from its low point. On that day the S&P closed at 376 and the conservative contrarian trader would have increased his stock market allocation to above-normal levels. Notice that he would have increased his stock market exposure at a point that was actually a new high level for the advance in prices that began in 1982. No matter. The conservative contrarian is not trying to buy near the low and sell near the high. His only objective is to beat the buy-and-hold strategy.

RALLY WITHOUT JOY, 1991-1994

From its October 1990 low at 295 the S&P 500 index advanced steadily for more than three years. It reached a temporary high point at 482 on February 2, 1994. This represented an advance of 63 percent from its 1990 low over a period of 40 months. Over the same period of time the Dow advanced 68 percent. The Contrarian Rebalancing strategy dictated a reduction of stock market exposure from above-normal to normal levels at this time because the bull market had met normal expectations for duration and extent.

A contrarian trader must always be contemplating his next move in every circumstance. In February 1994, with a normal stock market allocation going forward, he has to know how he will act should the 200-day moving average of the S&P drop 1 percent from any high level it attained during the bull market. The only circumstance in which this event calls for a reduction in stock market exposure is the presence of a bullish stock market crowd created by a bullish information cascade in the media. Had such a bullish crowd developed by early 1994?

My own media diary for the period shows that no bullish information cascade had even started by early 1994. This is easily seen from a sampling of magazine covers from 1991 to 1993.

The October 7, 1991, issue of *BusinessWeek* had a cover cartoon of a man thinking: "I'm Worried about My Job!" On November 4 *Newsweek* chimed in with a cover cartoon showing a family inside the jaws of a ferocious-looking wolf. The cover caption read: "What Recovery? The Bite on the Middle Class." Inside the magazine the lead story was headlined: "That Sinking Feeling—the recession that won't go away has average Americans spooked—and politicians running scared." On December 2 *BusinessWeek* published a "High Anxiety" headline that emphasized concerns about an elusive economic recovery. The November 29 issue of the *Economist* had on its cover a cartoon depicting stock traders tumbling down a graph of falling stock prices worldwide. The caption read: "And they all cried, 'Help.'" Finally, the December 23 issue of the *New Republic* was done with a completely black background with a pair of cartoon eyes peering upward from the bottom of an economic recovery. The caption read: "What's really wrong with our economy—and how to fix it." This was a remarkable gaggle of pessimistic economic cover stories within a short three-month span. It was proof positive that no bullish information cascade had begun by the end of 1991.

Not to be outdone, *Time* magazine chimed in with a depression cover for its January 13, 1992, issue. It showed a black-and-white, Depression-era photograph of a businessman buying an apple from an unemployed street vendor—except that the vendor's image was replaced by a 1992 color image of a man in a baseball cap holding an apple. The cover caption read: "How Bad Is It?"

As I write these paragraphs I find it jarring to recall that the 1990–1991 recession had already officially ended in March 1991, seven months before this sequence of cover stories appeared. The U.S. unemployment rate was still rising, however, and would reach a high of 7.8 percent in June 1992. To put this into historical perspective, the highest post–World War II unemployment rate was 10.8 percent, reached in December 1982. The highest recorded unemployment rate during the Great Depression of the 1930s was 25 percent. Two points are worth making here. First, it is highly unlikely that any bullish information cascade will develop in the stock market while unemployment rates are rising during a recession or its immediate aftermath. Second, in this particular case one gets the impression from these magazine covers that the U.S. economy was on the verge of collapse into Depression-era conditions. This illustrates the tendency of the media to exaggerate economic news, especially the worrisome kind, a tendency that helps start information cascades of one kind or the other. This tendency seems especially pronounced when the president of the United States happens to belong to the Republican party.

This intense pace of pessimistic cover stories slowed significantly in 1992 but did not halt entirely. The October 24, 1992, issue of the *Economist* showed a painting of shipwrecked sailors clinging to a rock in the ocean and was captioned: "Recession or Doom?" Remarkably, barely four months later and following the election of President Bill Clinton, a Democrat, the same magazine showed a cover cartoon of a joyful Uncle Sam springing up from his hospital bed, on which hung a chart of an upturn in economic activity. The cover caption read: "No Need for a Boost."

The magazine cover indicator was quiet for the rest of 1993. However, after a bearish information cascade that fairly can be said to have lasted nearly three years, the contrarian trader could rightly surmise that it would take at least a year and probably several before bullish animal spirits could revive and once more manifest themselves in the stock market. For this reason I think the conservative contrarian trader would have chosen to ignore any drop in the 200-day moving average of the S&P in 1994. In the event, this moving average did turn down but not by the full 1 percent required by the Contrarian Rebalancing strategy, so the issue was moot in any case.

THE STOCK MARKET BUBBLE INFLATES, 1995–2000

The very first convincing sign that a bullish information cascade had begun appeared on the cover of the November 13, 1995, edition of *U.S. News & World Report*. The cover caption read: "Gold Rush in Cyberspace—The Internet Will Change Everything—And Everyone Wants a Piece of the Action." The boom in Internet-related stocks had begun, but, as usually happens, no one could imagine the heights of overvaluation that these bubble stocks would reach. Note that this cover should have attracted the attention of aggressive contrarian traders because it was evidence that the internet stock bandwagon had started rolling. Bandwagon investors in this and related sectors did very well during the subsequent five years.

On June 3, 1996, *BusinessWeek* took note of the stock market upsurge with a cover captioned: "Our Love Affair with Stocks—Never before have so many people had so much riding on the market. Should we worry?" The September 30, 1996, cover of *Time* magazine showed a photograph of Ned Johnson, head of the mutual fund complex Fidelity Investments. Johnson is depicted holding a globe covered by ticker symbols. The cover caption read: "Can Fidelity Still Make Your Money Grow?"

This *Time* cover was definitive evidence that a bullish stock market crowd had formed. It demonstrated that the public mind was focused on the stock market, because *Time* is a general interest newsweekly. But the critical thing every contrarian must remember is that it is very difficult to predict just how big any bullish crowd will eventually grow. In this particular case the crowd continued to grow until the end of 1999, a full three years after the appearance of this *Time* cover. The fact that the *BusinessWeek* cover asked "Should we worry?" suggested to me that the bullish crowd would grow still bigger until worry was no longer associated with the stock market.

Recall that the Contrarian Rebalancing strategy called for the conservative contrarian trader to reduce his stock market allocation to normal levels in early 1994. From that point forward he maintained that normal allocation. Even after he had recognized this *Time* cover as strong evidence of a mature bullish investment crowd, the contrarian trader would continue holding a normal stock market allocation. Any reduction in stock market exposure would have to await a turn downward in the 200-day moving average of the S&P by 1 percent or more. When the *Time* cover came out, the S&P stood at 686. But the moving average sell signal did not occur until January 2, 2001, *more than four years later*. On the signal day the S&P closed at 1,283, 87 percent higher than on the date when that 1996 issue of *Time* hit the newsstands.

There was naturally much more evidence of this enormous bullish information cascade as it proceeded through 1997, 1998, and 1999. For one thing, stock market valuations as measured by dividend yields, price-earnings ratios, and Tobin's q ratio were literally off the chart. Even more telling were the frequent articles in the financial press explaining why traditional valuation measures were no longer useful in this new era bull market. The same kind of rationalizations appear to justify out-of-sight stock prices near the top of every extended boom and are always a sign of an inflated bubble and a mature stock market crowd.

Another interesting sign of the times could be found at your local bookstore. In sharp contrast to the situation in 1982, books about the stock market had become popular and were being published weekly. They occupied more and more retail shelf space. Especially popular were those books that married computer technology to stock market trading. Typical were three books reviewed by Christopher Byron in the June 28, 1999, edition of the *Wall Street Journal*. Their titles: *Day Trade Online, How to Get Started in Electronic Day Trading*, and *Electronic Day Traders' Secrets*.

The definitive history of the remarkable 1982–2000 bull market has yet to be written. As I mentioned in Chapter 5, I recommend that every contrarian trader read *Bull!* by Maggie Mahar. This book, published in 2004 by HarperCollins, does a fine job of recounting the history of the boom and bust from 1982 through 2002.

The conservative contrarian trader did reasonably well during the historic advance of 1987–2000. He certainly beat buy-and-hold investors by maintaining an above-normal stock market allocation during most of the 1991–1994 advance. At that point his allocation reverted to normal and he continued holding a normal allocation until January 2, 2001. While these are not spectacular results, one should keep in mind that the 1987–2000 period was one during which the buy-and-hold strategy outperformed virtually every other imaginable portfolio strategy. Even worse, many self-styled contrarians hurt themselves badly by remaining out of the stock market from 1996 or 1997 onward. Indeed, those who heeded Robert Shiller's 1996 warning (conveyed to the public by Alan Greenspan, chairman of the Federal Reserve) about the then-visible *irrational exuberance* of the stock market vastly underperformed buy-and-hold investors from that point forward. It was certainly true that in 1996 that stock market values were historically high and that a bullish stock market crowd had formed. But it is equally important to remember that bubbles can inflate much further than can be imagined by reasonable people. Our Contrarian Rebalancing strategy's 200-day moving average tactic is designed to take this fact of financial life in a bubble into account.

THE AGGRESSIVE CONTRARIAN FACES THE 1987 CRASH

In the rest of this chapter I am going to illustrate the use of the aggressive contrarian stock market strategy, described in Chapter 11, at three dramatic junctures during the 1987–2000 bull market. This recounting of an aggressive contrarian's actions during this 14-year bull market is therefore far from exhaustive. The complete story would take more pages to tell than anyone would want to read. I'll be content to convey the essence of an aggressive contrarian's market approach by describing only a few of the more important portfolio adjustments made by the aggressive contrarian trader during this time.

As explained earlier in this chapter, the contrarian trader had every reason to believe that a bullish stock market crowd had formed by the summer of 1987. The stock market averages were clearly overvalued by historical standards of dividend yield and price-earnings ratios. Sentiment was optimistic and bullish, largely because the averages had risen substantially since 1982. For example, from August 1982 through June 1, 1987, the S&P 500 had risen about 24 percent per year.

In March 1987, with the S&P trading a little below the 300 level, I decided to reduce substantially my portfolio allocation to the stock market. At the time I was measuring the S&P's progress from its July 1984 low at 148. By mid-1986 the average had advanced 65 percent from that low over a period of about two years. This met the minimum standard for potential market overvaluation. However, in 1986 I did not yet see convincing evidence of a bullish stock market information cascade. Moreover, at the time I thought that the advance from the 1982 lows would take about five years before significant levels of overvaluation could be reached. So I maintained an aggressively bullish stance until March of the following year.

Note that in March 1987 I reduced my own exposure to the stock market to well below normal levels, a tactic I do not recommend even to the aggressive contrarian trader. But I was confident that even if the S&P moved substantially higher I would get a chance to increase my stock market exposure to above-normal levels within a few months. In the event, the high close for the S&P was 337, reached on August 25, 1987.

On Friday, October 16, the S&P closed at 282, a level 5 percent below its 200-day moving average and a signal to the aggressive contrarian trader that a bear market had started. No bearish information cascade was visible at the time, so the aggressive contrarian would want to reduce his stock market exposure to below-normal levels on this signal. Why? A bullish stock market crowd had clearly formed by the summer of 1987. When such crowds disintegrate, the averages typically drop a minimum of 30 percent from their highs and sometimes more. Such a prospect justifies having only a minimal exposure to the stock market.

The next trading day, October 19, 1987, the major averages dropped an astounding 20 percent. The S&P closed that day at 225. I remember the following day as a completely chaotic one in the markets. Around midday on the 20th, there was effectively a trading halt on the New York Stock Exchange. There were no bids for stocks! This was the time of maximum panic. I estimate that the S&P had in fact fallen to 190 or so amidst this chaos, although the low for the day officially recorded in market statistics was 216. (The S&P futures traded as low as 181 on the 20th.) But then, as if out of nowhere, buyers appeared and a furious rally started. During the subsequent week the S&P fluctuated wildly in the 216 to 258 range. Bid-ask spreads for stocks and futures were enormous, reflecting the widespread shock and fear the crash had generated.

The bearish information cascade that developed in response to the crash was certainly visible a week afterward on October 26. The S&P closed that day at 227, more than 24 percent below its 200-day moving average. By all rights this was the definitive indication for the aggressive contrarian trader to increase his stock market exposure to above-normal levels.

Did I do so? No! I was as shell-shocked as everyone else at the time. I knew that at the October 19–20 low points the averages had fallen more than 30 percent from their high points. I knew that this was a typical bear market drop associated with the unraveling of a bullish stock market crowd. But the time element just didn't seem to fit. It usually takes many months for a bullish crowd such as the one evident during the summer of 1987 to unravel, but only two months had passed since the August 25 top. So I chose then to sit on my hands, do nothing, and await events.

I waited until May 1988, about nine months from the date of the August 1987 top. I estimated that this was the minimum duration of a bear market associated with the disintegration of a bullish stock market crowd. But in May the S&P dropped only as low as 248, a level well above its low of the previous October. It was then that I decided that the October low probably ended the bear market. If this was true, I had to increase my stock market allocation to above-normal levels. This I did. Since the hypothesis I adopted in May 1988 was that a bull market was under way, I wanted to follow the special rule appropriate for the first leg up in a bull market. One should wait for an advance of at least 25 percent from the low close, which takes at least six months. Then start watching the 50-day moving average. Cut stock market exposure back to normal levels when this 50-day moving average drops 0.5 percent from a high point.

A 25 percent advance on the bear market low close of 224 on December 4, 1987, would carry the S&P up to 280. This level was first reached on October 20, 1988, 10 months later. From the latter date the 50-day moving average continued to advance. Its first half percent drop became visible on November 6, 1989, when the S&P closed at 332. This was the point at which the aggressive contrarian trader would cut his above-normal allocation to the stock market back to normal levels.

THE 1990 LOW

Earlier in this chapter I explained how a bearish information cascade developed during the last quarter of 1990 in response to the S&L crisis and the threat of war in the Gulf. On August 21, 1990, the S&P 500 closed at 322, more than 5 percent below its 200-day moving average. At that juncture the aggressive contrarian trader would have moved to a below-normal stock market allocation.

A bearish information cascade would have been very evident by mid-October, which was also a time when the S&P spent several days more than 10 percent below its 200-day moving average. It would have been easy for the aggressive contrarian trader to move to an above-normal stock market allocation at a time when the S&P was trading below the 305 level.

The 1990 bear market was brief, carried the S&P down by 20 percent, and ended at the 295 level on October 11. At the time I was very bullish and believed that a new bull market had started. I reiterated this in several TV appearances on CNBC that fall. During the first leg of a bull market the aggressive contrarian wants to maintain an above-average stock market allocation for at least six months, awaiting an advance from the bear market low point of at least 25 percent. Six months after the October 1990 low the S&P closed at 378, more than 27 percent above that low point. At this juncture the aggressive contrarian trader would start watching for the first drop of 0.5 percent in the S&P's 50-day moving average, the signal to reduce his stock market allocation to normal levels. This happened on July 5, 1991, with the S&P at 374.

LONG TERM CAPITAL MANAGEMENT GOES BUST

We next fast-forward to 1998. It was a dramatic year in the world's financial markets. On August 17 the Russian government defaulted on its foreign debts. The ruble fell dramatically against other currencies. The global bond market was thrown into turmoil by the Russian financial crisis, and this caused enormous losses for a very big hedge fund, Long Term Capital Management. The fund's losses were so big that they threatened the solvency of several Wall Street banks. Because of this so-called systemic risk, the Federal Reserve orchestrated a buyout of the fund's portfolio by a consortium of these same banks. Not only that, the Fed cut rates substantially and added a great deal of liquidity to the money markets to prevent the panic from spreading.

The first sign of a bearish information cascade was the *New York Times* headline on the August 28, 1998, which read: "Markets Jolted, Dow Off 4.1% as the Russian Economic Slide Adds to Pressures on Yeltsin." On September 1, my local paper, the *Morristown Daily Record*, headlined: "Dow Wipeout—Gains for year lost in 512-point plunge."

The bearish information cascade was also prominent in weekly newsmagazines. On the cover of its August 8 issue the *Economist* showed a cartoon of a bear wearing sunglasses in which was reflected a chart of falling stock prices. The caption read: "Grin and Bear It." A month later, in its September 14 issue, *Time* magazine's cover asked: "Is the Boom Over?" and showed a graph of falling stock prices down which tumbled investors. On the cover of its October 12 issue *Newsweek* asked: "The Crash of '99?—It doesn't have to happen but here's why it might."

Prior to the Russian crisis, the S&P had reached its high close at 1,187 on July 17, 1998. It would fall to a low close of 957 on August 31 and an intraday low of 923 on October 8. This was a drop of nearly 20 percent on a closing basis, more on an intraday basis. Events moved so swiftly that the aggressive contrarian trader would not have been able to sidestep any of this decline. In fact, the first day on which the S&P closed at least 5 percent below its 200-day moving average was also the day of the low close, 957 on August 31. That was the first opportunity the aggressive contrarian could have taken to reduce his stock market exposure to below-normal levels.

The S&P first closed at least 10 percent below its 200-day moving average on the day of its intraday low, October 8. A bearish information cascade was clearly under way by then. The aggressive contrarian would have increased his stock market allocation to above-normal levels at the 959 level in the S&P.

At this juncture I was willing to bet that a new bull market was beginning. This was a gamble because it had been evident since 1996 that a substantial bull market crowd had developed. Since the S&P had dropped only 20 percent from its highs, there was every reason to think based on historical precedent that a bigger price decline would develop and carry the average down 30 percent or more.

Remember that the first leg of a new bull market generally sees the biggest percentage gains of the entire advance. I didn't want to take the chance of missing it. The aggressive contrarian, having guessed that a new bull market was under way, would want to wait for six months to pass after the bear market low and for the S&P to rise at least 25 percent from that low. Once these two criteria were met, he would watch for a half percent drop in the 50-day moving average to signal a reduction in stock market exposure.

I decided to adopt a compromise policy that would protect me if a bigger decline was at hand. I would stick with my above-normal stock market allocation until the 50-day moving average turned downward by 0.5 percent. If this happened, I would move back to a below-normal allocation even if six months had not passed and the market had not risen 25 percent.

In the event, it took only a little more than two months for the S&P to move above its July 17 high and at no time did the 50-day moving average drop 0.5 percent from a high during that rally. Once new highs were attained, I adopted the six-month, 25 percent rule appropriate for the first leg of a bull market. A move back down to a normal stock market allocation was triggered by a half percent drop in the 50-day moving average on September 20, 1999, with the S&P closing at 1,336. The bull market that started from the 1998 low would not end until the following March at a high close of 1,527 in the S&P.

CHAPTER 13

Collapse of the Bubble: The 2000–2002 Bear Market

End of the bubble bull market • the conservative contrarian stays until the lights go out • bear market signal in January 2001 • how far down? • bearish information cascade after the 9/11 terrorist attack • a long wait for a signal • the bears party in July 2002 • an amateur contrarian fades the crowd • the conservative contrarian waits until June 2003 • the aggressive contrarian trades the bear market • Wall Street wreck • Newsweek predicts a bear market • my thinking during the summer rally after the top • October 11 bear market signal • a chance to buy in March 2001 • out again in April • trading after 9/11 • buying near the bear market low • the first leg up in a new bull market

END OF THE GREAT BULL MARKET

The greatest bull market in the history of the United States began from the lows established in the Dow Jones Industrial Average and the S&P 500 index in August 1982. On August 12 the Dow closed at 776.92 and the S&P at 102.42. An astounding 18-year advance culminated on January 14, 2000, in the Dow when it closed at 11,722.98. The S&P reached its bull market peak on March 24, 2000, at 1,527.46. The home of the bubble stocks, the NASDAQ Composite index, moved up from 159 in August 1982 to a high close of 5,048 on March 10, 2000.

How would the contrarian trader have been positioned as these averages were ending this record-breaking bull market in early 2000? Keep in mind that the biggest mistake any contrarian trader can make is to be underinvested for any substantial period of time in an extended bull market. Beating the market means outperforming the buy-and-hold strategy, and it is during long bull markets that this strategy shines. So even after the contrarian trader had identified the bubble crowd in late 1996 he would only have maintained his stock market exposure at normal levels. A move to below-normal exposure for the conservative contrarian following the Contrarian Rebalancing strategy would await a turndown in the 200-day moving average of the S&P 500 by 1 percent from its bull market high. The aggressive contrarian would wait to see a drop in the S&P 500 of 5 percent below its 200-day moving average. These tactics would help both types of contrarian trader remain invested in the bubble bull market as long as was prudent.

CONTRARIAN REBALANCING DURING THE 2000–2002 BEAR MARKET

The 200-day moving average of the S&P 500 reached a peak of 1,447.54 on October 5, 2000, and had fallen 1 percent from that level by January 2, 2001. On January 2 the S&P closed at 1,283. At this juncture the conservative contrarian trader would have had ample reason to reduce the allocation to the stock market in his portfolio to below-normal levels. In our running example where normal is a 60 percent allocation, a below-normal allocation would perhaps be 30 percent or even less.

I want to emphasize here a very important point: The contrarian trader is emphatically *not* in the business of picking tops and bottoms in the stock market averages. Instead he is in the business of outperforming the buy-and-hold investment policy. Doing this does not require getting out of stocks close to the tops of bull markets and getting back in near the lows of bear markets. Rather it requires the contrarian trader to *lean against the crowd*, to invest opposite the preferences of well-established market crowds by identifying the point where these crowds are liable to begin disintegrating. It is very hard to identify the top of a bull market, but much easier to see when a bullish crowd is about to disintegrate after such a top has probably developed.

THE LONG WAY DOWN AGAIN

The most important feature of the 2000–2002 bear market from the contrarian trader's standpoint was that it developed from the collapse of a stock market bubble. The bubble had developed during the last years of the 1990s. The information cascade in the media that built the bubble's stock market crowd was easy to identify. By any historical standard the stock market was grotesquely overvalued at its high point in the year 2000.

Stock market bubbles do not develop very often, but when they do the ensuing bear market is likely to be long and severe. This bear market was no exception. By the time it ended in October 2002, the Dow had dropped 39 percent, the S&P 500 had dropped 50 percent, and the NASDAQ Composite nearly 80 percent from their high points in early 2000. Depending on which average is used as a measuring stick, the bear market lasted between 31 and 33 months. Historically, the last comparable drop in extent and duration was the Great Crash during 1929–1932, which ushered in the Great Depression of the 1930s.

The contrarian trader knows that the postbubble bear market is likely to be long and severe. For the conservative contrarian who is employing the Contrarian Rebalancing strategy, this has important implications. First, he knows that a severe bear market will probably last anywhere from 18 months to three years. He expects the market to drop at least 30 percent and probably closer to 50 percent during this time. He wants to take advantage of these historical tabulations and the information in his media diary to assume an above-normal stock market allocation as soon as is prudent—that is, as soon as he sees evidence that the bear market has ended.

Let's see how these goals could have been achieved during the 2000–2002 bear market.

CONTRARIAN REBALANCING DURING THE CRASH

In Chapter 11 I explained that a conservative contrarian trader should increase his stock market allocation to above-normal levels once he has evidence that a bear market is complete. This requires three conditions to be met. First, he must detect a bearish information cascade in his media diary, a cascade intense enough to build a substantial bearish stock market crowd. Second, the S&P 500 should have dropped as much as is typical for the type of bear market that is under way. So if it is a bear market attending the collapse of a bullish stock market crowd (associated with some sort of bubble), then he would expect a drop in the S&P of 30 percent or more. Otherwise, a normal bear market would drop the index only 20 to 30 percent. Finally, the 200-day moving average of the S&P 500 must turn upward by 1 percent from whatever low it made when the first two conditions were satisfied. Once this third condition is met, the conservative contrarian increases his stock market allocation to above-normal levels.

Since the biggest stock market bubble in U.S. history was associated with the 2000 high point in the market averages, the conservative contrarian trader would expect the subsequent bear market to drop the S&P at least 30 percent. Once this happens, he determines whether there is evidence of a bearish stock market crowd in his media diary. The high close in the S&P was 1,527 on March 24, 2000. A 30 percent drop from 1,527 would bring the average down to 1,069. On September 17, 2001, the S&P closed at 1,038, its first close below the 30 percent mark. Was there a bearish information cascade under way at the time? Was there a bearish stock market crowd visible?

My answer to both these questions is yes, but for reasons that are a bit unusual. The World Trade Center in New York City was attacked by terrorists on September 11, 2001. The stock market was closed for a week afterward and reopened on September 17. The S&P had been dropping steadily for almost four months from a short-term high point it made on May 21, 2001, at the 1,313 level. The impact of the terrorist blow on the financial markets was enormous, but it was not recorded on newspaper front pages or on magazine covers for obvious reasons. Instead it was political and military news that dominated the media. Even so, page 1 of the *New York Times* business section on September 12, 2001, was headlined: "The Financial World Is Left Reeling by Attack." The September 21 edition of the *Chicago Tribune* had a page 1 stock market story, complete with charts showing drops in all the averages during the preceding week. It was headlined: "America's Psyche Takes Another Blow, Old Assumptions No Longer Apply; 'There Is Fear in the Marketplace.'" The previous day the S&P had closed at 984. So I think it is fair to say that the conservative contrarian trader would have been justified in concluding that a bearish information cascade was under way. He would then await a move upward of 1 percent in the 200-day moving average of the S&P 500.

This would have been a long and trying wait, for the desired 1 percent upturn in the 200-day moving average did not develop until June 13, 2003, when the S&P itself closed at 988. There were fireworks in the marketplace in the meantime. The S&P moved as high as 1,178 in January 2002 and as low as 768 later in October that same year. These fluctuations occurred against the backdrop of a second bearish information cascade, which developed during the summer of 2002.

The first solid evidence for this second bearish information cascade appeared in the July 13, 2002, edition of the *New York Times*. This was a page 1 stock market story, although it was not the day's headline story. The story appeared above the fold and was accompanied by bearish charts of the S&P 500, the federal budget deficit, and plunging consumer confidence levels. The story's headline read: "Bears on Prowl As Market Ends a Dreary Week." The following day saw another above-the-fold, page 1 stock market story, again not the day's headline. The story was headed: "Stocks' Slide Is Playing Havoc with Older Americans' Dreams." Finally, on July 17 the stock market made it into the *Times*'s headlines: "Fed Chief Blames Corporate Greed; House Revises Bill—Greenspan Cites Cause for Investor Woes—Dow Drops Again." More evidence came from the *Times*'s July 20 page 1 headline: "Market Continues Four-Month Rout; Dow Plunges 390." That same day the *Chicago Tribune* chimed in with this headline: "Dow Dives to Four-Year Low." And on July 23 the *Tribune* headlined: "Dow Slides below 8,000 to '98 Level."

My wife, an amateur contrarian trader, increased her stock market allocation on July 22, 2002, the first market day after the two July 20 headline stories. The S&P closed on July 22 at the 820 level, her trade price since she was investing in S&P 500 index funds. My wife acted as an aggressive contrarian would, but when would a conservative contrarian assume an above-normal stock market allocation? Certainly the market had fallen far enough, almost 50 percent as measured by the S&P, to deflate the preceding bubble. There was a prolonged bearish information cascade, which had built a powerful bear market crowd. All that was necessary to trigger an allocation increase would be a turn upward by 1 percent in the 200-day moving average of the S&P 500. This happened on June 13, 2003, when the S&P 500 closed at 989. On that day the 200-day moving average of the S&P reached 887.96, a 1 percent move up from its bear market low point of 879.03 reached on May 1, 2003.

So we see that the conservative contrarian trader would have reduced his stock market allocation to below normal on January 2, 2001, with the S&P at 1,283. He then would have moved his allocation to above normal at S&P 988 on June 13, 2003. Notice two important things: He did not go to a below-normal allocation until the S&P had already dropped a substantial amount from its high close at 1,527. And he did not restore his allocation to normal and then to above-normal levels anywhere near the low bear market close of 777. This illustrates a very important point: It is not necessary to sell near the top or to buy near the bottom to improve one's investment performance relative to the benchmark buy-and-hold strategy. All that is needed is to buy at levels that are on average significantly lower than the levels at which you sell.

THE AGGRESSIVE CONTRARIAN DURING THE 2000–2002 BEAR MARKET

The 2000–2002 bear market years were punctuated by three very substantial rallies that carried the S&P up at least 20 percent. There were many wonderful opportunities for the aggressive contrarian trader to buy into these three big rallies and to sell or even sell short in anticipation of the subsequent declines. However, in this chapter I will pass over the short selling opportunities open to the aggressive contrarian trader during this postbubble bull market. Why?

I think that trading on the short side of the stock market, even via inverse exchange-traded funds (ETFs), is a game that should be played only by experts. It requires great flexibility of mind and a completely unbiased view of market opportunities. These characteristics are not well developed in a novice contrarian trader. Experts don't need my help, but I want to urge beginners not to get too far out over their skis. The stock market is a treacherous realm for any investor, and beginners are well advised to focus on the one activity that is favored by a secular uptrend in the U.S. stock market: buying and selling long positions. So in the rest of this chapter I point out some of the opportunities that were open to an aggressive contrarian trader who was content to manage only long positions during the 2000–2002 bear market.

A WALL STREET WRECK

The S&P 500 established its closing high for the bubble bull market on March 24, 2000, at the 1,527 level. Naturally no contrarian trader would have known then that 1,527 was destined to be the bull market's high close. But every contrarian trader would have seen plenty of evidence of extreme overvaluation in the stock market. And every contrarian trader's media diary would have contained plenty of evidence of the bullish information cascade that had created the bullish bubble crowd in the stock market. So, at the very least, every contrarian trader would have adopted a wary view of the market and would have been alert for signs that a bear market had begun.

In March 2000 I believed that despite these warning signs the bull market had further to run. My reasoning was based on my historical market tabulations. I thought that a mini-bear market had ended in October 1998 at the intraday 923 low in the S&P 500. From there I thought that a normal bull market would evolve, one that according to my tabulations would last about two years and carry the market up about 65 percent or perhaps a little more. A 65 percent advance from the 923 level was achieved on March 23, 2000, when the S&P closed at 1,527. But the two-year guideline would not be achieved until October 2000. So I expected the ultimate market top to occur sometime during the September–October 2000 time frame.

During bull markets the aggressive contrarian trader should always reduce his stock market allocation to normal levels once the S&P has rallied at least 15 percent from some short-term low and has made a new bull market high. In March 2000 the aggressive contrarian trader might have gotten lucky and reduced his stock market exposure to normal levels very near what proved to be the ultimate top. Why? There had been a short-term low on February 25, 2000, with the S&P closing at 1,333, about 2 percent below its 200-day moving average. That short-term low had been accompanied by a brief bearish information cascade, which was highlighted by a page 1 story in the February 26 edition of the *New York Times*. The story was headed: "Stocks in Turmoil as Worries Grow on Higher Rates—Dow Closes below 10,000." If an aggressive contrarian had taken an above-normal stock market allocation near the February 25 low close, he would have returned to a normal allocation after a 15 percent advance in the S&P (the 1,533 level, which was reached intraday on March 24, but never reached on a closing basis).

As mentioned, there was no way to know at the time that the March 24 close at 1,527 would be the bull market top. It is for this reason that I don't recommend going to below-normal stock market allocations during a bull market, even if you are an aggressive contrarian. Instead, the right policy for an aggressive contrarian trader in an ongoing bull market is to await an opportunity to increase stock market exposure to above-normal levels. As was illustrated in the case of the February 25 low at 1,333, this would require a drop in the S&P 500 to or slightly below its rising 200-day moving average at a time when a short-run bearish information cascade was under way. At that point the aggressive contrarian can assume an above-normal stock market allocation *even though* he knows full well that a bear market might begin at any time. The reason for this is that it is impossible to guess just how far a stock market bubble might inflate, and it is usually best for even the aggressive contrarian trader not to implement a bear market strategy until he sees the S&P drop 5 percent below its 200-day moving average, an event that did not occur until October of that year.

A short-run bearish information cascade developed quickly after the March top, in April 2000. The market averages, especially the NASDAQ Composite of bubble stocks, dropped sharply from their March high points. On April 5, the *New York Times* headlined on page 1: "Nasdaq Recovers after a Free Fall in a Wary Market." This headline story was accompanied by a color photo of a floor trader looking distressed as background to a graph showing the NASDAQ Composite's gyrations the previous day. At the close on April 4 the S&P stood at 1,494, a full 8 percent above its 200-day moving average. Moreover, it had dropped for less than two weeks from its March top and the drop had carried it down only about 2 percent on a closing basis. So while it appeared that a bearish information cascade may have begun on April 5, the market had not dropped near its 200-day moving average, nor had it dropped 5 to 10 percent for about one to three months from its high, these being the parameters for normal bull market reactions. So an aggressive contrarian trader would still be waiting for a better opportunity before increasing his long-side exposure to the stock market.

Things started to fall into place on April 13. The *New York Times* printed a page 1 stock market story, not the headline but appearing above the fold. The story's headline read: "In Only a Few Weeks, Nasdaq Falls 25.3% from Its Pinnacle—Steep Drop Suggests a Technology Bear Market." Then, on Saturday, April 15, the *Times* printed a multicolumn, bold print, page 1 headline: "Stock Market in Steep Drop As Worried Investors Flee; Nasdaq Has Its Worst Week." The local *Morristown Daily Record* had as its headline that day: "Wall Street Wreck."

Clearly a short-run bearish information cascade had taken hold and built up a short-lived bearish crowd, one typical of short-term low points in a bull market. Moreover, on April 14 the S&P 500 had closed at 1,357, 2 percent below its rising 200-day moving average, below its 50-day moving average, and nearly 12 percent below its March top at 1,527. This combination of circumstances made this an ideal buy spot for an aggressive contrarian trader, a place where it made sense to restore his stock market allocation to normal or even to above-normal levels. As far as anyone could tell, the bull market was still alive and well.

There is a magazine cover that appeared in April 2000 that merits the attention of an aspiring contrarian trader. On the cover of its April 24, 2000, issue, *Newsweek* magazine showed a photograph of a glass of water in which two antacid tablets were dissolving. The cover caption read: "Is the Bull Market Really Over?" This is an example of an eerily prescient magazine cover. Such covers are very unusual but do appear sometimes, and it is important for the contrarian trader not to be misled by them. A naive contrarian would be tempted to respond to the cover's question by guessing that the bull market was *not* over. And he would have been wrong! The point here is that the cover was trumped by the clear and overwhelming evidence that a stock market bubble had already formed. And historical experience suggested that it would take months and probably years to deflate.

THE SUMMER RALLY

The low close for the S&P 500 in April 2000 occurred on April 14 at 1,356. As I have pointed out, there was ample reason for the aggressive contrarian trader to move to an above-normal stock market allocation during the short-run bearish information cascade that developed that month. But there was no reason for him to believe that the bear market associated with the disintegration of the bullish bubble crowd had yet begun. The bull market that started from the October 1998 low had run only 17 months, well short of the average of 20 to 24 months. True, it had carried the S&P up 65 percent at the March 2000 top. But the contrarian is always acutely aware that stock market bubbles can inflate far beyond what is suggested by any historically based statistical projection. So at the very least the aggressive contrarian trader would await a drop of 5 percent in the S&P below its 200-day moving average before switching over to a bear market trading strategy. In the meantime his problem was to decide when to reduce his above-normal allocation to normal levels.

Here is how I handled this problem at the time. As I pointed out earlier in this chapter, I thought the bull market that started from the October 1998 low would continue into the September–October 2000 time frame. At that point I expected that the bubble crowd would begin to disintegrate and a bear market would take hold. I also knew the following important characteristic of the 1998–2000 bull market. There had been two short-term reactions prior to the one that developed during March–April 2000. After each of these two reactions had ended, the S&P 500 worked its way to a new high bull market close within six weeks. Thus I decided to use this six-week time interval as a measuring stick to gauge the strength of the rally from the April lows.

On June 19 the S&P reached a new closing high of 1,486 for the rally from the April low. Eight weeks had passed, but the average still had not managed to move above its 1,527 high close of March 24, 2000. This I took as a warning sign that the bull market top may already have been seen. But it was only a warning. I resolved to move into bear market mode if I saw a daily close in the S&P that was more than 1 percent below its 200-day moving average. Such a close would occur while the 200-day moving average was still *rising*, but I believed that an aggressively bearish stance would be warranted since it was clear that an enormous bullish crowd had formed and that the ideal time frame for a top, September–October 2000, was rapidly approaching.

On September 1, 2000, the S&P 500 reached a rally high of 1,521, close to but still below its bull market high close of 1,527. On September 26 the S&P closed at 1,427, more than 1 percent below its 200-day moving average, which then stood at 1,447 and was still rising. At that juncture I assumed a bear market posture for my contrarian trading. As a matter of fact, I had already reduced my above-normal stock market exposure to normal levels in July as the market rallied, this because more than six weeks had passed since the April low without a new bull market high. In late September I reduced my stock market exposure still further, to sub-stantially below-normal levels. This was a more aggressive approach than I recommended in Chapter 11, but then I have a lot more experience than a typical contrarian.

What would a typical aggressive contrarian have done had he reduced his allocation to normal levels by using the same tactic employed earlier that year on the rally from the February 25 low? The bull market top was already in place, and the S&P never rallied as much as 15 percent from its April 14 low. As was discussed in Chapter 11, one way for an aggressive contrarian to identify a new bear market is to watch for a move in the S&P that carries it 5 percent below its 200-day moving average after a normal bear market. On October 11, 2000, the S&P first dropped 5 percent below its 200-day moving average, closing at 1,365. At his juncture the aggressive contrarian trader would assume a below-normal stock market allocation. In particular he would sell whatever he had bought previously near the April 2000 low point, probably at a small loss.

THE MARCH 2001 PLUNGE

Beginning on October 11, 2000, with the S&P at 1,365, the aggressive contrarian would have had ample reason to think a bear market was under way. Since there was plenty of evidence that a stock market bubble had formed during the 1994–2000 stock market advance, the reasonable expectation was that this bear market would drop the averages at least 30 percent from their March high points.

On March 12, 2001, the S&P 500 dropped below the 1,200 level to close at 1,180, its lowest level in more than two years. The NASDAQ Composite average dropped 6 percent that day, bringing its total decline from its March 2000 top at 5,048 to 61 percent. Clearly the bubble had popped. The March 13 edition of the *New York Times* headlined: "Markets Plunge in Wide Sell-Off; Nasdaq Falls 6%." A bearish information cascade had begun, and the aggressive contrarian trader would immediately check the position of the S&P relative to its 200-day moving average. At its close on March 12 the S&P stood almost 16 percent below that moving average and thus justified increasing stock market exposure, provided that there was a well-developed bearish information cascade in progress and that the market had been falling for two months or more since its last short-term top (which in this case had occurred in late January). Had the cascade then gone far enough to indicate the presence of at least a short-term bearish crowd? My own answer to that question was that it had not. This was only the very first headline of a developing cascade. Moreover, the market had been dropping for less than two months after its top in late January. A substantial bear market appeared to be under way, especially in the NASDAQ Composite index. So I wanted to see more evidence than just a single headline in my media diary before concluding there was a bearish crowd big enough to justify increasing my stock market allocation.

Such evidence was not long in coming. The March 26 issues of *Time* magazine, *Newsweek*, and *U.S. News & Word Report* all had bearish stock market covers. These issues were on the newsstand about a week earlier than their publication dates. Both *Time* and *U.S. News* had photographs of growling bears on the cover. The *Newsweek* cover asked: "How Scared Should You Be?" It is very unusual, even in a bear market, to see three such magazine covers in the same week. I took this as solid evidence that a good-sized bearish crowd had developed and that a short-term stock market low was at hand. The average price of the S&P 500 during the 10 trading days ending March 26 was 1,153 and represents a fair estimate of the price at which an aggressive contrarian could easily have increased his stock market exposure. The actual short-term closing low for the S&P occurred on April 4 at 1,103. The intraday low occurred on March 22 at the 1,081 level.

Notice that the low close of 1,103 was *not* 30 percent below the March 2000 high close of 1,527. The drop in the S&P was not yet typical of a bear market accompanying the disintegration of a bubble crowd. Such bear markets typically drop the S&P at least 30 percent and often more. For this reason the aggressive contrarian would *not* interpret any subsequent move in the S&P to a point 5 percent above its 200-day moving average as a sign that a new bull market was under way. In this particular case this cautionary observation proved to be moot. In the event, the S&P never moved above its 200-day moving average until after it had fallen more than 30 percent from its bubble high point at 1,527.

Having increased his stock market exposure to above-normal levels in March, the aggressive contrarian trader would next be looking for an opportunity to sell his newly acquired long position and move back down to below-normal exposure. After all, as far as he could tell the bear market was still in progress because the S&P had not dropped at least 30 percent from its bull market top. The bear market trading strategy described in Chapter 11 for the aggressive contrarian dictates that he wait for the average to move 1 percent above its 50-day moving average. This happened on April 18 when the S&P closed at 1,238.

The interesting thing about April 18 was that it was the day of a surprise rate cut by the Federal Reserve. Since I watch the markets during the day, I was able to reduce my stock market exposure about an hour after the Fed made its announcement. This was an example of fading bullish news in a bear market if it generates a big rally. It made good sense at the time because the news itself sent the S&P 500 up almost 5 percent within about 30 minutes after the announcement. I knew that the market would be pushing above its 50-day moving average.

TERRORISTS ATTACK ON 9/11

With a below-average stock market allocation in place by the close on April 18, the aggressive contrarian trader would again be looking for another bearish information cascade to develop when the S&P was trading at least 10 percent below its 200-day moving average after a drop lasting at least two months from its last short-term high point. The price and time parameters were met on September 6, 2001, with the S&P closing at 1,106. But the average had not yet dropped back below its March 2001 low point, so it is not surprising that no bearish information cascade was then evident.

The terrorist attack on New York City's World Trade Center on September 11 changed the situation dramatically, as I described earlier in this chapter. Bearish sentiment became widespread. The aggressive contrarian trader would have easily been able to increase his stock market allocation while the S&P was trading below 1,000. The average reached its closing low at 966 on September 21 and its intraday low of 945 that same day.

Every trade requires a buy and a sell to be complete. The aggressive contrarian trader who bought below the 1,000 level would be looking for the S&P to move 1 percent above its 50-day moving average before again reducing his stock market allocation. This happened on November 5, 2001, when the S&P closed at 1,102. The rally from the September lows eventually carried the S&P 500 to a high close of 1,173 on January 4, 2002.

END OF A BEAR MARKET

During all of 2001 and 2002 the S&P 500 never closed as much as 5 percent above its 200-day moving average. Indeed, for most of this time it stayed below its moving average. The aggressive contrarian trader never had reason to doubt that a bear market was in progress. During this time his typical stock market allocation was at below-normal levels, but he took advantage of bearish information cascades to temporarily increase stock market exposure. He last did this in September 2001, but returned to a below-normal allocation in early November.

By June 21, 2002, the S&P had again dropped 10 percent below its 200-day moving average. However, the S&P still had not dropped below its September 21, 2001, low, so it was not surprising that no bearish information cascade was evident in my media diary at that date. By mid-July, however, that low had been broken and a bearish cascade was well under way. I explained the details earlier in this chapter. The closing low for the S&P was 798 on July 23. I think the aggressive contrarian trader had plenty of opportunity to increase his stock market exposure below the 900 level that July. For the sake of discussion, let's suppose he did so at an average price of 860.

This move to an above-normal allocation did not last long. The aggressive contrarian trader would have observed the S&P close at 951 on August 19, more than 1 percent above its 50-day moving average. Since the S&P was still below its 200-day moving average, he would then have reduced his stock market exposure to below-normal levels at that time.

During the entire July–October 2002 time frame the S&P 500 remained at least 10 percent below its 200-day moving average. Thus anytime that the bearish cascade again became visible the aggressive contrarian trader would be justified in once more increasing his stock market exposure after having reduced it on August 19. The only caveat I would add is that he would also want to be sure that the average was within a few percentage points of its July low at the same time.

As it happened, there was not much evidence for a renewed cascade when the S&P established its closing low for the bear market on October 9, 2002, at the 777 level. My media diary is filled with bearish news stories that were prevalent at the time, but there were no headline stories evident. However, there were some page 1 stories. The October 9 edition of the *Chicago Tribune* had a page 1, above-the-fold news analysis headlined: "Risk-Prone Economy Limps Along." The analysis was accompanied by graphs showing the downward course of the Dow Jones Industrial Average. The following day the *Wall Street Journal* had a significant page 1 story that was not a headline story. It appeared above the fold and was accompanied by charts showing dropping stock market prices. The story was headed: "Bears Claw Markets Yet Again, As Dow Industrials Fall Nearly 3%." At the time I underlined the opening sentence of the story, which read: "A harsh air of gloom hung over the markets, sending investors fleeing stocks yet again." The second paragraph began: "Why have things gotten so bad?"

At the time I took these two stories as evidence that justified an increase in stock market allocation, largely because the intraday bear market low on October 10 at 769 was a little below the intraday low reached on July 24 at 776. A big bearish crowd had been built up during repeated bearish information cascades in the previous two years. Moreover, the average had dropped nearly 50 percent from its March 2000 high point over a period of 31 months. Both parameters were near the outer limits reached by bear markets during the past 100 years.

The S&P quickly moved back more than 1 percent above its 50-day moving average on October 21 when it closed at 900. Since the S&P was still below its 200-day moving average, the aggressive contrarian trader may then have chosen to reduce his stock market exposure to below-normal levels. However, he would also have had good reason to believe that the move off of the October low point was the first leg of a new bull market. If so, following the method describe in Chapter 11, he would have ignored this October 21 sell signal. I personally did not adopt this view until after the March 2003 low had developed. In either case the investment results would have been the same and are described below.

From November 2002 through January 2003 the S&P remained below its declining 200-day moving average, but not by as much as 10 percent. But on February 7, 2003, the index dropped more than 10 percent below its 200-day moving average. This excursion lasted only a few days and was not accompanied by any bearish cascade. On March 10, 11, and 12 the S&P again traded at least 10 percent below its 200-day moving average. This time war with Iraq was imminent and was the focus of page 1 stories. The start of hostilities in a war can generally be taken as an indicator of bearish sentiment and of a bearish market crowd (see the discussion in Chapter 9). The outbreak of the Iraq war with the S&P 10 percent below its moving average justified an increase in stock market exposure by the aggressive contrarian trader. On March 11, 2003, the S&P established its 2003 low close at 800.

TRANSITION TO A NEW BULL MARKET

Contrarian strategies, like all other trading strategies, face their greatest challenge at the points of transition between bull and bear markets. It is especially important that a contrarian trader not be left on the sidelines during the early stages of a bull market, because that is when the stock market averages make their biggest percentage gains. The aggressive contrarian can recognize a new bull market by watching for the first close in the S&P that is 5 percent above its 200-day moving average. But this sort of signal always occurs well after the actual bear market low point. Consequently there is a significant danger that the aggressive contrarian will reduce an above-normal stock market allocation to below-normal levels just as the market accelerates upward in a bull market's early stages.

Here is how I dealt with this danger in 2003. First, stock market sentiment had been very bearish for eight months. Indeed, in March 2003 the weekly survey of investors conducted by the American Association of Individual Investors showed historically high levels of bearish sentiment. The bear market had carried the S&P down by nearly 50 percent and the NASDAQ down by 80 percent. It had lasted more than 30 months and thus exceeded the historical norm in duration and extent. With this as background, the fact that the market made a closing low in March 2003 at 801, visibly above the level of its October low at 777 and in a situation when war was imminent, made me suspect that better times were ahead. So I decided to defer selling my increased stock market allocation long enough to see if the S&P could trade above its 933 high of November 21. If it did, then I would take that as preliminary evidence that a new bull market had begun and switch to a bull market strategy.

In the event, the S&P rallied strongly as the Iraq war began and moved above the 933 high on May 6. On May 2 the S&P closed at 930, more than 5 percent above its 200-day moving average. At that point every contrarian trader would have hard evidence that a new bull market had begun.

CHAPTER 14

The Postbubble Bull Market of 2002–2007

Bears at the 2002–2003 low points • the conservative contrarian increases his stock market exposure • 30 months later he reverts to a normal stock market exposure • looking for a bullish information cascade • Google's IPO • the housing bubble • the aggressive contrarian during the bull market • avoid below-normal stock market allocations during a bull market • May 2004 buying opportunity • March 2005 buying opportunity • trading during 2006 and 2007

ESCAPING THE BEAR'S CLAW

Like all bull markets, the big advance that began from the October 2002 low started amidst conditions of fear and loss of confidence in the U.S. economy. The stock market spent nearly eight months trading sideways near the low points of the 2000–2002 bear market. The S&P 500 traded as low as 771 in July 2002, then as low as 768 in October 2002, and finally as low as 789 in March 2003.

During that eight-month period, the bearish stock market crowd that had formed during the bearish information cascade of May–October 2002 remained strong. Indeed, some polls of investor sentiment showed the maximum bearish sentiment at the March 2003 low point which occurred at a higher price level in both the Dow Jones Industrial Average and the S&P 500 index than the October 2002 lows. For example, the weekly sentiment poll conducted by the American Association of Individual Investors showed nearly 60 percent of respondents bearish during the week of the

169

March 2003 low point. This was a greater bearish percentage than was seen at any time during the 2000–2002 bear market. This fact convinced me then that the bearish crowd was on the verge of disintegration.

By 2007 the Dow and S&P 500 would double from their 2002 lows at 7,181 and 768 respectively. How would the conservative contrarian trader have positioned his portfolio to take advantage of this advance? In Chapter 13 we saw that on January 2, 2001, the 200-day moving average of the S&P had dropped 1 percent from its bull market high. That day the S&P closed at 1,283 and the Contrarian Rebalancing strategy called for a reduction of stock market exposure to below-normal levels, this because all the signs of a bubble were evident near the 2000 top.

During a bear market that follows a bubble, the conservative contrarian maintains a below-normal stock market exposure. He expects to see a drop in the S&P 500 of at least 30 percent. Once such a drop has developed, he looks for a bearish information cascade to occur near a potential bear market low point. If one develops and if the 200-day moving average of the S&P subsequently advances 1 percent from a low point, the conservative contrarian has his signal to increase his stock market allocation to above-normal levels.

By October 2002 the S&P had fallen nearly 50 percent. The May–October bearish information cascade had built the bear market crowd until its views dominated in the media. Then on June 13, 2003, the 200-day moving average of the S&P turned up by 1 percent. That day the S&P 500 closed at 988. This upward turn in the 200-day moving average was the first to occur during the entire 2001–2003 period. On that day the conservative contrarian would have increased his stock market exposure to above-normal levels.

The Contrarian Rebalancing strategy calls for a reduction of stock market exposure to normal levels once the bull market has continued for 20 to 24 months and the S&P has advanced 65 percent from its low point. The low close for the S&P was 777 on October 9, 2002. A 65 percent advance on that low would carry the index to 1,282. On January 6, 2006, the S&P closed at 1,285, its first close at or above 1,282, and had advanced for more than three years. At that juncture the conservative contrarian trader would have reduced his portfolio allocation to the stock market to normal levels.

WHAT BULL? LOOKING FOR SIGNS OF A BULLISH INFORMATION CASCADE

As I have already pointed out, the 2002–2007 postbubble bull market nearly doubled both the Dow and the S&P and lasted five years. One normally would expect to find an enthusiastic bull market crowd form in such circumstances. But the trauma of the previous bear market, which had sent the S&P 50 percent lower and lasted nearly three years, apparently had very long-lasting effects on investors. Perhaps this was because the bubble stocks that led the market to its top in 2000 suffered even more than the average stock in the S&P. The bubble stocks for the most part were traded on the NASDAQ. The NASDAQ Composite average dropped 80 percent during the 2000–2002 bear market!

For whatever reason, the signs of a bull market crowd and a bullish information cascade never appeared in my media diary during the 2002–2007 bull market. Let's recall the signs.

First of all, magazine covers that favorably (even heroically) depict corporate leaders of prosperous industries generally appear during a bullish information cascade. During this bull market I noticed only one such cover story, which appeared in the October 24, 2005, issue of *Time* magazine. The cover was a photograph of Apple Computer's founder and CEO, Steve Jobs, and was captioned: "The Man Who Always Seems to Know What's Next."

Another kind of bullish cover story conspicuous by its absence was one discussing the "new" role of money and wealth in our culture and economic environment. Typically these tell the story of the newly rich entrepreneurs who have become wealthy by riding the tide of rising stock market prices and spectacular initial public offerings (IPOs).

A second sign of a bullish information cascade is a series of well-publicized and very profitable (for the corporate insiders at least) initial public offerings. These were very prominent during the 1994–2000 bubble bull market but almost entirely absent during the 2002–2007 bull market. The single exception was Google's IPO, which I will discuss shortly.

A third sign of a bullish information cascade is the emergence of one or more pied pipers—financial commentators, market strategists, or industrial leaders who are thought to have predicted the bull market and are constantly being quoted in the press and other media cheerleading for rising prices and predicting more to come. Many such gurus became prominent during the 1996–2000 period, which saw the inflation of the prices of many bubble stocks. None were featured in the media during the 2002–2007 bull market.

A fourth sign indicating the presence of a big bullish stock market crowd is a general sense of well-being and optimism on the part of the public. This generally shows up in opinion polls of various kinds, in measures of consumer sentiment, and in discussions found in the media and in ordinary, everyday sorts of conversations about economic and stock market prospects. Far from showing any signs of such optimism, public opinion during the 2002–2007 bull market was generally pessimistic about the economy and the prospects for the United States. This may have been due in large part to the prosecution of the Iraq war and the general concerns about terrorism, but opinions are what they are whatever their genesis.

A final sign of a bullish information cascade is the very well publicized bullish performance of one or more innovative business sectors and their common stocks. During the 1994–2000 bubble bull market these were the computer, communications technology, and Internet-related sectors. During the 2002–2007 bull market, the best-performing stock market sectors were related to housing and finance, but these sectors did not attract nearly the public attention that the dot-com stocks had done during the preceding bubble bull market. Indeed, it is likely that the only significant bullish investment crowd of 2002–2007 occurred not in the stock market but in the housing market. The great advance in home prices during the 1995–2005 period certainly created the belief that investment in owner-occupied housing was a sure road to wealth. It would turn out that the collapse of this housing market investment crowd would have serious consequences in the stock market in 2008, but the crowd itself was not a stock market crowd. I'll have more say about the investment crowd in the housing market later.

Since no bullish stock market crowd developed during the 2002–2007 advance, the conservative contrarian trader should have maintained his normal stock market allocation even after the averages started to decline from their October 2007 high points. In the event (see Chapter 15), this involved suffering through a drop in the S&P of more than 50 percent during the panic of 2008. However, there is good reason for adopting such a strategy, even when it can expose the trader to such risks. The long-run investment odds in the United States favor owning common stocks. The Contrarian Rebalancing strategy takes these odds into account by being very careful before adopting a below-average allocation to the stock market.

The most damaging mistake a contrarian trader can make is to maintain a below-average allocation to the stock market during an extended period when the stock market averages are advancing. This would guarantee portfolio returns inferior to those generated by the buy-and-hold strategy. Therefore, the Contrarian Rebalancing strategy demands a reduction of stock market exposure to below-normal levels only if the contrarian trader sees convincing, affirmative indications of a bullish stock market crowd in his media diary.

THE STORY OF GOOGLE'S IPO

On August 18, 2004, the search engine company Google conducted an initial public offering (IPO) of its common stock. This offering was unusual in two respects: It was conducted by Google itself via an unusual Dutch or reverse auction, and this auction was conducted online. Google had hoped to sell 25.7 million shares in a range of $108 to $135, but in fact was able to sell only 19.6 million shares at $85. At the time, Wall Street gloated at the apparent disappointing outcome of the auction. Of course it was the Street's investment bankers whose ox was gored by Google's decision to conduct the IPO itself instead of giving the Street's underwriters a substantial piece of the pie.

But it was Main Street's reaction to the prospect of this IPO and to the event itself that I found more interesting and significant. Investors had been burned so badly by the collapse of the dot-com bubble that they seemed to actually *hope* that Google's IPO would fail. They wanted the price of Google's newly issued common stock to drop following the offering. Such hopes about a widely anticipated IPO are highly unusual. As a rule, there is a bullish anticipation of the IPO of any company in the technology or computer sector, especially one as successful as Google had been in dominating the online search market. Investors hope to make some quick profits on the IPO as it is oversubscribed. But bullish sentiment toward Google's IPO was nowhere to be found.

Instead the public's attitude seemed to be that investors who bought Google's IPO deserved to lose money. After all, hadn't everybody been hurt by the big drop in the prices of the bubble stocks during the 2000–2002 bear market? The same thing would happen again, and would justify these investors' sour attitude toward the stocks of all tech and communication companies and toward the stock market in general.

In August 2004 I found this public attitude toward the upcoming Google IPO astounding. It seemed that the bull market that had started from the 2002 lows had not yet entered a zone of overvaluation, and neither had a bullish stock market crowd been evident from the material I preserved in my media diary. Google was the leading company in its field. The bull market was still going strong, and it would tend to lift the price of Google's stock along with the general market. Add these considerations to the evidence of the public's highly unusual bearish hopes and expectations about Google's offering, and you have a classic opportunity to fade this bearish stock market crowd that formed around expectations for Google's stock performance.

I told my friends and clients at the time that for these reasons Google was a buy at its IPO. After the stock advanced from $85 to $200 I went out on a limb and predicted a move to the $500 level before the bull market ended. Events proved me too conservative, for by the end of October 2007 Google had risen to $747. The 2008 bear market dropped Google to a low price of $247, but this was still nearly three times its IPO price of $85.

The day after Google's IPO the public's attitude could be seen reflected in the *New York Times* and the *Wall Street Journal*.

On page 1 of the *Times*'s August 19 edition there was a story headlined: "Weak Demand Leads Google to Lower Its Sights." The story was accompanied by a color photo of the news ticker in Times Square, which read: "Google Slashes Price Range." The story's lead sentence read: "Google, conceding that demand for its long-awaited public stock offering had fallen far short of the company's hopes, slashed the number of shares yesterday and concluded its unorthodox online auction by accepting a price well below its original target."

The August 19 edition of the *Wall Street Journal* had two Google stories. The first was headlined: "Is Now the Time to Buy Google?" Its subhead: "Though Price Is Now Lower, History Suggests Waiting Six Months to Grab an IPO." (Six months later Google's stock was trading at $190.) A second story in that day's *Wall Street Journal* said even more about the public's attitude. The story's headline was: "How Miscalculations and Hubris Hobbled Celebrated Google IPO," and its subhead read: "Euphoria Ebbed, Tech Stocks Sagged, Till Firm Cut Size; Priced at a Low $85 a Share, Blow to Dutch-Auction Method."

A few days later the *Wall Street Journal* published a column about the outlook for IPOs in general. Its headline read: "Gloomy IPO Market Wonders About Life After Google's Entry." The theme of the article was the difficulty of selling stock offerings to the public in the current market environment. This was another solid piece of evidence that no bullish stock market crowd had formed yet.

The public attitude toward Google's stock was nicely reflected in a *Newsweek* column by Allan Sloan that appeared in the October 11, 2004, edition. When Sloan wrote his story, Google was selling near $130. A week earlier five analysts had come out with their initial opinions of Google's prospects. Sloan wrote:

> *Surprise! All five gave Google high ratings, even though it was a far more expensive stock than at the IPO just six weeks earlier, having risen almost 40%. Why investors took these opinions seriously is a mystery to me.*

Later in that story Sloan said:

> *At this point, Google's stock is going up because it's going up—not because its fundamentals are 60% better than when it sold its initial offering in mid-August. ... At some point, reality will seep in ... and investors will begin wondering whether Google can earn enough to justify its $40 billion market value.*

The story of Google's IPO in 2004 and of the public attitudes toward it and toward the entire IPO market then offers an important lesson for the contrarian trader. In August 2004 the market averages had not yet entered zones of potential overvaluation, according to my historical tabulations. There was no indication of a bullish stock market crowd in my media diary. These two indications were strongly reinforced by the public reactions to the Google IPO and attitudes toward the IPO market in general at the time. The conservative contrarian trader would have found it easy to sit with an above-normal stock market allocation during this time because public attitudes toward the stock market were skeptical if not outright bearish. Even better, here was an opportunity to fade a bearish crowd focused on a single company in the context of a bull market in the averages. The aggressive contrarian trader has to be on the lookout for these kinds of opportunities, because they will offer chances to enhance his performance relative to what is possible using only exchange-traded funds (ETFs), which follow the broad market.

THE HOUSING BUBBLE

The U.S. stock market indexes all reached their bubble high points during the first quarter of 2000 and then dropped to low points in October 2002. Remarkably, the market for owner-occupied housing actually strengthened during the 2000–2002 bear market and the associated economic weakness. In fact, housing prices accelerated their upward trend during that time. The Case-Shiller index of U.S. home prices rose nearly 90 percent between the first quarter of 2000 and the second quarter of 2006. This should be compared with a rise of 30 percent during the six-year period prior to 2000. The interesting thing about the housing bubble is that it was widely recognized as a bubble by many commentators at the time it was inflating, but as with all bubbles this offered no clue about how high home prices would rise and how long the bubble would inflate.

This is a lesson for contrarian traders. Bubbles are *always* recognized as such by wise observers at the time the bubble is inflating. Sadly, this is no help to the investor; it doesn't tell you when the bubble is about to pop. Bubbles as a rule inflate far beyond any reasonable expectation. This is why we call them bubbles. The most stunning example of this phenomenon in recent memory was the Japanese stock market and real estate bubble of 1980–1990.

Japan's Nikkei stock market index had risen nearly 350 percent during the 1970s. As the market rose even higher during the 1980s one could read frequent commentary on Japan's stock market bubble and predictions of its imminent demise. Yes, the bubble did pop in 1990, but not before the Nikkei had advanced another 490 percent during the 1980s. This ended a two-decade bull market, which had sent the Nikkei up an astounding 1,850 percent! If you studied the Japanese market in mid-1985 when the Nikkei reached the 13,000 level, it having doubled in the previous five years, you would have been tempted by market commentators and by the historically very high level of prices to think the bubble was about to pop. But you would have had to wait another five years and watch the market advance another 200 percent before you actually heard the popping sound!

The contrarian trader would have gotten some early warnings that the U.S. housing bubble was in its terminal phases. The clues came to him via cover stories in weekly and monthly newsmagazines.

The first housing market cover I have in my media file was the *Fortune* magazine cover of its September 20, 2004, issue. It shows a cartoon of a man sweating and saying: "They said prices would go up forever!! . . . and we believed it!!" The cover headline asked: "Is the Housing Boom Over?"

This cover expresses skepticism about the housing boom. Sometimes a bearish cover like this *does* come near the end of a bubble. This in fact happened in April 2000 for the stock market bubble. As explained in Chapter 13, *Newsweek* published a cover story then asking if the bull market in stocks was over! In general, however, a bearish cover in the midst of a bubble is something that coveys little information to the contrarian trader. If anything, it means that the bubble is not yet ready to pop.

The next two covers in my files tell quite a different story. The May 30, 2005, issue of *Fortune* is headlined: "Real Estate Gold Rush." It shows photographs of individuals and couples who have apparently made a lot of money in the real estate market. The subhead reads: "Inside the Hot-Money World of Housing Speculators, Condo Flippers, and Get-Rich-Quick Schemers (Is It Too Late to Get In?)." Two weeks later, in its June 13 issue, *Time* magazine published a cover story showing an illustration of a man hugging his home. The headline read: "Home $weet Home—Why We're Going Gaga Over Real Estate."

At the time these two covers appeared, in the second quarter of 2005, the Case-Shiller housing price index stood at 176.70, up 76 percent from its level of 100.00 in the first quarter of 2000. By the second quarter of 2006 the index reached its high point at 189.93. During the subsequent two years the index fell 20 percent to the 140 level.

While these two cover stories gave fair warning of the end of the housing boom, they appeared a full year before the actual peak in home prices. This is quite a common phenomenon. Market tops tend to lag bullish magazine covers by anywhere from four to 12 months, while market lows tend to lag bearish covers by only a month or so, if that.

These covers timed the top of the housing sector of the stock market much more exactly than they did the price of housing. The housing stock price indexes maintained by Standard & Poor's and by the Philadelphia Stock Exchange reached their housing bubble tops in July 2005, barely a month after the magazine cover stories appeared. By July 2008 these indexes had fallen 85 percent and 70 percent respectively from their 2005 high points.

The contrarian trader should always be on the lookout for media clues indicating a mature bullish or bearish crowd. These can arise in unexpected places. The housing bubble is a case in point. The year 2005 saw the debut of two television series devoted to real estate speculation. "Flip That House" on the Learning Channel and "Flip This House" on the Arts & Entertainment network drew growing and enthusiastic audiences. Interestingly enough, both shows continued to air through the housing downturn as the flippers whose activities they recorded began losing money. Apparently misery loves company.

AGGRESSIVE CONTRARIAN TRADING DURING THE 2002–2007 BULL MARKET

Unlike his conservative cousin, the aggressive contrarian trader expects to make adjustments to his stock market allocation at least a couple of times each year during both bull and bear markets. His goal is to use his media diary and his market tabulations to take advantage of the short-term market swings that develop within the context of any longer-term, multiyear trend. In a bull market, for example, a typical short-term upswing might carry the averages upward by 15 to 25 percent and last four to nine months or even longer. A typical short-term downswing might last anywhere from one to three months (and in extreme cases as much as six months) and carry the averages downward by 5 to 15 percent. In a bear market the extent and duration of short-term upswings is similar to that of short-term downswings in a bull market. A similar reversal of parameters applies to short-term downswings in a bear market.

Ideally, the aggressive contrarian trader will have an above-normal portfolio allocation to the stock market near the low points of short-term downswings and a normal or below-normal allocation to the stock market near the high points of short-term upswings.

At this juncture let me say that below-normal stock market allocations can be dangerous. I don't think any contrarian trader should have a below-normal exposure to the stock market during a bull market. Remember that having a below-normal stock market allocation during an extended upswing in prices is a recipe for ensuring that your portfolio's performance will be inferior to that of the buy-and-hold benchmark policy. I urge all aggressive contrarian traders to allow their bull market stock market allocations to fluctuate between normal and above-normal levels only. The aggressive contrarian would move to a below-normal allocation only after he sees the S&P drop 5 percent below its 200-day moving average. A below-normal stock market allocation is justified only in a situation where a stock market bubble has likely formed and is probably about to pop. In all other situations, leave below-normal stock market allocations to expert contrarian traders.

Let's see what tactics an aggressive contrarian trader might have used in pursuit of this objective during the 2002–2007 bull market. The S&P 500 index began its bull market from a low at 768 (intraday) on October 10, 2002. The aggressive contrarian trader would have had very strong evidence that a new bull market was about to begin. Certainly media evidence that appeared during the summer of 2002 revealed a massive, bearish information cascade, one that was stronger than those evident at the March 2001 and September 2001 low points. By October 2002 the bear market in the S&P had lasted 31 months and carried the average down nearly 50 percent, thus making it bigger than any other bear markets of the preceding 50 years. I think the conjunction of these two facts made it reasonable for the aggressive contrarian trader to act on the assumption that a new bull market was about to begin.

The most important thing to remember about the early stages of a bull market is that the first short-term swing upward is generally the biggest one of the bull market in percentage terms. It is also often the longest in duration. It is doubly important for the aggressive contrarian trader to maintain his above-average stock market allocation during this upswing, because this is an opportunity to improve substantially his portfolio's performance relative to the buy-and-hold strategy.

How may this important objective be achieved? As a rule you cannot expect much help from your media diary in identifying the end of this first short-term upswing of the bull market. Even though the bearish stock market crowd that existed at the start of the bull market is disintegrating rapidly, no bullish crowd is likely to be evident yet and no bullish information cascade is likely to be visible in your media diary.

To solve this problem I suggested in Chapter 11 a rule based on my market tabulations coupled with the use of the 50-day moving average of the S&P 500 index. My market tabulations suggest that one should wait for the averages to rise at least 25 percent from the preceding bear market low in an upswing that lasts at least six months. Once this has happened, start watching the 50-day moving average. (This is just the sum of the preceding 50 daily closes divided by 50.) Look for a new bull market high in this moving average that occurs after the six-month advance of at least 25 percent. Once the moving average turns downward by at least 0.5 percent of that high, you have a signal to cut back your stock market allocation to normal levels.

I want to emphasize that this rule, like every other one you find in this book, is not some magical formula to be applied slavishly by every reader. There is lots of room for creative thought—for modifications of the basic idea that these rules embody. Every trader has skills, knowledge, and experience that are unique. It would be silly not to take advantage of your own knowledge to improve or modify the rules I suggest so that they fit better with your own style and market knowledge.

Let's apply my rule to the initial upswing of the 2002–2007 bull market. The low was at 777 on October 9, 2002. The aggressive contrarian trader waits for the average to advance 25 percent and for a period of six months after this low. This requires an advance to the 971 level, which achieves a new high for the upswing after April 10, 2003. These two conditions were jointly met on June 3, 2003, when the S&P closed at 972. That same day the 50-day moving average established a new high for the move up from its bear market low of 846 established on April 4, 2003. The aggressive contrarian trader is now watching for a drop of 0.5 percent in the 50-day moving average as a signal to return to a normal allocation to stocks. On April 28, 2004, with the S&P closing at 1,128 this event occurred.

Once the aggressive contrarian trader has reduced his stock market exposure to normal levels near the top of a short-term upswing, he starts looking to his media diary for evidence that a short-lived bearish crowd is developing near the low of a short-term downswing. His hope is that his media diary will help him to identify a short-lived bearish information cascade developing near the low point of the short-term downswing. For this purpose he is looking for page 1 stock market headlines in major newspapers, or several page 1 stories that may not be major headlines. Even better would be a magazine cover taking bearish note of the short-term downswing in the stock market.

He may not get this opportunity right away and the averages may continue higher for a while. No matter. His allocation is normal and his performance will match that of the buy-and-hold investor while he waits for a short-lived bearish crowd to develop.

In May 2004 the only page 1 story I put into my media diary was from the *Chicago Tribune*'s May 18 edition. The story appeared above the fold but was not a headline: "Investors Shaken by War Woes." It was accompanied by a table headed "Dow in Decline." This table recorded the extent of the previous three weekly drops in the Dow Jones Industrial Average. The preceding day, May 17, the S&P closed at 1,084 and had dropped as low as 1,079 during that day. These levels should be compared with those that ended the preceding short-term upswing: an intraday high of 1,163 with a close at 1,157 on March 5. The drop subsequent to that high lasted more than two months and carried the average down 7 percent by May 17, a short-term downswing well within normal expectations within a bull market context. At the May 17 close the S&P 500 was not quite 1 percent below its 200-day moving average and was also below its 50-day moving average. Such a combination in a bull market should alert the aggressive contrarian trader to a potential opportunity for increasing his stock market exposure. At the time I was very bullish, partly because of the *Tribune*'s story but mainly because of generally gloomy, nonheadline commentary in the press.

Another factor in my bullishness was a dramatic rise in bearish sentiment that was apparent in the weekly poll of individual investors conducted by the American Association of Individual Investors. This was consistent with a rise in put option buying (by investors betting on further market declines) in the options markets, which also became evident at the time.

But let's suppose you didn't act on this information because you were looking for stock market headlines in the *New York Times*. None appeared, so you maintained your normal allocation to stocks. You would stick with this allocation until a short-term drop in the S&P was accompanied by a bearish information cascade. As it happened, this opportunity would take almost another year to develop. But this is not a bad thing since during this waiting period the aggressive contrarian trader would have matched the performance of the buy-and-hold policy.

To make sure we cover all the bases, let's consider how an aggressive contrarian trader who *did* increase his stock market allocation to above normal in May would have acted during the next upswing. The short-term downswing ended in the S&P at the 1,063 level on August 12. At what point during the subsequent short-term upswing should he move his stock market allocation back down to normal levels?

Here is the way I answer this question. Before I consider moving my stock market allocation back to normal levels, I want to see the S&P advance 15 percent from its short-term low and make a new high for the bull market. The 15 percent number is not a magic one. I generally adjust it as the bull market ages, generally in a downward direction. You may want to modify this policy by incorporating other contrarian information or technical indicators you are skilled in using.

The aggressive contrarian who is following the strategy outlined in Chapter 11 might time his reduction of stock market exposure to normal levels in a different way by using the 50-day moving average of the S&P.

For the short-term upswing that developed from the August 2004 low at 1,063, a 15 percent advance would take the S&P to 1,222, which was also a new high for the bull market. On March 4, 2005, the S&P closed at 1,222 and the aggressive contrarian trader would revert back to a normal stock market allocation if he had been so fortunate as to maintain an above-normal allocation during the upswing.

APRIL 2005—A BUYING OPPORTUNITY

At this juncture the aggressive contrarian trader may have been sitting with a normal stock market allocation since April 28, 2004, when the S&P closed at 1,128. If he was very skilled he may have gone back to an above-normal allocation on May 18 at the S&P 1,084 level and then reverted to a normal allocation on March 4, 2005, with the S&P at 1,222.

Traders would now be looking for a short-run bearish information cascade to indicate the presence of a bearish crowd near the lows of a normal short-term downswing within the ongoing bull market. This generally requires one or more page 1 stock market stories recounting the drop in the averages or at least one newspaper headline doing so. Even better would be one or more magazine covers expressing bearish attitudes about the stock market.

On April 16, 2005, the front page of the *New York Times* featured a stock market story that wasn't a headline story but did appear above the fold at the top left accompanied by a chart of the falling Dow Industrials. The story's headline read: "Stocks Plunge to Lowest Point Since Election." The positioning of this story and the headline's use of the word *plunge* and the phrase *lowest point* all added significance and weight as indicators of a bearish information cascade. On April 18 the *New York Times* page 1 headline read: "As Stocks Slide Investors Focus on Earnings Data." And then in the April 21 edition of the *New York Times* we find an above-the-fold story headlined: "Inflation Fears Pummel Stocks; New Lows for '05." Any of these three stories would have sufficed to move the aggressive contrarian trader to an above-normal stock market allocation. On April 15 (a Friday) the S&P closed at 1,143 and on April 20 it closed at 1,138. The drop from the March high at 1,225 had lasted more than a month and carried the average down more than 6 percent, well within normal parameters for short-term drops in a bull market. Moreover, on April 15 and for a few days afterward the S&P was trading not quite 1 percent below its 200-day moving average and also below its 50-day moving average.

Having established an above-normal stock market allocation, the aggressive contrarian trader would wait for an advance carrying the market up 15 percent from its 1,138 low established on April 20, 2005. This happened on April 6, 2006, with the S&P closing at 1,311. At that time the aggressive contrarian trader would move back to a normal stock market allocation. He then would await evidence from his media diary that another short-run bearish information cascade was under way.

JUNE 2006—ANOTHER BUYING OPPORTUNITY

The S&P established a short-term swing high on May 8, 2006, at the 1,327 level. The subsequent short-term drop ended at an intraday low of 1,219 on June 14. This was a drop lasting a little more than a month and carrying the S&P down about 8 percent, a perfectly normal short-term downswing in a bull market. The evidence for a short-run bearish information cascade during this short-term downswing was not as neat as during the March–April 2005 downswing, but it was clearly there to see.

The single most significant piece of evidence was a magazine cover story. The May 27 issue of the *Economist* had a cover showing a photograph of a brown bear standing on its hind legs and peering out from behind a tree. The cover caption read: "Which Way Is Wall Street?" By the time this issue appeared on May 26 the S&P had already dropped as low as 1,245 on May 24. This was a 6 percent drop from its May 8 high over a two-week period—all in all a bit brief for a normal short-term downswing. Even so, the S&P 500 was again trading a little below its 200-day moving average and below its 50-day moving average. The aggressive contrarian trader could have justified increasing his stock allocation to above normal as soon as the S&P returned to or fell below its May 24 low. This happened on June 8 when the average dropped as low as 1,235 intraday and closed at 1,258.

More evidence for a short-run bearish stock market crowd was to follow. The June 11 Sunday edition of the *New York Times Magazine* had on its cover a cartoon of a hairy, red bogeyman labeled "debt" and crowds of people running from him in terror. The caption read: "America's Scariest Addiction Is Getting Even Scarier." While this cover didn't deal with the stock market directly, I felt at the time that it reflected fairly the tenor of public attitudes toward the stock market and the economy and so interpreted it as part of a short-run bearish information cascade.

The final piece of evidence was also delivered by the *New York Times*. In its June 16 edition there appeared on page 1, below the fold, a graph of the Dow Jones Industrial Average that emphasized the big decline from its May 10 high. Its caption read: "Relief, at Least for Now." The explanation below the caption ended with the sentence: "But the increased volatility in the markets suggested that *their troubles may not be over*" (my emphasis). The low for this short-term downswing in the S&P had occurred two days earlier.

We see then that an aggressive contrarian trader would have had good reason to move his stock market allocation up to above normal somewhere below the 1,260 level in the S&P. The low close was 1,224 on June 13. Adding 15 percent to this yields 1,408. The S&P reached this level on December 4, 2006. At that time the aggressive contrarian trader would have cut back his stock market allocation to normal levels.

AGGRESSIVE CONTRARIAN TRADING IN EARLY 2007

The next opportunity for the aggressive contrarian occurred during February–March 2007. The February 28, 2007, edition of the *Chicago Tribune* was headlined: "China Market Plunges, Dow Follows. Now What?" The headline was spread across the entire front page of the paper in bold lettering and was accompanied by a line chart that recorded the progress of the steep, 416-point drop in the Dow Industrials the previous day. It was subheadlined as the worst day since 9/11 (the date of the 2001 attack on New York's World Trade Center). The stock market drop was also headlined that day by the *New York Times*: "Slide on Wall St. Adds to Worries About Economy ... Fears of Recession Grow." This headline was not nearly so dramatic as the *Tribune*'s; it appeared only over the first column in normal headline type. It was, however, accompanied by a chart depicting drops in the world's stock markets that spread across most of the top part of the front page.

Media interest in the stock market break fell off after February 27, but did not disappear entirely. The March 11 edition of the *New York Times* printed a "News Analysis" by Gretchen Morgenson on page 1, above the fold and right next to that day's headline story. The analysis was headlined: "Crisis Looms in Mortgages." It detailed the financial tribulations of mortgage lenders, in this case New Century Financial, which had specialized in the subprime segment of the mortgage market. On March 14, the day of the market low, the *Wall Street Journal* headlined: "Subprime Fears Spread, Sending Dow Down 1.97%." These two stories are among several in my diary associating the February–March stock market drop with a subprime mortgage crisis. They illustrate the fact that there is a cascadelike aspect to even very brief bearish stock market episodes. One news story feed inspires the next as journalists race to comment and explain the latest developments.

Sometimes important contrarian clues are more ephemeral than the ones I have just mentioned. On February 27 and again on March 2 I noted in my media diary that Jay Leno had made the stock market drop part of his opening monologue on the *Tonight Show*. On February 27 he opened by observing that people didn't have any money anymore *because the stock market just dropped 500 points* (his emphasis). Even a comedian's jokes can tell you something about the temper of the crowd!

The 7 percent drop in the stock market averages that ended at the March 14 low lasted barely three weeks. It was mild and brief in any historical context. But much to my surprise at the time there were three weekly newsmagazine covers that either mentioned or focused on this stock market drop.

The first was the March 3, 2007, issue of the *Economist*. Its cover was headlined "A Walk Down Wall Street." The semiotic interpretation of this cover was easy. First, it was in black and white, a depressing combination for any cover story. Second, it depicted the feet of a person walking a tightrope, a very dangerous, potentially deadly activity. Finally, the headline itself used the word *down*. All in all, this was a cover with a clear bearish bias. However, I think that among all bearish cover stories I have seen this one was only mildly so.

The second cover mentioning the stock market was that of the March 12 issue of *Time* magazine. The cover itself was devoted to food, but in smaller green print against a white background at the top of the cover was the question "Is the Stock Market Getting Too Risky?" Here I note the use of the negative word *risky*. This was evidence of something we already knew from newspaper headlines and from the *Economist*'s cover a week earlier—the stock market drop had investors worried. Even so, the fact that *Time* magazine noted the drop on its cover was a modest bullish clue for the aggressive contrarian trader.

The March 12 issue of *BusinessWeek* also had a stock market cover. But the cover had little emotional content, and it is the emotional content of a magazine cover that reveals information about and conveys information to investment crowds. This cover was headed "What the Market Is Telling Us." But you had to open the magazine to find the answer, making this particular cover insignificant from a contrarian trader's perspective.

An aggressive contrarian trader would have found a trading opportunity in these headlines and cover stories. The S&P had established a new high for the bull market at the 1,460 level on February 20. It is certainly true that a week is never enough time for an honest bearish crowd to develop via an information cascade, even amidst an ongoing bull market. But by mid-March, after a three-week, 7 percent decline, the situation had changed. A bearish information cascade was under way, although it was a relatively mild one. And the S&P had dropped enough to pique my interest in increasing my stock market allocation.

I noticed in my tabulation of reactions within the 2002–2007 bull market that the median drop during the bull market thus far had been about 100 S&P points and that the minimum duration of such drops was about three weeks. (Note that these numbers are specific to the 2002–2007 bull market and will be different in other contexts.) The S&P 500 had reached the 1,462 level intraday on February 22 and dropped to 1,389 on February 27. This was a 73-point drop in only five days. At the time I believed that while it was likely the market was close to its low, there was probably more to come on the downside. Indeed, the actual intraday low occurred on March 14 at 1,364, 18 days after and 98 points below the February 22 top. From the moving average perspective, the closest the S&P got to its 200-day moving average was at the March 13 low close of 1,378, where it was 2.16 percent above the moving average. At the same time it was below its 50-day moving average. I believed then that this combination of circumstances justified going to an above-average stock market allocation.

The aggressive contrarian who assumed an above-average stock market allocation in March 2007 would expect to reduce this allocation to normal levels after a 15 percent advance from the closing low of the reaction. In this case that level was 1,584 and was never reached before a new bear market began. Had the aggressive contrarian chosen to adopt the 1,364 *intraday low* as the starting point for his measurement, he would have reverted to a normal stock market allocation on October 11 when the S&P reached an intraday high of 1,576. But let's suppose he decided to act only on closing prices instead. What might the aggressive contrarian have done then?

Of course the simplest thing to do would be to follow the strategy described in Chapter 11 exactly. Thus the aggressive contrarian would resolve to cut his stock market allocation to normal after a 15 percent advance on the low reaction close or to below normal if the S&P should drop 5 percent below its 200-day moving average. In the event, it was the latter condition that first obtained, and the aggressive contrarian would have reduced his stock market exposure to below-normal levels on November 26, 2007, when the S&P closed at 1,407, more than 5 percent below its 200-day moving average.

A more sophisticated approach to this kind of situation would rely on bull market tabulations. In this case, by mid-2007 the bull market had lasted nearly five years and had not seen any reaction of as much as 10 percent. This was an extraordinary run of positive returns, one that was unlikely to last much longer. I think in view of these circumstances it would have been perfectly logical for the aggressive contrarian to adopt a more conservative profit-taking tactic and to reduce stock market exposure to normal levels as soon as the S&P rallied only 10 percent or so (instead of waiting for a full 15 percent) to a new high for the 2002–2007 bull market. This event occurred on May 15, 2007, with the S&P at 1,514.

Before leaving the events of February–March 2007 I want to mention another aspect of this bearish information cascade that impressed me. I was surprised to find three stock market covers generated by a relatively modest drop in stock prices. Normally one needs a much more long-lasting and extensive decline before newsweeklies put it on their covers. I interpreted this as further evidence that there was no significant bullish stock market crowd in existence at the time. Not only was there no bullish theme evident, but there was a decided media tendency to print bearish stories at the drop of a hat. People were willing to express pessimism and negative emotions on the slightest market pretext. This reaffirmed my view at the time that there was no bullish stock market information cascade in operation.

JULY–OCTOBER 2007

On July 17, 2007, the S&P closed at 1,553. It was about to drop some 10 percent during the subsequent month, a bigger short-term downswing than any during the preceding four years. This decline presented the aggressive contrarian trader with another opportunity similar to the one he exploited in March.

The progression of page 1 stories during this July–August decline is instructive. The *New York Times* printed stock market stories on page 1 at the top left on both July 27 and July 28. Both noted the stock market drop, which by then had lasted for about 10 days and dropped the averages about 4.5 percent, not enough to attract the interest of an aggressive contrarian. The drop was explained by the reemergence of credit market fears.

The first headline story appeared in the August 4 edition of the *New York Times*. The headline read: "Markets Tumble As Lender Woes Keep Mounting." As headline stories go this was a mild one. The language used was conservative—the markets "tumbled"; they didn't "plunge" or "crash." The print size was normal, and the headline appeared over only a single column.

The previous day (Friday) the S&P closed at 1,433, about 8 percent below its high close. The decline had lasted 16 days, still shy of the three-week tabulation standard and even shy of the duration of the February–March 2007 break. Still, the S&P was trading about 1 percent below its 200-day moving average and below its 50-day moving average at the time. I think an aggressive contrarian trader would be justified in increasing his stock market allocation at this juncture, and this could have been done early Monday morning at a level close to Friday's close.

The drop in stock prices from the July top ended on August 16 at the S&P's 1,371 level. There was one more headline story before the low, this one in the August 10 issue of the *New York Times*. The headline read: "Mortgage Losses Echo in Europe and on Wall St." The previous day the S&P closed at 1,453, a level above that which preceded the August 4 headline. So the aggressive contrarian trader would have gained nothing by waiting past August 6 to increase his stock market allocation.

The end of this drop in stock prices on August 16 can clearly be associated with a crystallizing event that had occurred a few days earlier. This was a massive credit market intervention by the Federal Reserve and other central banks that took place on August 10 and was recorded in newspaper headlines on Saturday, August 11. That day the *New York Times* headlined: "Central Banks Intervene to Calm Volatile Markets." This headline was spread over two columns, as opposed to the single column occupied by the August 4 and August 10 headlines, thus showing more emotional intensity. This event was also headlined by the *Chicago Tribune* that day with "Jittery Markets Look to the Fed" in bold letters, spread across the top of page 1 and accompanied by a photograph of a worried trader at the New York Stock Exchange.

The July–August stock market drop also prompted some magazine cover stories, but, like those associated with the February–March decline, these appeared only in business-focused magazines, not those of general interest like *Time* or *Newsweek*. The August 13 issue of *Barron's* had a cover announcing "Market Turmoil" in bold red letters against a black background. From a semiotic point of view I note that red and black are colors associated with fear and danger. The August 18 issue of the *Economist* showed a cartoon of an investor surfing shark-infested waters and about to suffer a surfer's wipeout (note the double meaning). The headline read "Surviving the Markets." Finally, the September 3 issue of *Fortune* (which would have been in subscribers' hands around August 24) sported a black cover that shouted "Market Shock 2007" in bold red and white lettering. Compared to the March 2007 magazine covers I discussed earlier, these covers conveyed somewhat stronger bearish sentiment. This would have further reinforced the aggressive contrarian trader's choice to increase his stock market exposure earlier in August.

After assuming an above-normal allocation to the stock market in August, the aggressive contrarian would probably have reduced his exposure to normal levels on a 10 percent advance from the closing low at 1,406 on August 15. This occurred on October 1 when the S&P closed at 1,547. The S&P reached its high close for the 2002–2007 bull market on October 9 at the 1,565 level. The curtain was about to rise on the panic of 2008.

CHAPTER 15

The Panic of 2008

The remarkable 2002–2007 bull market • no bullish crowd evident at the top • the bullish crowd in the housing market • bear market signal • when will the conservative contrarian increase his stock market exposure? • the mortgage mess • a debt-deflation spiral • the government steps in • credit crisis and the aggressive contrarian trader • breaking below the moving average • failure of Bear Stearns in March 2008 • Fannie and Freddie in July 2008 • the crash • world panic in October 2008 • an amazing sequence of magazine covers • the aggressive contrarian contemplates a new bull market

THE CONSERVATIVE CONTRARIAN DURING THE PANIC

From its low at 777 in October 2002 to its high at 1,565 in October 2007, the S&P 500 index more than doubled. This was an unusually long bull market, exactly five years in duration—longer than the typical bull market, which lasts two or three years. The 100 percent gain in the averages was not as unusual, although a 65 percent gain would have been closer to the average.

To me as a contrarian trader the remarkable thing about the 2002–2007 bull market was the persistent pessimism expressed in the media about the U.S. economy and the stock market during those five years. There was never any indication in my media diary that a bullish stock market crowd had formed.

However, as I pointed out in the previous chapter, a very big, bullish investment crowd had formed in the residential housing market, not just in the United States but around the world. In October 2007 it was hard to imagine that the collapse of this housing bubble would have the devastating consequences for the world's economy, financial markets, and banking system that developed during the subsequent 12 months.

From its closing high of 1,565 on October 9, 2007, the S&P dropped to a closing low of 752 on November 20, 2008, a decline of 52 percent in barely more than a year. A conservative contrarian trader who followed the Contrarian Rebalancing strategy would have reduced his stock market allocation to normal levels on January 6, 2006, with the S&P at the 1,285 level. The 200-day moving average of the S&P turned downward from its bull market high by 1 percent on February 20, 2008, when the S&P closed at 1,360. But this event would cause a further reduction in stock market exposure only if the conservative contrarian believed that a bullish stock market crowd had formed by 2007. I for one did not think so, but I know other investors who did. Consequently I did not interpret the 1 percent turndown in the 200-day moving average as a signal for the conservative contrarian to move to a below-normal stock market allocation.

In either case, it is important to remember that the panic of 2008, as terrifying as it was, did not hurt the conservative contrarian's portfolio performance relative to the buy-and-hold benchmark. And it is only his performance relative to this benchmark that matters. The name of the game every contrarian trader plays is beating the benchmark, not being right about the stock market's direction.

As this is being written (in late November 2008), the conservative contrarian is awaiting a turn upward in the 200-day moving average in the S&P 500 by 1 percent. This will be a signal that the panic of 2008 is history and that a new bull market has begun. An enormous bearish stock market crowd has formed in the stock market, not just in the United States but around the world. So when the moving average turns up by 1 percent, the conservative contrarian should plan to increase his stock market exposure to above-normal levels.

There is no way to predict when and at what price level this moving average upturn might develop. At the moment the 200-day moving average of the S&P stands at 1,244 and is dropping at the rate of about 50 points per month. No turn upward in the moving average is likely until the S&P rises above it. Currently the S&P stands at 800. From this data it is reasonable to conclude that the moving average upturn lies several months in the future.

In the rest of this chapter I follow the development of the panic of 2008 through the eyes of the aggressive contrarian trader. First, though, I want to explain just how and why the panic arose from the collapse of the housing bubble.

THE MORTGAGE MESS

What caused the panic of 2008? In a word, mortgages. When the housing bubble burst, the resulting unexpected drop in residential home values led many borrowers to default on their mortgages. But these mortgages had been packaged into bonds called *mortgage-backed securities*. Worse, even more complicated securities called *collateralized debt obligations* were manufactured from mortgage-backed securities by Wall Street banks in order to satisfy the demand by investors for higher yields in a low-yield bond market. Mortgage defaults arising from falling home prices made it very difficult to determine the value of these complex securities. There simply was no historical precedent for what was happening. Residential home prices had not declined nationally in real terms since the 1930s and even that decline was smaller that the one experienced in the U.S. between 2006 and 2008. Because these complex securities were so hard to value objectively the bond market assumed the worse and consequently traded them at very low prices. This raised the specter of mass insolvency for banks and other financial institutions that owned them.

What is a mortgage-backed security? It is a long-term bond created when an investment bank buys portfolios of home mortgages from the mortgage originator (usually a commercial bank or mortgage loan company) and bundles them into a single portfolio. It does this by transferring ownership of these mortgages to a special purpose entity (sometimes called a Specialized Investment Vehicle or SIV—this is usually a trust or nonprofit corporation). This special purpose entity then issues bonds (mortgage-backed securities) whose sale finances the investment bank's original purchase of these home mortgages. Mortgage-backed securities promise their owners a series of payments from the pool of monthly interest and principal payments made by the mortgage borrowers, homeowners like you and me.

So far this seems a straightforward process of financial intermediation. Securitization of portfolios of illiquid home mortgages converts them into a more liquid asset and at the same time reduces the risk to mortgage lenders that can arise from, say, economic difficulties specific to a single geographic housing market. In this way mortgage securities make home financing cheaper and easier for the average home buyer.

The value of a mortgage-backed bond depends on the interest and principal payments homeowners are expected to make on the mortgages that make up the portfolio backing the bond. It was from the process of evaluating these expected payments that trouble arose. The trouble was greatly amplified by the fact that mortgage-backed securities were often repackaged into even more complex securities, collateralized debt obligations, in a process called structured finance.

The dramatic increase in U.S. home prices during the 1996–2006 period moved them to levels at least 30 percent above construction costs, a divergence that in the long run was unsustainable. Even so, people began to believe that the price of owner-occupied housing could only go up. This made the prospective mortgage borrower see a home purchase as an essentially riskless investment. Worse, mortgage lenders viewed mortgage loans in essentially the same way, as riskless assets whose value would be protected by ever-rising real estate prices. The convictions of both borrowers and lenders that the price of owner-occupied real estate would only go up reinforced each other. Not only did the demand and the supply of mortgage loans go up, but this increase in mortgage credit further fueled the advance in home prices. A real estate bubble was the result.

As in any credit bubble, lenders gradually lowered their lending standards in competition to originate more and more mortgage loans and earn the resulting fees. It was here that the financial technology of the mortgage-backed security short-circuited prudent mortgage lending standards. No longer did loan originators—banks and home-loan institutions—have to keep mortgages on their books. Instead they bundled these mortgages and sold them to investment banks. Since they did not retain the mortgage loans they originated in their own investment portfolios, they had little incentive to make sure such loans could be serviced and repaid by the borrowers.

As long as home prices went up, these lax lending standards caused no problems. In fact, the historical data used to estimate the chances of the mortgage loans being repaid showed that even low-quality borrowers, the so-called subprime borrowers, had good repayment records. After all, home prices only went up, didn't they? This data was used by ratings companies like Standard & Poor's (S&P) and Moody's Investors Service to justify rating even those securities backed by subprime mortgages as AAA quality, especially after they had been repackaged into collateralized debt obligations.

Few people thought to ask what would happen if home prices stopped going up and, worse, started to fall. Even those who did ask this question and knew that problems would arise did not have any idea of just how destructive to balance sheets the drop in the value of mortgage-backed bonds would be, and of the complex securities that structured finance would produce from them.

According to the S&P/Case-Schiller index of U.S. home prices, the value of owner-occupied housing peaked in mid-2006. During the subsequent two years home prices dropped more than 20 percent nationally. People who had purchased homes at the height of the boom during

2003–2006 with small down payments were in financial trouble. In many cases the drop in home prices made their mortgage debt exceed the value of their homes. This led to an increase in mortgage defaults, especially among subprime borrowers. Suddenly the repayment expectations that supported the beliefs about the value of mortgage-backed bonds were proven wrong by events.

But the situation was much worse than that. The real estate market had entered truly uncharted territory. There was no historical basis for estimating the rate at which subprime borrowers would default as housing prices fell and put them in negative equity situations. The same was true for other mortgage borrowers as well, for the United States had never experienced an extended period of time when the real price (i.e., the inflation-adjusted price) of owner-occupied housing had fallen substantially. When the fair value of any security cannot be compared to any historical norm at all, the security is prone to be priced on the basis of fear. This is what happened during 2008 in the market for mortgage-backed securities and collateralized debt obligations. The values of many of these securities were set at levels often 70-90 percent below their purchase prices of only a year or two earlier.

THE DEBT-DEFLATION SPIRAL TAKES HOLD

Once the value of mortgage-backed bonds began to fall, fear cascaded through the world's financial markets. Any bank, insurance company, hedge fund, or other financial institution with a substantial portfolio of mortgage-backed bonds saw the equity of its shareholders plummet as these securities were marked down to values that were much lower than their purchase prices. In many cases there was no market for such securities at all. Consequently, other securities that had viable markets were sold in order to finance holdings of the mortgage-backed securities that had no market.

As the net worth of institutions with substantial holdings of mortgage securities dropped, the value of their bond and short-term loan liabilities naturally was called into question. This was an especially dangerous turn of events because no one seemed to know which financial institutions were about to take substantial losses on these mortgage securities.

Safety at any price became the byword. Deleveraging became the operational policy of financial institutions. Banks refused to lend to one another or to their business customers. Corporations could not borrow in the commercial paper market. The normal business of financial intermediation ground to a halt as the demand for immediate loan repayment spiraled upward. This was the start of a classic debt-deflation spiral, so feared by economists who study the business cycle. Such spirals begin when there is a sudden rush to sell assets to repay loans. This drives the price of assets downward, making it even more difficult to repay loans, thus spurring further asset sales. The entire process, if left alone, will drive the economy into a depression from which it will be very difficult to recover. The Great Depression of the 1930s is the classic example of a debt-deflation spiral.

LENDERS OF LAST RESORT

As the panic of 2008 began to affect markets worldwide, central banks and government financial regulators stepped in. During the July–October 2008 period large numbers of government-financed lending programs were announced and implemented. If banks and other financial institutions would not lend to one another, then perhaps they would be willing to lend to or borrow from the government or from the central bank. In this way central banks and national treasuries around the world assumed the role of financial intermediation that had been temporarily abandoned by the private sector. They had become the true lenders of last resort in the world economy.

Has government action halted the debt-deflation spiral in time to prevent a worldwide depression? As I write this in November of 2008 my view is that it has, but only time will tell. In this regard it is important to compare the events of 2008 with the events that accompanied the onset of the Great Depression in 1929.

Then as now there was a financial bubble whose unwinding caused bank failures and mortgage defaults. The big difference can be found in the governmental response to these developments. Government spending now is a much bigger part of the world economy that it was in the 1930s, and this makes fiscal policy now much more potent and able to cushion economic downturns. Of even more importance is the widely held belief that intervention to control the business cycle is appropriate, especially in downturns. In the 1930s few policy makers held this view, especially because they believed that adherence to the gold standard was essential to long-run prosperity.

Finally, central banks, especially the U.S. Federal Reserve, are now taking very seriously their responsibilities as lenders of last resort, of acting as financial intermediaries in times of crisis. This, after all, was the reason that most central banks were created. Moreover, the current Fed chairman, Ben Bernanke, is an expert on the policy failures that created the Great

Depression and is determined to avoid them. If only for this reason, I think that things will turn out differently this time and that the United States and the world economy will recover relatively quickly from this financial fiasco.

THE CREDIT CRISIS AND THE CONTRARIAN TRADER

It is unusual for any economic crisis to last as long as the panic of 2008 has done. It has been a financial crisis in several acts. The curtain first rose in July–August 2007 with the failure of two hedge funds sponsored by the investment bank Bear Stearns that invested in mortgage-backed securities. Each subsequent act of this terrifying play had its own bearish information cascade, which focused on a new set of financial fears and dangers. Each ended with a crystallizing event in which what had been feared became a fact. After a brief intermission of investor relief and market rallies, the curtain would go up on the next, even more fearful act. As this is being written, in late November 2008 shortly after the election of Barack Obama to the presidency of the United States, no one can be sure whether the curtain will rise yet again to reveal yet another unanticipated financial disaster.

I have never witnessed so many intense, bearish information cascades during a 12-month period during my 40 years of involvement in the financial markets. As we shall see, these cascades were created and accompanied by many dramatic newspaper headlines and by an unprecedented torrent of bearish magazine covers.

As I pointed out earlier in this chapter, the conservative contrarian trader has only matched the performance of the buy-and-hold strategy during 2007 and 2008. As this is written, the conservative contrarian is awaiting a 1 percent upturn in the 200-day moving average of the S&P 500. When this occurs he will move from a normal to an above-normal stock market allocation.

In contrast to his conservative cousin, the aggressive contrarian has been far more active throughout the crisis. In the rest of this chapter we follow him as he reacts to the information cascades occurring during late 2007 and the first 11 months of 2008.

BULL MARKET TOP AND THE FIRST STEP DOWN

The S&P 500 started its 2007–2008 bear market from a closing high of 1,565, reached on October 9, 2007.

The first subsequent indication that a bearish information cascade had begun was the headline for the November 8, 2007, edition of the *New York Times*. It read: "Markets and Dollar Sink As U.S. Slowdown Grows." I note that on the semiotic scale of bearishness this was a very mild headline. Why? First, it does not mention the stock market explicitly—note the use of the plural form *markets*. There was a first column subheading mentioning the Dow, but that same subheading also mentioned the prices of oil and natural gas. There was also a subheading mentioning that homeowners were feeling the pinch of reduced equity. The words *pinch* and *sink* convey only mild bearish emotions. Overall I would say that this was not a headline that indicated anything like a mature bearish stock market crowd in existence. It only shows that a bearish information cascade was under way.

About three weeks later, the aggressive contrarian adopted a bear market stance when the S&P closed at 1,407 on November 26, 2007. That was the first time in nearly five years that the S&P closed at least 5 percent below its 200-day moving average. At this juncture the aggressive contrarian would assume a below-normal stock market allocation.

Seven more weeks passed before a second bearish stock market headline appeared in the *New York Times*. In the January 17, 2008, edition, over two columns, the headline read: "Fed Chief's Reassurance Fails to Halt Stock Plunge." The use of the word *plunge* and the explicit mention of the stock market make this a more decisively bearish headline than the one that appeared on November 8. The only semiotic consideration diminishing its bearish message is that the stock market is the object of the sentence, not its subject.

After the January 17 close, the aggressive contrarian would note that the S&P 500 was trading more than 10 percent below its 200-day moving average. If he were to judge that the bearish stock market crowd had grown big enough, this would justify increasing his stock market exposure to above-normal levels on the S&P close at 1,333 that day.

There was only one thing that might have caused the aggressive contrarian trader to delay increasing his stock market commitment at that juncture. He believed that a bear market was in progress. There was as yet only this single headline suggesting that a bearish stock market crowd had formed, and there was as yet no magazine cover commenting on the drop. This lack of evidence, despite a substantial drop in the averages during the preceding three months, would have made some aggressive contrarians defer action.

Only a few days later, on January 22, the situation had changed. The U.S. markets had been closed the previous day, Martin Luther King Day. But overseas markets were open. The headline of the *New York Times* read: "World Markets Plunge on Fears of U.S. Slowdown." This headline was very dramatic, spread across four columns and accompanied by several color photographs. One was a chart showing the previous day's minute-by-minute drop in the Nikkei 225 index of the Tokyo Stock Exchange. The other showed a worried crowd of investors in India and turmoil on the floor of a Brazilian stock exchange.

A semiotic interpretation of this headline reveals its very bearish quality. First, "world markets" is the subject of the sentence, which also uses the words *plunge* and *fears* to describe the situation. The headline appears across four columns and with color photographs. One photo shows a chart of the drop of the Tokyo stock exchange index. The others show worried and frantic investors. Overall, I take this headline as very convincing evidence that a bearish stock market crowd had formed. This was good reason for the aggressive contrarian trader to increase his stock market exposure, something he could have done near the opening of trading that day when the S&P stood near 1,280.

The next day's headlines provided more evidence that a bearish stock market crowd had formed. "Fed, in Surprise, Sets Big Rate Cut to Ease Markets" read the headline of the January 23 edition of the *New York Times*. The *Chicago Tribune* chimed in with its headline: "Fed Jolts Stock Market." The previous day the U.S. Federal Reserve had cut the overnight lending rate by 75 basis points from 4.25 percent to 3.50 percent, and the stock market averages had responded by rallying from the low points they had reached near the opening of trading on January 22. The *Times*' two-column headline stood next to a pair of graphs, one of which recorded the behavior of several stock market averages the previous day. It also appeared next to a news analysis by David Leonhardt entitled: "Worries That the Good Times Were a Mirage." The analysis opened with the sentence: "So, how bad could this get?"

If the aggressive contrarian trader had not already increased his stock market allocation to above-normal levels on January 17, he certainly would have done so on January 22 or 23. The headline material in his media diary presented strong evidence for an ongoing bearish information cascade, one that had already built up a substantial bearish crowd. The stock market had been dropping for three months, and the Dow and the S&P showed their biggest percentage drops in five years. Moreover, the Fed's interest rate cut on January 22 was in this instance an example of a crystallizing event, something that serves to focus emotions in a single (in this case bearish) direction. Such events are generally closely associated with market turning points.

The evidence for a bearish stock market crowd became even more definitive late in January with the appearance of several magazine cover stories. Two that especially attracted my attention were the covers of the February 4 issues of *BusinessWeek* and of the *New Yorker*.

The latter was especially significant because the *New Yorker* is a general interest magazine that rarely runs a cover related to the financial markets. Its February 4 cover depicted a worried Humpty Dumpty wiping his brow as he sat atop the New York Stock Exchange building on Wall Street. As we all remember from the childhood story, Humpty Dumpty is an egg-shaped fellow who shattered into innumerable tiny pieces in a great fall, never to be put back together again. From a semiotic point of view this is a very powerful and discouraging bearish image.

The *BusinessWeek* cover was less dramatic. Black letters on a green-lit screen announced: "Market Reckoning." The cover depicted a trader in shirtsleeves, his hands clenched to his head as he stared at the headline.

THE BEAR STEARNS FAILURE

Over the subsequent two months the stock market moved sideways, not dropping below its January low points but not rallying much, either. The aggressive contrarian would be waiting for the S&P to move 1 percent above its 50-day moving average, but this did not happen before another bearish information cascade took hold. During this cascade the aggressive contrarian would maintain an above-normal stock market allocation even as the S&P fell back down to the 1,256 level on March 17.

In its Saturday, March 17, edition the *New York Times* headline read: "Run on Big Wall St. Bank Spurs U.S.-Backed Rescue." The Wall Street bank in question was Bear Stearns. Bear Stearns had achieved some notoriety nine months earlier on June 23, 2007, when the *New York Times* headlined: "$3.2 Billion Move by Bear Stearns to Rescue Fund." Bear Stearns found it necessary to bail out a hedge fund it had sponsored that had gone belly-up because of losses from mortgage-based securities.

Evidently Bear's exposure to mortgage losses was even more substantial than was evident in June 2007. The March 17 headline does not mention the stock market explicitly and so normally would not part of a stock market information cascade. But I made an exception to this rule here for two reasons. First, the headline mentions a bank run. This run was not one that affected depositors, but the emotional content is the same in either case. Worse, it was a Wall Street bank that needed to be rescued. The association of Wall Street with a bank run and a rescue makes this headline part of a bearish stock market information cascade. It provides more confirmation that a mature bearish stock market crowd exists.

The *Times'* headlines for March 17 and March 18 were of similar if less dramatic import. On March 17: "In Sweeping Move, Fed Backs Buyout and Wall St. Loans." On March 18: "Plunge Averted, Markets Look Ahead Nervously." These headlines are all associated with a crystallizing event, the rescue (which was in fact a government-financed sale) of Bear Stearns.

More evidence for a mature bearish stock market crowd soon followed. The March 22 issue of the *Economist* depicted a wall with a jagged crack running through it. The wall was embossed with gold lettering reading "Wall Street." The subheading read "A Ten-Page Special Report on the Crisis" in red lettering. Needless to say, a widely recognized crisis on Wall Street is generally a good buying opportunity.

The *Weekly Standard* chimed in with its March 31 issue. This weekly magazine is devoted to conservative politics and opinion and generally does not pay any attention to financial markets. But this particular issue was an exception. It showed a black-and-white photograph of an older man dressed in a suit, tie, and hat holding an old-style ticker tape in his hand. The man is frowning, his hat is set back on his head, and his palm is slapped against his forehead. The whole effect evokes memories of the 1929 crash. The headline simply reads: "YIKES."

FANNIE AND FREDDIE

From its low point on March 17 at 1,256 intraday, the S&P rallied to a high at 1,440 on May 19. On April 1 the S&P closed at the 1,370 level, more than 1 percent above its 50-day moving average. This signaled to the aggressive contrarian that it was time to again reduce his stock market allocation to below-normal levels.

During April, May, and June 2008 the stock market stayed out of the headlines of major newspapers. It wasn't the focus of any magazine cover stories, either. Nonetheless, when I read through my media diary for this period I am struck by the continuous flow of bad news about the housing market and the economy. But perhaps the biggest single story was the spectacular rise in crude oil prices, from $99 on March 4 to $147 on July 15. This 50 percent increase in crude oil prices was accompanied by a sharp increase on gasoline prices during the summer driving season in the United States. Moreover, this was only a part of a general increase in the cost of living for most Americans. All in all, this was a news background that investors found very discouraging.

The June 7 edition of the *New York Times* was headlined: "Jobs Down for 5th Month; Oil's Rise Adds to Gloom." Note the use of the word *gloom* in this headline, a very strong indicator of the public's mood at the time. On June 24 the Conference Board announced the June reading of its index of consumer confidence: 50.4, the lowest reading in 16 years; lower readings had been seen only twice in the prior 34 years. These two items illustrate the tenor of virtually all media discussion of the state of the economy during the April–June period. An enormous bearish economic crowd had developed. Its themes were falling housing prices, tight credit conditions, imminent failures of financial institutions, inflation, and increasing unemployment. Yet the stock market was still trading above its January low point!

The Dow and the S&P 500 started another decline from their highs on May 19. By early July both indexes had dropped below their January–March lows. Even so, the stock market stayed out of the headlines until July 8. That day the *New York Times* headlined: "Mortgage Fears Depress Shares at Two Agencies—Fears of Worse to Come." The story concerned the condition of two government-sponsored corporations, Fannie Mae and Freddie Mac, both responsible for financing home mortgages for U.S. homeowners. The stock market as a whole had become very sensitive to the fortunes of Fannie and Freddie, because their debt was held by so many banks and financial institutions. Failure of Fannie and Freddie would result in an economy-wide credit crisis and economic contraction. From a semiotic point of view this headline conveyed extremely bearish sentiments. Note the two appearances of the word *fears* and the use of the word *depress* and the phrase *worse to come*. A week later on July 15 the *New York Times* headlined: "Confidence Ebbs for Bank Sector and Stocks Fall—Lines Form at Lender." The story's opening paragraph said in part: "[C]onfidence in the banking sector spiraled downward Monday." It went on to note that the shares of regional banks "plunged in one of the sharpest declines since the 1980's."

These two headlines, a week apart, both concerned the stock prices of banks and financial institutions. They indicated that a bearish crowd had developed in this sector of the stock market. It is important to keep in mind that financial institutions keep the economy functioning. In a banking panic the prices of all shares, not just those of the banks, will fall. For this reason it seemed to me at the time that this was a buying opportunity for the aggressive contrarian trader. This was another bearish information cascade, and on July 14 the S&P had closed at 1,228, which was more than 10 percent below its 200-day moving average and a new low for the ongoing bear market. Here the aggressive contrarian had ample reason to increase his stock market allocation to above-normal levels. Moreover, the S&P had dropped for about two months since its last short-term high on May 19.

Magazine covers provided more evidence for the existence of a bearish stock market crowd. The July 7 issue of *Barron's* was headlined: "The Bear's Back." It showed a cartoon of a ferocious snarling bear with its teeth bared. The July 14 issue of *BusinessWeek* was even more significant. It was headlined: "Retirement Strategies for Tough Times" and showed a man and a woman trying to find their way through a maze. Of course the phrase *tough times* conveys a definite bearish sentiment. But of much more importance is the subject of the headline, retirement. When contemplating retirement from the workforce, people see themselves as being at the mercy of financial market fluctuations. When they start to worry about retirement, it is generally because the stock market has fallen enough to attract their attention and focus their fears. Remember that the low of the 2000–2002 bear market coincided with a July 2002 *Time* magazine cover story about retirement fears.

The July 19 issue of the *Economist* had on its cover a depiction of two tornadoes, which were sucking up currency, houses, and piggy banks (savings). It was headlined: "Twin Twisters: Fannie Mae, Freddie Mac and the Market Chaos." Tornadoes represent disaster, and the word *chaos* is about as bearish a word as can be used to describe markets. The July 28 issue of *BusinessWeek* depicted a snake eating its own tail. It was headed, in red capital letters (the color of fear and danger): "How Wall Street Ate the Economy."

As if to summarize Americans' feelings about the state of the economy, the *Economist*, in its July 26 issue, depicted the Statue of Liberty sitting and staring dejectedly at the New York skyline. The headline read: "Unhappy America."

There were still other signs that an enormous bearish stock market crowd had developed. On August 3 the Conference Board released its latest consumer confidence report. For the first time in 20 years the majority of respondents expected stock market prices to decline over the subsequent 12 months. The bearish stock market crowd was accompanied by an equally bearish economic crowd. On August 3 the Gallup poll showed that 77 percent of Americans held negative views of the economy, while only 7 percent held positive views!

On August 28 the aggressive contrarian would have seen the S&P close at 1,301, for the first time since mid-July at least 1 percent above its 50-day moving average. As it happened, this signal occurred after the actual short-term high, which was on August 11 at the 1,305 level. At this juncture a move back to a below-normal stock market allocation was called for. It was hard to believe then, but worse was still to come.

THE CRASH: BANKRUPTCY OF LEHMAN BROTHERS

In September the collapse of the Wall Street investment banks began and this time a worldwide panic enveloped the financial markets. The first sign of new trouble (and a new bearish information cascade) was the one-column headline of the September 10 edition of the *New York Times*. It read: "Wall St.'s Fears on Lehman Bros. Batter Markets." Two days later the *New York Times* published a three-column headline: "Financial Crisis Reshapes Wall Street's Landscape." It appeared that Lehman Brothers was on the verge of bankruptcy. Much to the surprise of Wall Street and the banking industry, the U.S. Treasury and the Federal Reserve refused to rescue Lehman Brothers and on September 15 the investment bank entered bankruptcy.

The Lehman Brothers bankruptcy triggered a financial panic. The solvency of virtually every large financial institution was now called into question. The venerable brokerage firm Merrill Lynch had suffered such losses in mortgage-backed securities that it had to be sold to Bank of America. On September 16 we had the first headline featuring stock prices as the subject of the sentence. In its September 16 edition the *New York Times* headlined: "Wall St. in Worst Loss Since '01 Despite Reassurances by Bush." The next day the *New York Times* headlined more bad news: "Fed in $85 Billion Bailout Plan of Faltering Insurance Giant." The American International Group (AIG) insurance company was in danger of bankruptcy because of losses incurred on its issuance of credit default derivatives. Finally, on September 18 the *New York Times* published a four-column headline: "New Phase in Finance Crisis As Investors Run to Safety."

Note that in only one of this sequence of headlines was the stock market itself the subject of the headlining sentence. So whereas a bearish information cascade was under way, I think the aggressive contrarian would have had reason to delay any decision to increase his stock market exposure even though the S&P was trading 10 percent below its 200-day moving average. More important, barely a month had passed since the last short-term top on August 11. Generally, buying opportunities in bear markets develop only after the market has dropped for at least two months.

During the next two weeks the newspapers were filled with stories and headlines describing the U.S. government's efforts to develop a plan for rescuing Wall Street and the economy. Things came to a head on September 29 when the first legislative rescue effort failed in the U.S. House of Representatives. The next day's headlines recounted the event. From the *New York Times* we have: "Defiant House Rejects Huge Bailout; Stocks Plunge; Next Step Is Uncertain." The *Chicago Tribune* that same day headlined: "The House Says No. Fear Grips Investors."

Clearly a very big bearish stock market crowd had developed, one even bigger than at the temporary July low point. But the S&P was in a bear market, not a bull market. In bear markets, history recommends waiting for two months or so to pass after a short-term top before increasing long positions in a bear market even when a bearish information cascade has developed sooner.

The next stock market headlines appeared on October 7, a total of 57 days after the August 11 short-term top and close enough to the two-month guideline to get the attention of the aggressive contrarian trader. The *New York Times* published a four-column headline, complete with photographs of fearful investors and charts of plunging stock prices: "Fed Weighs Bid to Spur Economy As Markets Plummet Worldwide." That same day the *Chicago Tribune* headlined all across its front page: "Crisis Goes Global," and helpfully provided inset photographs purporting to show fearful investors in various world stock markets accompanied by a down arrow labeled by that particular market's percentage drop the previous day. The *Tribune*'s biggest contribution to this bearish information cascade came with its October 10 headline spread entirely across page 1 and accompanied by down arrows describing the market drops of the preceding seven trading sessions: "All Signs Pointing to Panic." The S&P reached an intraday low at 839 that day.

Starting on October 7 the aggressive contrarian would have been justified raising his stock market allocation to above-normal levels. The S&P was trading more than 10 percent below its 200-day moving average. An unprecedented bearish information cascade had built up a strong bear market crowd. And about two months had passed since the last short-term top in this bear market. On October 6 the S&P 500 closed at 1,056, but closed much lower at 996 on October 7. Nonetheless, I think it is best to assume that the aggressive contrarian would have increased his stock market allocation to above-normal levels at the S&P 1,056 close.

So far I have documented the September–October bearish information cascade solely through newspaper headlines. But an unprecedented avalanche of magazine covers did its part in building up the bearish stock market crowd. The first was the September 29 cover of *Time* magazine. It depicted a businessman headfirst in a hole with only his legs showing. The caption read: "How Wall Street Sold Out America." The September 29 issue of the *Weekly Standard* was captioned "High Anxiety" and showed cartoon characters fleeing the New York Stock Exchange. The September 29 issue of the *New Yorker* showed a businessman talking on his cell phone while walking down Wall Street and about to fall into a manhole. The October 13 issue of *Time* showed a Depression-era breadline and was captioned "The New Hard Times." The October 13 issue of *U.S. News & World Report* showed a cartoon of part of a dollar bill with a likeness of George Washington wide-eyed. The caption read: "How Scared Should You Be?"

Finally, the October 20 issue of the *New Yorker* featured on its cover a stunning cartoon of Death, dressed in a red robe and wearing a black-plumed red hat. He gripped a staff with a skull at its top, and held a chart on which a jagged red graph line depicted dropping stock prices. Beneath his gaze stood a group of agonized bankers and brokers, apparently bleeding losses in red from their eyes. Yikes! A fitting insight into and summary of the psychological tenor of the time!

As I write this, the aggressive contrarian is still sitting with the above-normal stock market allocation he assumed on October 7 at the S&P 1,056 level. At its November 20 low close the S&P stood at 752, so he has suffered through a seven-week, 29 percent drop. He has underperformed the buy-and-hold strategy since early October. But another bearish information cascade has now developed in the *New York Times'* headlines. Its November 20 edition headlined: "Stocks Are Hurt by Latest Fear: Declining Prices." This headline conveyed only mild bearish sentiment; it covered a single column and used the verb *hurt* instead of the more emotional possibilities like *plunge* or *plummet*. A much more emotional headline appeared the following day, though, spread across four columns and accompanied by a chart of the Dow: "Stocks Drop Sharply and Credit Markets Seize Up."

As we have seen in this and previous chapters, headlines like these are usually published within a day or two of a short-term stock market low. For this reason I think the aggressive contrarian would now be looking for an upward move in the S&P. The real question he must confront is the tactic he should use to restore his current stock market allocation to normal or to below-normal levels.

Normal bear market tactics would demand he wait for the S&P to close at least 1 percent above its 50-day moving average and then restore a below-normal stock market allocation. But there is an important issue that the aggressive contrarian must address at this market juncture. From its October 9, 2007, high at 1,565 to its current 752 low close on November 20, the S&P 500 has dropped 47 percent over a 12-month period. The bear market has thus far been above normal in extent and about normal in duration. What are the odds that the up move from the November 20 low at 752 is actually the first leg upward of a new bull market?

The strength of bearish sentiment about the stock market and the economy argues for the start of a new bull market from the November 20 low. But the aggressive contrarian currently has an above-normal allocation to the stock market and shows a substantial loss relative to his buy at the 1056 level in early October. In such situations I have always found it best to "play defense" to avoid losing too much ground to the buy-and-hold strategy. So I think the right choice here is to follow the normal bear market tactic by waiting for an S&P level close at least 1 percent above its 50-day moving average and then restoring a below-normal allocation the stock market.

CHAPTER 16

Vignettes on Contrarian Thought and Practice

A 1912 gem • Humphrey Neill • two great books on tape reading • Neill's contrary opinion writings • American's love opinion polls • Investors Intelligence fills a gap • No Free Lunch • Garfield Drew and the odd lotter • the finest book on speculation ever written • Paul Montgomery invents the magazine cover indicator • histories of bubbles and crashes • irrational exuberance finds its nemesis • Robert Shiller • a contrarian looks at value investing • three pages from the value investor's handbook

Every contrarian trader eventually constructs his own unique way of taking advantage of the market mistakes crowds make. In the preceding chapters I explained the methods I have developed over the past 40 years. But there is a lot more to say about the contrarian approach to markets than I have discussed so far. In this chapter I am going to try to fill this gap.

What follows is a sequence of short memos I have written for my own benefit over the years I have spent developing my approach to contrarian trading. These memos were written for various reasons. Sometimes I would come across a thought-provoking book and would then write a short review attempting to put it into a broader context within contrarian theory. Occasionally I would learn of a contrarian method that wasn't explained in any book I had read and would write a short essay explaining its connection with my own approach. The following are several of these vignettes on contrarian thought and practice.

THE PSYCHOLOGY OF THE STOCK MARKET

The Psychology of the Stock Market is the title of a short book written by George C. Selden and first published in 1912. It originated from a series of magazine articles that had appeared a few years earlier in the *Ticker* magazine. The *Ticker* was founded by the legendary Richard D. Wyckoff just after the turn of the century and eventually became the *Magazine of Wall Street*. Amazingly enough, this book it is still in print and available from Cosimo Classics.

Selden describes in detail the ebb and flow of investor emotions and thinking during a typical speculative cycle. His observations are as relevant today as they were when first made nearly 100 years ago. I was particularly struck by this passage on page 22:

> *[M]ost of those who talk about the market are more likely to be wrong than right, at least so far as speculative fluctuations are concerned. This is not complimentary to the "molders of public opinion," but the most seasoned newspaper readers will agree that it is true. The daily press reflects, in a general way, the thoughts of the multitude, and in the stock market the multitude is necessarily ... likely to be bullish at high prices and bearish at low.*

Here is the genesis of the idea that investment crowds, especially in the stock market, can be detected by carefully tracking the content of the media. Over the next 100 years this idea would be developed in several different directions, each leading to a particular method for beating the market by leaning against the crowd.

THE GODFATHER OF CONTRARY OPINION

The torch lit by G. C. Selden was passed to the man I think of as the godfather of contrary opinion, Humphrey Bancroft Neill (1895–1977). A wonderful 32-page biography of Neill appears as Chapter 5 in the book *Five Eminent Contrarians* by Steven L. Mintz, which was published in 1994 by the Fraser Publishing Company of Burlington, Vermont.

Neill wrote three books, each of which is still in print and remains an outstanding contribution to contrarian theory and technique.

The first of these, *Tape Reading and Market Tactics*, is probably the best single work on the technique of tape reading in print today. It was first published in 1931. In it Neill explains the methods a tape reader uses to evaluate and make deductions from the volume of trading associated with stock price movements. (I should add that the best work on tape reading ever written is Richard D. Wyckoff's *Tape Reading and Active Trading*. This was published as part of his 1930s stock market course *The Richard D. Wyckoff Method of Trading and Investing in Stocks*. Sadly, this course is no longer in print. However, one can still purchase Wyckoff's 1910 book, *Studies in Tape Reading*, which contains his early thoughts on tape reading.)

Neill's second book is *The Art of Contrary Thinking*. It first appeared in 1954 and it is still his most popular work. In its first 46 pages Neill articulates his theory of contrary opinion. He explains it as a dialectical approach to thinking about markets and more generally about social and political affairs. One starts from a *thesis*, which is the current opinion of the crowd. The contrary step is then taken to the *antithesis*, which is a view in some substantial way contrary to the view held by the crowd. There follows the *synthesis*, in which one traces out the implications of facts that the crowd has overlooked. This results in an assessment of the extent and ways in which the crowd's opinion could prove to be mistaken. In the book's final 150 pages Neill develops his theory in a number of directions through a sequence of short essays. Stock market investors often find this book quirky because, while it offers much food for thought, it is not focused on the applications of contrary opinion to investing.

The Ruminator, Neill's third book, is of much more interest to traders and investors. First published in 1975, it contains a number of short essays describing the contrarian's take on stock market and economic events during the 1968–1973 period, described by Neill as a time of great emotional turmoil in the United States and around the world.

OPINION POLLS: WHAT DO *YOU* THINK?

It is interesting to contrast Neill's approach to contrary thinking to another that has become popular over the past 40 years. Neill emphasized the importance of assessing the crowd's view by culling information from the print media. He often referred to the files he kept of newspaper articles, magazine commentary, brokerage firm recommendations, and the like. It is Neill's approach for gathering information that I have taken in this book.

But it wasn't long before the opinion poll supplanted Neill's method for assessing the beliefs of the crowd. This development may reflect a peculiarly American trait. In his 1936 classic, *The General Theory of*

Employment, Interest, and Money, John Maynard Keynes observed (section VI of Chapter 12):

> *Even outside the field of finance, Americans are apt to be unduly interested in discovering what the average opinion believes the average opinion to be; and this national weakness finds its nemesis in the stock market.*

In 1963 an American advisory firm, Investors Intelligence, led by its founding editor A. W. Cohen, began a weekly polling of newsletter writers and other investment advisers about their current stock market views. The results were summarized by the percentages of advisers who were then bullish, bearish, or neutral on the stock market. The Investors Intelligence poll has had many imitators. Some of these have focused on the futures markets. Another is a weekly poll sponsored by the American Association of Individual Investors. This is a survey of its members, a much bigger swath of nonprofessional investors, and has been conducted at least since 1987.

Opinion polls like these have a 45-year history. There was a time when I paid a lot of attention to these polls. But I grew disenchanted with them. I found that indications of an ongoing information cascade were far more significant than are the opinions of investment professionals offered on a weekly basis. Moreover, the results of these weekly polls are highly correlated with shorter-term movements in the stock market itself, showing high bullish sentiment after an extended rise in the averages and high bearish sentiment after an extended drop. Consequently, there are no set levels of bullish or bearish sentiment that give reliable clues to the market's subsequent movements.

This is not surprising. These polls are all in the public domain. They make it easy to be a contrarian by, say, turning bullish when 50 percent or more of those polled express bearish views. But the No Free Lunch principle implies that such a strategy cannot beat the market, because it uses information that must already be incorporated into the current level of stock prices.

Why doesn't the same argument imply that the contrarian trader's media diary will similarly be useless? The No Free Lunch principle tells us that any successful contrarian trading strategy must use information that is outside the public's purview. Now, it is true that all the content recorded in a contrarian's media diary is in the public domain. But the diary *itself* is not! The trader's selection of content to retain in his diary will reflect his grasp of the life cycles of investment crowds and his understanding of the types of opinions that reveal an ongoing information cascade. The semiotic interpretation a skilled contrarian makes of his diary material will develop his insight into the nature and intensity of an investment crowd's beliefs. A contrarian trader's media diary thus becomes a highly personalized tool for beating the market and as such is not information available to the investing public.

Is there any danger that media diaries will become popular among investors who fancy themselves contrarian traders? I think not. First, it is a lot of work to maintain such a diary. Second, acting on the information contained in one's media diary means investing against widely held popular beliefs, something beyond the capacity of most investors. This is the source of the contrarian trader's *edge*.

IS THE ODD LOTTER ALWAYS WRONG?

In 1941 the first edition of the book *New Methods for Profit in the Stock Market* was published. Its author, Garfield A. Drew, was asked at the time why he would write a book about stock market profits when there were no profits to be had in the stock market. Drew simply smiled, for he knew that his odd lot indexes were sending a different message. The Dow Jones Industrial Average then was trading near the 105 level, down from its 1929 peak at 381, which had occurred 12 years earlier. The 1929 crash and the Great Depression of the 1930s had soured the nation on the stock market. Yet the April 1942 low in the Dow Jones Industrial Average at the 92 level was then just a few months away, and this average has never again been that low at any time during the subsequent 67 years!

Drew himself was a committed contrarian at a time when the theory of contrary opinion didn't even have a name. The revised 1955 edition of his book sits on my shelf and is of great interest to anyone curious about the historical development of Neill's theory of contrary opinion. Its section VI, entitled "Measures of Psychology," takes up 68 of the book's 383 pages. In this section Drew explains Neill's work on the theory of contrarian opinion and illustrates its use in the stock market during the 1936–1948 period. Drew also explains his particular implementation of Neill's theory, his famous *odd lot* indexes.

Odd lots are orders for less than 100 shares (a *round lot*) and customarily did not appear on the New York Stock Exchange ticker tape. The ticker tape was a paper-based, telegraphic reporting method for transactions (later was supplanted by the so-called Trans Lux, an electronic version of the paper tape that used to be displayed in all brokerage offices). Nowadays reporting is done electronically on all individual stocks, and no human being could possibly process the torrent of trades if presented to him in the sequence in which they occurred.

In any case, when Drew developed his odd lot indexes it was widely believed that people who traded in odd lots were ill-informed and most prone to be trading on emotions instead of economic fundamentals. But in the late 1930s the Brookings Institution published a study of odd lot behavior as shown by monthly transaction totals over the 1920–1938 period. This study concluded that odd lot transactions tended to move toward buying on balance as stock prices declined and toward selling on balance as they advanced. Contrary to the popular conception, odd lotters seemed to act more rationally than the investment advisers polled nowadays by Investors Intelligence: They grew more bullish as prices dropped and less bullish as they advanced!

But Drew had noticed two subtle features that he felt could be used to quantify the then conventional wisdom about odd lot behavior. Near the extremes of price swings, odd lotters would temporarily take leave of their senses! Just before low points occurred, the odd lotters who had been steadily increasing their ratio of purchases to sales would temporarily take fright—one would then observe a temporary decrease in their purchase-sale ratio. Just before high points in the averages, the opposite phenomenon could be observed. Drew also noted that the number of odd lot short sales would often show dramatic and sudden increases near low points of price swings, behavior that is similar to the behavior of the bearish sentiment percentage in investor polls nowadays.

Drew's odd lot indexes represented a significant advance in the theory of contrary opinion. For the first time an objective measure of the market sentiment of a specific segment of the investor population, the odd lotters, had been constructed. This was possible because there was no need for the number of shares purchased in odd lots to equal the number of shares sold. Drew applied his theory with generally good forecasting results until the end of the 1960s. Of course, his odd lot indexes needed a great deal of interpretative skill on Drew's part to be effective.

But in 1973 stock market trading changed dramatically. The Chicago Board Options Exchange was established and spurred the development of exchange trading in put and call options. Now a significant part of the volume of trading on the stock exchanges and options exchanges arose from hedges and spreads, transactions in which traders attempted to profit from mispricing of put and call options. The purchase of a call option can be seen as a bet that a stock will rise in price, whereas the purchase of a put option can be seen as a bet on a price decline. This was both good news and bad news for contrarians.

The bad news was that the advent of exchange-traded put and call options affected the amount of and the motivation for odd lot trading. Where odd lot transactions had previously been investment choices of small investors, now they included a large number of transactions that were part of hedges involving put or call options. At this juncture the odd lot indexes quickly lost most of their value as market clues for the contrarian.

The good news was that now there was a new opportunity to observe the opinions of investors as reflected in the activity of put and call options traded on options exchanges. The theory was that near market lows the ratio of put volume to call volume should be high and the converse should occur near market highs. This put-call ratio has many variants, but they all show strong (negative) correlation with the levels of the stock market averages, just as do the opinion survey numbers. Moreover, the volume of put and call trading is information that is freely available to the public. Consequently, the No Free Lunch principle tells us that these put-call ratios will not be good predictors of subsequent price movements. I believe that this implication has been supported by the evidence.

A FORECASTING GIANT OF THE PAST

The finest book on speculation ever written is *Investment for Appreciation* by Lawrence Lee Bazley Angas. First published in 1936, it describes Angas's theory of the business cycle and the steps investors may take to profit from the associated swings in the prices of stocks, bonds, and commodities.

Angas himself developed an extraordinary forecasting record during the 1920–1940 period, when he was invariably right about stock price movements in England and the United States and their associated economic fluctuations. In his later years his forecasting record became more erratic. Angas perished in a hotel fire in 1972. A brief biography of the man can be found included in the biography of Neill (Chapter 5 in *Five Eminent Contrarians*) cited earlier in this chapter. As it happened, Neill and Angas had developed a friendship, and in the early 1950s Neill persuaded Angas to move to Neill's hometown of Saxton's River in Vermont.

While it would not do to call Angas a contrarian trader, even a casual reading of his book reveals a man who believed that investment success only comes to those who are willing and able to cross the crowd, to buy when investors are temporarily discouraged and to sell when they are enthusiastic. Angas advocated an investment policy similar to the one that I have suggested for the aggressive contrarian trader—take advantage of shorter-term upswings and downswings that occur in the context of bull and bear markets. In his book Angas also discussed the art of chart reading and advocated its use in conjunction with his economic theories. In fact, he asserted that chart reading by itself was slightly more effective as an investment tool than economics used alone! In any case, a careful look at his chart reading theory shows that it has much in common with the market tabulations I have discussed in Chapter 6 of this book.

PAUL MONTGOMERY, THE MAGAZINE COVER CONTRARIAN

Paul Macrae Montgomery is the most innovative thinker the world of contrary opinion has seen in the past 40 years. It was from Montgomery that I learned the importance of magazine cover stories for detecting information cascades and the associated investment crowds. In the mid-1970s Montgomery studied the *Time* magazine archive containing the covers of all its issues from 1923 to the present. He found that those covers that had some sort of financial market theme often pointed to an imminent top or bottom either in the stock market averages or in the stock of some specific company or industry group.

The general rule he deduced was that bullish or optimistic covers or covers highlighting the success of a prominent CEO or financier generally preceded the development of an important top within the four months subsequent to the cover story. Conversely, covers that conveyed a pessimistic attitude or fear about financial affairs or that highlighted the failure of some prominent financier's policy preceded the development of an important low point within a month.

The passing years have been very kind to Montgomery's magazine cover theory. As an active money manager and market commentator, he has used it to make spectacular market calls over the past 30 years. Montgomery stands with Neill, Drew, and A.W. Cohen (the founder of Investors Intelligence) as a guiding light for all contrarian traders.

IRRATIONAL EXUBERANCE AND OTHER BUBBLES

Bubbles and the crashes that inevitably follow are frequently revived dramas played on the stage of free markets. They are the greatest opportunity and at the same time the greatest danger to the contrarian trader. In this book I have tried to show how monitoring the progress of information cascades can alert the investor to the existence of investment crowds whose growth and disintegration cause bubbles and crashes. And I have shown how to use simple tactics utilizing moving averages of the S&P 500 to time portfolio adjustments suggested by the existence of these cascades.

But the essential nature of any market economy is described by Joseph Schumpeter's wonderful phrase, *creative destruction*. The only thing we can be sure of is that financial markets and the media will be organized differently 50 years from now than they are today. The basic principles of contrarian trading will not change during the next 50 years, if ever. They are timeless and rooted in the nature of free markets. But the specific sources of media content and possibly also the nature and identity of the markets most prone to bubbles and crashes probably will evolve in unexpected ways.

To cope with and adjust to changing conditions, the contrarian trader must have a good grasp of the way bubbles and crashes typically develop, a grasp that is attained by studying historical instances of these phenomena. Of course it is better to have lived through and invested during them, but even then a historical perspective reveals details and relationships that are obscure at the time events are unfolding.

I think a good way to start this project is by reading a book entitled *Devil Take the Hindmost* by Edward Chancellor, subtitled *A History of Financial Speculation*. This was published in 2000 by the Penguin Group. Sadly, it was written before the stock market bubble of 1994–2000 burst, although it does contain some last-minute comments on this episode on pages 150–151, at the end of the section devoted to the railway mania of the 1830s in England! Among this book's highlights is a long chapter on the boom in the Japanese economy during the 1980s and on the subsequent bust.

One of my favorite books is one by David N. Dreman, published in 1977 and entitled *Psychology and the Stock Market*. Dreman has since become a well-known and very successful money manager and value investor. He also has written a number of other books, but I think this one is his best. In it Dreman explains how Wall Street groupthink feeds stock market bubbles and why no investment professional is immune to its effects. He illustrates his thesis with detailed historical accounts of a number of bubbles and a very close look at the U.S. stock market during the 1960s and early 1970s, especially the Nifty Fifty, two-tiered stock market of 1972.

The 1994–2000 stock market bubble in the United States and the subsequent bear market are covered nicely in a book by Maggie Mahar, published in 2003 by HarperCollins and entitled *Bull!* While I like this book, I think it is necessarily incomplete as a historical document since it was published so soon after the bubble burst. Perhaps someone is even now at work on a definitive history of that bubble.

Charles P. Kindleberger (1910–2003) was an eminent economic historian. Perhaps his most popular work is the book *Manias, Panics, and Crashes*, which was first published in 1978 and most recently in a revised 2005 edition. In this book Kindleberger not only recounts the facts detailing historical episodes of market manias and crashes, but also explains his views on their underlying causes and on the appropriate responses governments should make to these phenomena. This is deeper water than the previous three books I have mentioned, but the reader will be repaid for his effort to navigate in and out of its many historical bays and inlets.

The economist and author with the best literary market timing is without doubt Robert J. Shiller. In March 2000, the exact peak of the 1994–2000 stock market bubble, his book *Irrational Exuberance* was published by Princeton University Press. In it Shiller argued that only the irrational exuberance of investors could explain the unreasonably high stock market valuations then current. He went on to predict an imminent return to more normal valuations and an attendant substantial drop in stock prices. It should be pointed out that the phrase *irrational exuberance* first entered the public consciousness when Alan Greenspan, the chairman of the Federal Reserve, used it in a speech in 1996. It was Shiller who had suggested this phrase to Greenspan as a description of the stock market psychology of that time.

Shiller then repeated this coup of precise publication timing in the 2005 revision of this book, which included an expanded look at and analysis of the bubble in housing prices. The following year saw the peak in housing prices in the United States, and the collapse of this real estate bubble eventually brought on the crash of 2008. In 2008 Shiller published *The Subprime Solution*, in which he presents his analysis of the collapsing real estate bubble and suggests solutions for managing the crisis.

I believe that every contrarian should read and reread both of these books. In them Shiller offers a wealth of information on historical bubbles in stocks and real estate, as well as detailed explanations for the psychological mechanisms that cause them. There can be no doubt that Shiller is the world's reigning expert on the formation of investment crowds, the theme of the book you are reading.

VALUE INVESTING—A BACK-OF-THE-ENVELOPE APPROACH

It may seem strange to include a short essay on value investing in a book about speculation. But I think a moment's reflection shows that there is a close connection between value investing and the growth and disintegration of investment crowds. Warren Buffett, the most successful value investor of all time, puts it best when he says that the time to sell is when people are greedy, and the time to buy is when they are fearful. Investment crowds, especially bearish ones, create opportunities for value investors as well as for contrarian traders. So it makes sense that indicators that help value investors determine whether the stock market is far over or far under fair value would be useful to the contrarian trader, too.

A value investor does not pay much attention to crowd psychology. Instead, and above all else, a committed value investor wants to form a reliable estimate of a business's fair value. This generally means trying to determine the rate of return it earns on its invested capital, and whether this rate of return can be sustained and/or improved. A value investor wants to hold shares in companies that earn the highest rate of return on their invested capital, for these are almost by definition the best businesses in the economy. Note that the rate of return earned on invested capital may differ from the rate of return on shareholder equity, because of debt financing. A value investor is generally much more concerned about the former than about the latter, even though both do matter.

Having identified suitable businesses using the rate of return on capital criterion, the value investor then concerns himself with the price at which shares in the business can be purchased. It is at this juncture that value investing becomes as much art as science. What is a fair price for the equity in a good business? There is no definitive answer to this question. One generally seeks guidance from the historical data on valuations of similar companies to estimate some normal range of fair prices for a business with similar characteristics. Intuition, together with business vision, generally plays an important role, too, as does an ability to evaluate whether corporate management is committed to maintaining and improving its rate of return on invested capital.

The formal aspects of this process, those that have to do with balance sheets and income statements, are explained thoroughly in the investment classic *Security Analysis* by Benjamin Graham and David Dodd. This book was first published in 1934 and is still in print in revised editions. Benjamin Graham is widely acknowledged as the father of value investing and was Warren Buffett's mentor. He is credited with articulating the concept of the margin of safety, which describes the situation in which the market price for a security is sufficiently below its fair value that unforeseen events will not cause loss to the investor.

An excellent introduction to Benjamin Graham's thinking can be found in his book *The Intelligent Investor*, which was first published in 1949. I highly recommend the 2006 paperback edition (HarperCollins) containing commentary by Jason Zweig as well as a preface and appendix by Warren Buffett. The story of how Graham's thinking influenced Buffett and of the innovations Buffett made security analysis is told expertly in a wonderful biography, *Buffett: The Making of an American Capitalist*, by Roger Lowenstein (Random House, 1995).

Is it easier to be a value investor than a contrarian trader? In a word, no. Both need the ability to stand aside from the crowd's influence, to buy when others are fearful, and to sell when others are cheerful. The value investor's skill in assessing the likelihood that the rate of return on capital will stay high or improve uses insights that are difficult to teach. Similarly, the contrarian trader's skill in culling suitable media content that accurately reflects the tenor or the time is built only through experience. Both types of investors can carve profitable niches into the slippery slope of the investment mountain. But in neither case is this process easy or simple.

I'd like to offer the interested contrarian three methods that help value investors detect extreme over- or undervaluation in the stock market. These tools need only the back of a handy envelope for calculations. In fact, if you make use of your favorite Internet search engine, you won't even need an envelope. The calculations I am about to describe are often done by dedicated investors who maintain blogs or home pages, and you will probably be able to piggyback yourself on their work.

I should say that you won't be able to become a successful value investor using only these simple methods. They speak only rarely. But when they do they identify situations in which investment crowds have pushed stock market valuations so high or so low that the correct long-term investing stance becomes obvious. This can be very valuable information to a contrarian trader as well.

The first method is simplicity itself. Just calculate the current value of common stocks of publicly traded U.S. corporations and divide this number by the dollar value of gross domestic product (GDP). This stock market/GDP ratio fluctuates above and below its average value of 0.6. In 1929 and 1972, two instances of extreme overvaluation, this ratio stood at 0.8 or higher. In 1932 and 1942, both instances of extreme undervaluation, the ratio stood at 0.2. In 1974 and 1982 the ratio dropped a little below 0.4, showing an undervalued condition that was not as extreme as that associated with the Great Depression. At the peak of the 1994–2000 stock market bubble the ratio reached 1.7. My rough calculation shows that the ratio stood near 0.6 in late November 2008, at its historical norm and not showing clear undervaluation.

The second method is similar in spirit to the first. It involves calculating Tobin's q ratio. If you want to learn more about Tobin's q, I suggest you read *Valuing Wall Street* by Andrew Smithers and Stephen Wright, a book first published in 2000 by McGraw-Hill. Tobin's q is the ratio of the market value of common stocks to the replacement value of the capital employed by the associated corporations. This is more difficult to calculate, but the raw data are published by various government agencies. Values of q substantially above 1.0 indicate an overvalued stock market, while values substantially below 1.0 indicate an undervalued stock market. At the peak of the 1994–2000 bubble the q ratio stood at a record high of 2.9. I estimate that on November 20, 2008, with the S&P 500 closing at 752, the q ratio stood at 0.65. While it would need to fall to 0.5 to match the undervaluation levels seen in 1932, 1974, and 1982, the ratio indicated that the U.S. stock market was substantially undervalued in late November 2008.

The third method was advocated by Benjamin Graham and popularized in Shiller's book *Irrational Exuberance*. It is the classic price-earnings ratio for the S&P 500, but one that uses the 10-year moving average of reported earnings as the denominator. The average value of this ratio during the past 120 years has been 16. It generally drops below 10 during times of significant undervaluation. By contrast, at the 1929 peak this ratio was over 30, and at the 2000 bubble top it stood at a historical high of 44. At the November 20, 2008, S&P low of 752 this price-earnings ratio stood at 11, well below its historical average but not yet below 10.

These three pages from the value investor's handbook will help the contrarian trader identify the bullish crowds that create stock market bubbles as well as the bearish crowds that seem willing to give away their stock market holdings for a song. Back-of-the-envelope calculations like this won't make you the next Warren Buffett, but they will help you to avoid the mistakes that make stock market investing so frustrating for so many.

About the Author

C arl Futia is a stock index futures trader with more than 25 years of experience. An economist with a Ph.D. from the University of California at Berkeley, he also has published a number of articles in academic journals. He currently writes one of the most popular investment blogs on the Internet.

Index

Above-average returns, 4–5
Acampora, Ralph, 54
Advances in Behavioral Finance (Thaler and Barbaris), 14
Agriculture, 106
AIG. *See* American International Group
Al-Qaeda, 102
Amazon.com, 49, 114–115
American Association of Individual Investors, 169–170
American International Group (AIG), 202
America Online (AOL), 49, 58, 72, 105
Angas, Lawrence Lee Bazley, 211–212
AOL. *See* America Online
Apple Computer, 49, 171
The Art of Contrary Thinking (Neill), 207
Assets, 125

Bandwagon strategy, 134–135
Bankruptcy, 103, 201–204
Barbaris, Nicholas, 14
Barone, Michael, 90
Barron's, 82, 90, 91, 92, 94, 95, 113, 114, 200
Bartiromo, Maria, 54
Bear market, 86–87, 132, 133
    1921–1929, 69
    1942–1966, 69
    1976–1978, 69
    1982–2000, 69

2000–2002, 160–162
aggressive contrarian trading during 2000–2002, 157–158
collapse of the bubble, 2000–2002, 153–167
crowd, 54–55, 56
end of, 54, 164–165
extended, 68–69
normal tactics, 204
during the 2001 plunge, 162–163
rebalancing during 2000–2002 market, 154
short, 69
S&L crisis and, 141–143
transition to a new bull market, 166–167
Bear Stearns, 198–199
Behavioral finance, 14–16
exploitable market mistakes and, 16–17
predictions, 17
Bernanke, Ben S., 91, 117. *See also* Volcker, Paul
Bezos, Jeff, 114–115
Biggs, Barton, 21
Bikhchandani, Sushil, 39
Black Gold, 75
Blodget, Henry, 54
Blogs, 56–57, 75, 90
Bloomberg, 74
Bond market, 89
    interest rate movements and, 107
    mortgage backed securities, 191
Brimelow, Peter, 90
Browning, E. S., 90

Bubbles, 58–59, 138, 212–214
   1994–2000, 72, 81
   1995–2000, 145–147
   2000–2002 collapse, 153–167
   development, 155
   history, 77
   housing, 175–177
   markets, 66
   peak oil, 70
   postbubble bull market of
      2002–2007, 169–188
*Buffett: The Making of an American
   Capitalist* (Lowenstein), 215
Bull! (Mahar), 47, 58, 147, 213
Bull market, 66, 132
   1982–2000, 137–152
   1991–1994, 143–145
   1995–2000, 145–147
   2005, 181–182
   2006, 182–183
   2007
      early, 183–186
      late, 186–188
   aggressive contrarian trading in the
      2002–2007 market, 177–181
   1990 bear market crowd and,
      141–143
   1929–1932 crash, 140–141
   1987 crash, 138–140, 147–149
   decline of, 153–154
   duration, 67
   information cascade and, 170–172
   long-term capital management,
      150–152
   1990 low, 149–150
   panic of 2008 and, 195–198
   postbubble during 2002–2007,
      169–188
   1987–1990 S&L crisis, 141–143
   transition from a bear market,
      166–167
BusinessWeek, 74, 88, 114, 137, 142,
      144, 146, 184, 197, 198
Byron, Christopher, 147

Capital gains taxes, 128
Capital management, 150–152

Cara, Bill, 90
Case-Shiller housing price index, 176,
      192–193
CDs. *See* Certificates of deposit
Certificates of deposit (CDs), 89
Chancellor, Edward, 213
Chart Store, 77
Chicago Board of Trade, 117
Chicago Board Options Exchange, 210
Chicago Tribune, 73, 82–83, 84–85, 91,
      156, 157, 165, 179–180, 183, 197,
      202, 203
Civil War, 100
Clinton, President Bill, 145
CNBC, 102, 143, 150
Cohen, A. W., 208, 212
Cohen, Abby Joseph, 54
Collateralized debt obligations, 191
Collective wisdom equilibrium, 38–41
Commodities, 106–107
Commodity Systems Inc., 64
Communication, 71–77
   mass media and, 73–75
Contrarian trader
   aggression and, 130–131, 134–135,
      157–158, 177–181, 195, 201
   during the 2000–2002 bear market,
      157–158
   capital gains taxes, 128
   1987 crash and, 147–149
   credit crisis and, 195
   difficulty being, 89
   edge and, 28
   goals, 64–65, 126–127
   investment planning, 123–124
   investment portfolio, 125–126
   mistakes, 172
   novice, 64–65
   during the panic of 2008, 189–190
   strategies, 123–135
      bandwagon, 134–135
      investment with a crowd, 129
      long-only, 131–134
      rebalancing, 129–130
      speculation, 128
   thoughts and practice, 205–217
   vision of, 27–29

Credit, 99
The Crowd (Le Bon), 55
Crowds, 31–42, 154, 214–215. *See also*
    Social groups
  behavior of investment, 40
  collective judgment, 33
  collective wisdom, 32–34, 35–36
  forecasting market psychology,
    36–38
  independent decisions in the
    financial markets, 34–36
  market, 118
  members, 31–32
  speculation and, 38–41
Cuban missile crisis, 101

Debt-deflation, 193–194
Dell Computer, 49, 105
Demuth, Phil, 82
Devil Take the Hindmost
  (Chancellor), 213
Discounted future dividends, 3
Dividends, 13
Dodd, David, 215
Dot-com companies, 59
  bubble of 1994–2000, 72
Dow Jones Industrial Average, 46, 65,
    69, 83, 91, 98–99, 101, 103, 113,
    137, 140–141, 153, 183
Dreman, David N., 213
Drew, Garfield A., 209–211
Druckenmiller, Stanley, 57
Dudack, Gail, 58

Earnings, 13
eBay, 49
Economics
  considerations for uncovering
    mistakes, 4
  globalization, 48
  new economy, 48
Economist, 74, 94, 114, 144, 145, 151,
    182, 184, 199, 201
Edge, 1–2, 19–29, 79–81, 209
  of the contrarian trader, 28
EFTs. *See* Exchange-traded funds
Elves Index, 58

Employment rates, 144
Enron, 49
Equilibrium price, 3
European War, 101
Exchange-traded funds (ETFs),
    125–126, 130–131, 134, 135, 158,
    175
Eyeball count, 100

Fair value price, 3, 44–45
  versus mistakes, 62–63
Fama, Eugene, 16–17
Fannie Mae, 104, 199–201
Financial Institutions Reform,
    Recovery, and Enforcement Act
    of 1989, 141
Financial markets
  crises and crowds, 102–104
  independent decisions, 34–36
  subprime crises of 2008, 103–104
Financial Review, 5–6
Five Eminent Contrarians (Mintz),
    206
Ford, Bill, 93–94
Ford Motor Company, 93–94, 105
Forecasting, 36–38
Fortune, 74, 88, 94, 114, 176
Franklin National Bank, 103
Freddie Mac, 104, 199–201
Fundamentalist investors, 6–7

Gale of creative destruction, 3
GDP. *See* Gross domestic product
Genentech, 105
General Motors Corporation, 94, 105
*The General Theory of Employment,
    Interest, and Money* (Keynes),
    21, 36–38, 207–208
Gladwell, Malcom, 40
Globalization, 48
Gold, 89, 106
Google, 94, 105
  initial public offering, 171, 172–175
Graham, Benjamin, xii, 215, 217
Granville, Joe, 113
Greenspan, Alan, 54, 147, 214
Gross, Daniel, 89

Gross domestic product (GDP), 216
Grubman, Jack, 54
Gulf War, 69, 101–102, 142, 150, 166

Harper's, 74
Haugen, Robert A., 92
Hedge funds, 103, 150
Hedgehogging (Biggs), 21
Hirshleifer, David, 39
Housing bubble, 175–177, 190. *See also* Mortgages
Hulbert, Mark, 87–88, 89, 92
Hulbert Financial Digest, 87
Hussein, Saddam, 101–102

IBM, 105
Inflation, 66
Information cascades, xii–xiii, 39
  behavior of investment crowds, 40
  effect on market, 41
  information technology, 48
  investors and, 71–73
  as living history, 110
  media and, 109–110
  new information economy, 48–49
  sequence of choices, 39
  signs of a bullish market, 170–172
Initial public offering (IPO), 88, 105, 171
  Google, 172–175
Instincts of the Herd in Peace and War (Trotter), 51–52
Intel, 49
The Intelligent Investor (Graham), 215
Interest rates
  bond market and, 107
  cuts, 163
Internet, 75, 86, 105
Investment crowds, 19, 25–27
  bear market of 2001–2002, 49–51
  communication, 71–77
  contrarian trading and, 129
  eyeball count, 100
  financial crises and, 102–104
  history of bubbles and crashes, 77

identification of, 20
information transmitted, 72
instincts and the search for certainty, 51–53
life cycle and psychology of, 43–60
  birth and death cycle, 44–46
life within, 56
mass media and, 73–75
mature investment and, 61–62
mental unity of, 55–59
mistakes versus fair value, 62–63
monitoring the markets, 76–77
new information economy, 48–49
personal flexibility and, 76
pied pipers of, 54–55
recognizing, 71–72
stock market bubble of 1994–2000, 46–48
suggestibility, volatility, and disintegration, 59–60
tolerance, 57
Investment for Appreciation (Angas), 211–212
Investment goals, 126–127
Investment planning, 123–124
Investment portfolio, 125–126
Investment theme, 23, 55–56
Investors, 2–4, 33
  behavior, 40
  exposure, 148, 161–162
  fundamentalist, 6–7
  information cascades and, 71–73
  social groups and, 25–27
  value, 215
Investors Intelligence, 208, 212
IPO. *See* Initial public offering
Iraq, 101–102, 142
Irrational Exuberance (Shiller), 11, 12, 214, 217

James, William, 52
Japan, 175–176, 197, 213
Jobs, Steve, 171
Journal of Political Economy, 39
JPMorgan Chase, 104

Keynes, John Maynard, 21–22, 36–38, 207–208
Kindleberger, Charles P., 213–214
Knight, Frank, 15
Korean War, 101

Le Bon, Gustav, 55, 56
Legislation. *See* Financial Institutions Reform, Recovery, and Enforcement Act of 1989
Lehman Brothers, 104, 201–204
Lenders of last resort, 194–195
Lincoln, President Abraham, 100
Long-only strategy, 131–134
Long Term Capital Management (LTCM), 103, 150
  crisis of 1998, 69
"A Long Way Down" (Stein and Demuth), 82
Lowenstein, Roger, 215
LTCM. *See* Long Term Capital Management
Lucent Technologies, 49, 105

Magazine covers, 92–95, 137, 200–201, 212
  stories, 114–116
Magazine of Wall Street, 206
Mahar, Maggie, 47, 58, 147, 213
Maine, 100–101
Malkiel, Burton, 5–6
Manias, Panics, and Crashes (Kindleberger), 213–214
Market data
  creative destruction, 213
  market semiotics, 109–121
  monitoring, 76–77
  sources, 63–65
Market-investment-themed social groups, 23
  effect by information cascade, 41
Market Volatility (Shiller), 12
MarketWatch, 74, 86, 87–88, 90
Mass media
  future of, 76
  investment crowds and, 73–75

MCI WorldCom, 49
Media diary, 79–95. *See also* individual newspapers
  in 2002, 81–83
  in 2005, 86–89
  in 2006, 89–92
  construction, 83–86
  edge, 79–81
  magazine covers and, 92–95
  market semiotics, 109–121
  newspapers, 85–86
  novices and, 113
  purpose, 79–80
  stock market and, 97–98
  to track investment themes, 107–108
  weight of the evidence, 119–120
Meeker, Mary, 54
Microsoft, 49
Mintz, Steven L., 206
Mistakes, 3, 4–5, 9–17, 19–21, 172
  creation, 22–25
  versus fair value, 62–63
  historical context, 61–70
  identification, 62
  market data sources, 63–65
  statistically exploitable, 10
  undervaluation in the stock market, 67–68
Money market funds, 89
Montgomery, Paul Macrae, 92–93, 114, 212
Moody's Investors Service, 104, 192
Morgan, John Pierpont, 10
Morgenson, Gretchen, 183
Morristown Daily Record, 82, 150, 160
Mortgage backed securities, 191–193
Mortgages. *See also* Housing bubble
  during the panic of 2008, 191–193

NASDAQ Composite index, 11–12, 25, 49, 51, 57, 81, 115, 138, 153, 159–160, 162
Neill, Humphrey Bancroft, 206–207
New Century Financial, 183–184
New Methods for Profit in the Stock Market (Drew), 209–211

New Republic, 74, 142, 144
Newspaper headlines, 116–118,
    138–139, 156–157, 186–187.
    See also individual newspapers
Newsweek, 58, 74, 87, 113, 114, 115,
    119–120, 139, 142, 151, 160, 163
New Yorker, 74, 197–198
New York magazine, 74, 142
New York Times, 73, 82, 83, 84–85,
    86–87, 88, 89, 91, 92, 116–117,
    138, 142, 150, 156, 157, 159, 160,
    162, 174, 183, 186–187, 196, 197,
    198, 200
New York Times Magazine, 95, 182
Nikkei stock market, 175–176, 197
9/11, 102, 156, 164, 183
Nixon, President Richard, 103
No Free Lunch Principle, 7–8, 10, 17,
    20

Oil
    inflation, 70
    prices, 70, 106
    prognosis, 70
Opinion polls, 207–209
Oracle, 49

Panic of 2008, 189–204. *See also*
    Fannie Mae; Freddie Mac
    Bear Stearns and, 198–199
    bull market and, 195–198
    conservative contrarian during,
        189–190
    credit crisis and, 195
    debt-deflation spiral, 193–194
    Lehman Brothers and, 201–204
    lenders of last resort, 194–195
    mortgages and, 191–193
Paper trading, 124
PC. *See* Personal computer
Peak oil investments, 23–24, 70
Penn Central Corporation, 103
Penn Square Bank, 103
Personal computer (PC), 105
Politics, effect of war and
    international political crises
    stock market, 100–102

Priceline.com, 49
Principles of Psychology (James), 52
Profits, 9
Psychology, 36–38
    of an investment crowd, 43–60
Psychology and the Stock Market
    (Dreman), 213
The Psychology of the Stock Market
    (Selden), 206
Publishing industry, 120–121, 146–147

Q ratio, 3, 46–47, 49–50, 216–217
Quantum Fund, 57
Quattrone, Frank, 54
Qwest Communications, 49

Railroads, 105
Rational expectations equilibrium,
    35–36
Rational expectations theory, 35–36
Rebalancing, 129–130, 139–140, 146,
    154, 170
    during 2000–2002 bear market, 154
    during the crash, 155–157
Retirement, 82, 115, 116
Risk, Uncertainty, and Profit
    (Knight), 15
Risks, 14–15
    lunatic factor, 15–16
    "the last one to know," 15
    unknown unknown, 15
Robertson, Julian, 57
Rukeyser, Louis, 58
The Ruminator (Neill), 207
Russia, 103, 151

Samuelson, Robert J., 87
Saudi Arabia, 142
Schiller, Robert J., 214
Schumpeter, Joseph, 3, 213
Security Analysis (Graham and
    Dodd), 215
Selden, George C., 207
Semiotics, 109–121. *See also* Magazine
    covers
    definition of, 111
    events, 118–119

front page stories and editorials, 118
market, 120–121
newspaper headlines, 116–118
price chart, 112–114
S.G. Warburg, 58
Shiller, Robert J., 11, 12, 217
Silicon Graphics, 49
SIV. *See* Specialized Investment
Vehicle
Sloan, Allan, 58–59
Smithers, Andrew, 46–47, 216–217
Social groups, 21–22. *See also* Crowds
"black hole," 19
collective behavior, 32
eccentric people in, 22
investment themes and, 25–27
membership in, 20, 22
SPDRs. *See* Standard & Poor's
Depositary Receipts
Specialized Investment Vehicle (SIV),
191
Speculation, 1–2, 128
Standard Oil, 105
Standard & Poor's Depositary Receipts
(SPDRs), 126
Standard & Poor's (S&P) 500 index, xi,
5–6, 12, 50, 75, 81, 83, 104,
116–117, 189
Statistically exploitable mistakes, 10
Stein, Ben, 82
StockCharts.com, 77
Stock market
during 2000–2002, 158–160
bear market in 2000–2002, 25, 49–51,
50
boom in 1996–2000, 25
bubble of 1994–2000, 46–48, 54,
145–147
bull market
in 1921–1929, 98–99
in 1949–1966, 99
in 1994–2000
crashes, 77
disintegration in 2003, 25
effect of war and international
political crises on, 100–102
efficient markets, 9–10

evidence, 5–6
exposure, 148, 161–162
fluctuations in stock prices, 12–14
industry groups, 74–75
media diary and, 97–98
mistakes, 3, 4–5, 9–17, 19–21,
22–25
No Free Lunch Principle, 7–8, 10, 17,
20
overvaluation, 65–67
panic of 2008, 189–204
psychology, 36–38, 206
risks, 14–15
roller coasters and, 10–12
speculation, 1–2
timing, 6–7
undervaluation, 67–70
unstable nature of, 35
Studies in Tape Reading (Wyckoff),
207
The Subprime Solution (Shiller), 214
Surowiecki, James, 33–34, 34–36

Tape Reading and Active Trading
(Wyckhoff), 207
Tape Reading and Market Tactics
(Neill), 206–207
Taxes, capital gains and, 128
Technology, 50, 57, 104–106, 105
Terrorism, 102, 156, 164
Thaler, Richard, 14
"A Theory of Fads, Fashion, Custom,
and Cultural Change as
Information Cascades"
(Bikhchandani, Hirshleifer, and
Welch), 39
Ticker, 206
Tiger Management, 57
Time, 74, 82, 92–93, 103, 114, 115,
119–120, 127, 142, 144, 146, 151,
163, 212
The Tipping Point (Gladwell), 40
Tobin, James, 46, 216–217
Tonight Show with Jay Leno, 75, 82,
184
Treasury bonds, 107
Trotter, Wilfred, 51–52, 52–53, 56

U.S. Congress, 141
U.S. Federal Reserve, 103, 104, 115, 147, 187, 194–195
   rate cut, 163
U.S. News & World Report, 74, 145, 163, 203

Valuing Wall Street (Smithers and Wright), 46–47, 216
Vietnam War, 101
Volcker, Paul, 115. *See also* Bernanke, Ben

Wall Street Journal, 74, 87, 88, 89, 90, 91, 147, 165, 174
Wall $treet Week, 58

War, effect of political crises on stock market, 100–102
Watergate scandal, 101
Weekly Standard, 199, 203
Welchi, Ivo, 39
Wilson, President Woodrow, 101
The Wisdom of Crowds (Surowiecki), 33
WorldCom, 105
World War II, 101
Wright, Stephen, 46–47, 216–217
Wyckhoff, Richard D., 206, 207

Yahoo!, 49, 72, 76
Yahoo! Finance, 64

Zweig, Jason, 215